Bewitching Development

CHICAGO STUDIES IN PRACTICES OF MEANING

A Series Edited by Jean Comaroff, Andreas Glaeser, William Sewell, and Lisa Wedeen

ALSO IN THE SERIES

Producing India: From Colonial Economy to National Space
by Manu Goswami

Parité! Sexual Equality and the Crisis of French Universalism
by Joan Wallach Scott

Logics of History: Social Theory and Social Transformation
by William H. Sewell, Jr.

Inclusion: The Politics of Difference in Medical Research
by Steven Epstein

The Devil's Handwriting: Precoloniality and the German Colonial State in Qingdao, Samoa, and Southwest Africa
by George Steinmetz

Bewitching Development

Witchcraft and the Reinvention of Development in Neoliberal Kenya

Develop 5 questions
for ch. 5-8
"worksheet!

JAMES HOWARD SMITH

THE UNIVERSITY OF CHICAGO PRESS   CHICAGO AND LONDON

JAMES HOWARD SMITH is assistant professor of anthropology at the University of California, Davis.

The University of Chicago Press, Chicago 60637
The University of Chicago Press, Ltd., London

Printed in the United States of America
17 16 15 14 13 12 11 10 09 08   1 2 3 4 5

ISBN-13: 978-0-226-76457-3 (cloth)
ISBN-13: 978-0-226-76458-0 (paper)
ISBN-10: 0-226-76457-5 (cloth)
ISBN-10: 0-226-76458-3 (paper)

Library of Congress Cataloging-in-Publication Data

Smith, James Howard.
Bewitching development : witchcraft and the reinvention of development in neoliberal Kenya / James Howard Smith.
p. cm.—(Chicago studies in practices of meaning)
Includes bibliographical references and index.
ISBN-13: 978-0-226-76457-3 (cloth : alk. paper)
ISBN-10: 0-226-76457-5 (cloth : alk. paper)
ISBN-13: 978-0-226-76458-0 (pbk. : alk. paper)
ISBN-10: 0-226-76458-3 (pbk. : alk. paper) 1. Taita (African people)—Social life and customs. 2. Taita (African people)—Rites and ceremonies. 3. Witchcraft—Kenya—Taita Hills. 4. Economic development—Kenya—Taita Hills. 5. Taita Hills (Kenya)—Economic conditions.
I. Title.
DT433.545.T34S65 2008
305.896′395–dc22

2008000461

♾ The paper used in this publication meets the minimum requirements of the American National Standard for Information Sciences—Permanence of Paper for Printed Library Materials, ANSI Z39.48-1992.

Contents

PREFACE

Escaping Development

To find it, to find the right thing, for which it is worthy to live, to be organized, and to have time: that is why we go, why we cut new, metaphysically constitutive paths, summon what is not, build into the blue, and build ourselves into the blue, and there seek the true, the real, where the merely factual disappears—*incipit vita nova.* —Ernst Bloch, *The Spirit of Utopia*

This book concerns the ongoing struggle over "development" in Kenya, approaching this concept as a prism through which to understand diverse African efforts to bring such powerful forces as neoliberal globalization, the past embodied in place, and even time itself under personal and social control, in part by projecting images of violence and disorder outside these emergent social orders. My interest in these issues dates back to my earliest experiences of Kenyan society and politics, in which I witnessed a widespread feeling of rising hope, global interconnection, and infinite possibility against powerful, repressive forces rapidly give way to an equally ubiquitous feeling of decline, isolation, and confusion. I was an undergraduate exchange student at the University of Nairobi when I first visited the Taita Hills, the setting for most of this book. I left the university after only one semester there, in early 1991, after my closest Kenyan friend at the time, a Luo political science major by the name of Owidi mak Ogega Sila, was expelled. The circumstances surrounding Owidi's expulsion were complicated, and deeply political, for he was an outspoken critic of President Daniel arap Moi's regime and also openly rejected the conservative, upwardly mobile culture of the university under President Moi's chancellorship. It was a period when governing authorities were paranoid about the rapid spread of what came to be called "multiparty," the push for political alternatives to Moi's Kenyan African

National Union Party. I had arrived in Nairobi at a very tense time, shortly after the murder of Foreign Minister Robert Ouko, the mysterious death by car accident of the outspoken Bishop Alexander Muge, and the riots that later came to be known as "Saba Saba Day" (July 7, 1990), when more than a dozen civilians promoting multipartyism were killed in a violent clash with the police. President Moi had long blamed the United States and other European "foreign masters" for corrupting the *wananchi*, or citizens, with notions of democratic pluralism, which, he maintained, were inimical to peace, development, and the African cultural preoccupation with unity.

Owidi, a self-professed radical, often talked about development himself; his was a utopian vision of a future in which the inequalities fostered by the Jomo Kenyatta and Moi regimes would finally be redressed. Particularly pivotal, according to Owidi, was Kenyatta's early decision to deny Mau Mau insurgents' claims to land in favor of the Kikuyu elite, who alone could afford to purchase land from an already indebted independent government.[1] Owidi believed that Kenyatta's disavowal of the anticolonial Mau Mau insurrection was treason against the nation and that it paved the way for the cynical rapaciousness that characterized the Moi regime. Once, in a heated debate with another student, he insisted that Kenyatta's body should be "disinterred" (his word; it was the first time I had heard it) and put on trial for crimes against the nation. Owidi was not simply ranting; his argument was that Kenyatta should be ritually alienated from the land, so that generative value would be separated from the false development that this putative national hero had engendered by redistributing national property to elites.

Owidi echoed other Kenyan "dissidents" of the time, like the Kikuyu novelist Ngugi wa Thiong'o, when he claimed that Kenyans had turned their backs on African principles of reciprocity and egalitarianism, and that to save themselves from tyranny they first had to abandon their slavish dependence on Western aid and cultural values, such as individualism. Owidi was trying to achieve a kind of lumpen authenticity himself, and he dressed like an urban version of a Mau Mau forest fighter: short dreadlocks, sandals, jeans, and a pullover sweatshirt that was always dirty. His appearance was in stark contrast to the obsessive cleanliness of the majority of students who, much to my chagrin, rose as early as 5:00 a.m. to noisily shine their shoes. And he frequently chewed *miraa* (or *qat*), the low-class stimulant of choice for bus drivers and *matatu* "touts," which most University of Nairobi students considered too *kichafu*, or unclean, to touch. This was a time when police regularly arrested those few people who dared to have dreadlocks, and cut them off summarily. Also, several years earlier, Ngugi had been detained without trial, in part for implying that the postcolonial government's selfish greed mocked the earnest, heroic, and communitarian visions that had allegedly sustained Mau Mau insurgents in the forest. Such were the punishments for publicly invoking the memory of this guerilla insurgency, and so it is not surprising that Kenyan religious countercultures in the 1990s, the era of political liberalization, were fated to seize upon Mau Mau symbols in that moment of promise and danger.

Owidi chastised the smartly dressed university students who sometimes questioned him about his clothes or his unkempt hair, for he was fond of reading while lying on the grass. We used to sit on the dormitory rooftop drinking *chang'aa*, the illegal gin we purchased in Nairobi's slums, and talking about Marxism (I remember him telling me a joke about Moi's Minister Kariuki Chotara, who allegedly suggested that the Kenyan government should detain Karl Marx for subversive activities). Owidi was particularly fond of paraphrasing former Communist China Chairman Mao Tse-tung's suggestion that revolutionaries read Karl Marx, but not too closely, and he was passionate in his conviction that someday he would be president of a detribalized, socialist Kenya. Once, we went to Tanzania on a field trip by bus with the university's Archaeology Club so I could see "African socialism" at work. Observing a well-maintained market in Arusha, Owidi proclaimed with simultaneous pride and envy, "Now, this is an African society! Here you will not find Africans eating ice-cream cones!" Later, we students on the bus got into a big argument that reiterated the so-called Kenya Debate of the 1970s: which was the greater paragon of development, capitalist Kenya or socialist Tanzania? The debate, which focused on the relative virtues of growth and equality, got out of hand and culminated in the graduate student director of the Archaeology Club being put on "trial" for embezzling from the undergraduates and kicked off the bus, which was rerouted from Ol Luvai Gorge to Dar es Salaam (so we could visit the University of Dar es Salaam, supposedly a genuine institution of free, leftist thought).

Owidi's iconoclastic, confrontational style, and his insistence that to change the present one had to lay hold of the past, appropriate it, and put it to work for the future, challenged the comfortables, and landed him in a great deal of trouble. His extreme views and style, his habit of putting his political opinions in writing at every opportunity (including in examinations and class essays), and no doubt his friendship with an American eventually attracted the attention of student informants and secret police posing as students during this time when the government was still able to employ such people. One day, the University of Nairobi senate and members of Kenya's security forces (the Special Branch) interrogated each of us separately about our friendship, our political views, and our topics of conversation. I am not entirely sure what happened during Owidi's impromptu hearing, but at its end he was informed that he was to be expelled immediately and would be taken the next day by police escort to his home near Kisumu. Instead, the chief security officer (CSO) drove him directly to the police station, where he was arrested on trumped-up marijuana possession charges, thrown in jail, and almost immediately released by the police for lack of evidence (the CSO had failed to produce the marijuana). The university later claimed that marijuana had been found in Owidi's room "in an American container, with an American dollar price tag," a statement whose blithe disregard of plausible truth unnerved me at the time.

My own hearing had gone somewhat better. At first the university expelled me as well, but later it amended the decision, allowing me to finish the semester and complete my exams, so long as I did not step foot in the men's residences or return the following semester. I stayed in Nairobi for nearly a month afterward, waiting for the semester to finish, and each evening I made my way quickly and nervously down Nairobi's dangerous River Road to stay in a seedy hotel-cum-brothel that was home to other foreign exiles. Anxious to leave the city and Kenya's tense politics, I followed the advice of Dr. Tom Wolfe, an American professor at the university who had lived in the Taita Hills as a Peace Corps volunteer and researcher: after finishing the semester exams, I made the 200-kilometer bus trip to the southeast, near the Tanzania border, and within a few days I was trying to explain to Taita high school students the geopolitical significance of the assassination of the Archduke Franz Ferdinand in exchange for room and board.

Six years later, in 1997, Kenya's political climate seemed completely transformed, at least if one were to judge from the proliferation of newspapers critical of the government; the dizzying number of new political parties, nongovernmental organizations (NGOs), and churches on the local scene; and the open discussion of corruption, which took place on a variety of secular and religious registers. Under these new conditions, the passing whims of a powerful few would not materialize so easily as permanent fact. I had returned to Kenya to conduct doctoral research on the dialectics of witchcraft and development in Taita, and found Owidi by accident, lounging under a tree in Nairobi's Uhuru, or Independence, Park with the *wakora* (thugs) whose lifestyles he had formerly emulated from afar. The story Owidi told me was confused and difficult to follow. Over the years he had been active in politics with the now legal opposition party Forum for the Restoration of Democracy (FORD), had been thrown in and out of detention, and had been occasionally tortured in dark chambers where he was forced to sit in the same stagnant water in which he defecated. Though surprising, given the fact that he was expelled and never reinstated, Owidi was elected president of a revitalized University of Nairobi student union in 1992 and, in 1994, ended up in law school at the University of Sao Paulo, Brazil, on a University of Nairobi scholarship. But the Kenyan state had apparently changed its mind and, according to Owidi, sent security personnel to Brazil to pick him up and escort him back home; Owidi spent the next year in detention without trial and, according to him, had been regularly beaten and injected with what he called "psychotic drugs." Owidi's papers, passport, and identification card had been taken from him, and he no longer had any official existence. To make matters worse, he refused to return home because, perhaps in his neurosis, he suspected that his misfortunes had been facilitated by jealous kin back home.

Owidi's eyes were insane and bloodshot, his speech confused and inarticulate, and his body filthy. He laughed maniacally at inappropriate times while fixing his eyes on mine as if he possessed a great secret; at one point he tauntingly informed me that he was now a ghost, and I let my silence serve as consent. I took him to lunch, but he was so afraid that the waiter had been sent by a prominent opposition politician to kill him that we had to leave before the meal arrived. Somewhat unsettled, I gave him some money and, after securing his assurances that he had some people to stay with for at least the next couple of weeks, took my leave, promising to get in touch. Though I tried to find Owidi again, and asked his former friends of his whereabouts, I never succeeded, and for years I was not certain that he was even alive.

Development, and the struggle over its meaning, was the leitmotif of Owidi's life, and he ended up sacrificing this life for the particular vision of development that he tried to inhabit. Stories such as his testify to the fact that African politics is meaningful, that it consists in efforts to construct viable moral and social orders in contexts that are often ridden with conflict and venality. Owidi's form of social critique and his embodied reconfiguration of development—indeed, his development work—were poetic in their considered contrariness and their formalized, parodic dissembling of respected narrative and political structures. His actions were also constructive, in that development was the idiom through which he articulated the desire for a utopia, and through which he generated an alternative, critical model that energized and incited others—in part because it did strike a common, recognizable chord, even among, and perhaps especially among, those who governed. This consideration of Owidi highlights the point that, in Kenya, the historically loaded concept of development (*maendeleo*), and historically layered debates about it, permeates all levels of existence, encompassing everything from geopolitics to ice cream. All meaningful action is forced to confront it and respond to it, in one way or another. Because it is bent on nothing less than changing the world, the concept inhabits the world of religion and art as much as politics and economics (Ngugi wa Thiong'o's novels are clear evidence of that). The project of this book is to trace the development imagination as it unfolds, and is materialized, in a specific region, often in response to state and international development interventions, thereby showing how people generate models of possibility and mechanisms for positive social transformation that can only be grasped in the particular.

This is a good time to point out, by way of segue, that I went to the Taita Hills after spending a great deal of time listening to University of Nairobi students' apparently contradictory rants about the need to educate and revolutionize "the peasantry" on the one hand and the need to draw on their received values to generate an authentic cultural revolution on the other hand. When I first went to Taita, I had expected to get away from what I took to be this derivative, elite discourse about development and find something more authentically "cultural." But I found instead that development was what Wataita, the people who inhabit the Taita Hills, wanted to talk about, and that they would not shut up about it. When they were not talking about development, or maendeleo, they were enacting and transforming the concept in ways that were constantly in motion, in opposition to the equally shifting category of witchcraft. Wataita live in temperate hills surrounded by a game park (a major source of foreign exchange revenue and a particular model of national development) from which they are effectively excluded; their home, now the seat of the district's governmental and development offices, has long been favored by Christian missionaries and, more recently, international NGOs. It became clear to me over time that "maendeleo" had become their historically derived word for a promise constantly threatened by the manipulative actions of others, epitomized in witchcraft.

Finally, I want to point out that Taita has always represented a refuge for me from Nairobi's gritty meanness and crime and Kenya's at times frightening politics. When I arrived there, I looked down from my stunning vantage to the plains below me, and it was hard to believe that I was in the same country I had been in a mere eight hours earlier. The people seemed different as well—gregarious and genteel. This sense of cool calm stayed with me despite the fact that I eventually came to know the Taita Hills as a deeply troubled place and the Wataita as an oppressed people whose actions nevertheless caused their existence to flow over the historical fact of their oppression. Wataita are familiar with this contrast between the cities of Nairobi and Mombasa and their home, the hot plains below and their cool mountain air, and feel that it is reflected in their disposition: they refer to it as moistness (*kinyoshi*), and it is central to Taita visions of the good life and civic peace (*sere*). "Kinyoshi" is an ecological, social, and psychic condition that those who live in the hills argue is being eradicated by powerful exogenous forces that Wataita to seek to control.

The research for this project was carried out primarily in the Taita Hills, supplemented by frequent visits to Nairobi and Mombasa, where I stayed with Taita civil servants, labor migrants, and preachers, as well as Kikuyu and Luo friends from my University of Nairobi days. After teaching in Taita for four months in 1991, I returned for one month in 1995, and then for twenty months between 1997 and 1999. Since then, I have returned for short periods every other year. In Taita, I lived in the highlands and spent most of my time in the administrative division of Wundanyi, though I traveled throughout the hills and to small towns and villages in the semi-arid lowlands, near the border of Tsavo National Park, where I would camp outside for a few days at a time.

Over the course of a long project such as this, one incurs many debts and obligations, and I would like to take this opportunity to thank as many people as possible. In particular, I would like to express my gratitude to the people of the Taita Hills, especially in the administrative locations of Mgange, Mwanda, Wundanyi, Werugha, Mbololo, and Wesu, for inviting me into their communities and homes with generous enthusiasm, and for helping me whenever possible. Ralph Faulkingham, in the Department of Anthropology at the University of Massachusetts, Amherst, made it possible for me to study abroad in Kenya as an undergraduate, and without his influence my life would have certainly taken a very different trajectory. Dr. Tom Wolfe, formerly of the University of Nairobi Department of Political Science and the United States Agency for International Development, was the person who directed me to the Taita Hills in the first place, and knows far more about the intricacies of Kenyan and Taita politics than anyone I have ever met, myself included.

While countless Kenyans were of assistance, I would like to thank a few in particular. I benefited greatly from the tireless efforts of my research assistant, translator, and great friend, Ngeti Mwadime, who is currently an unemployed, aspiring entrepreneur in Mombasa, and without whose efforts this book never would have been written. I would also like to thank another research assistant of mine, Mathius Ng'ombe, who extended his home in Werugha to me, where I lived for some months. Chombo Shete, formerly headmaster of St. John's Secondary School, offered me the job teaching there when I was an undergraduate student. Chief Clement Hesabu of Mgange Location was extremely encouraging of my research and generously allowed me to attend meetings and juridical disputes concerning a countless array of issues. Edward Mighanyo, who was the first person to instruct me in Kidabida, taught me about Taita culture and history by serving as a constant embodiment of its moral virtues; his sons, Steven and Sebastian, were among my great companions. Eloji the Bartender taught me everything I know about Taita farming and business practices, and Shako the Elder, probably the greatest electrician and radio repairman in the hills, was an unparalleled expert in local politics and history, who always had time for me. My friend Scott Sweet, a Peace Corps volunteer, helped me develop connections in a part of the hills that was new to me. In Nairobi, Dr. Kimani Njogu, formerly of Kenyatta University, helped me to develop contacts and find a place to stay in Nairobi while I was writing parts of the dissertation. His friend, Dr. Njoroge Njenga of Kenyatta Hospital, generously invited me into his home and introduced me to a new network of friends and colleagues, for which I am forever grateful.

I conducted the research with grants from the Wenner Gren Foundation and the Fulbright-Hays Foundation. While in Kenya, I was affiliated with the Institute of African Studies at the University of Nairobi, and I benefited greatly from my interactions with the faculty there. The Spencer Foundation for research related to education helped fund the writing of the dissertation upon which this book is based. I finished the manuscript while on a Rockefeller Fellowship in Religion, Conflict, and Peace-building at the Joan Kroc Institute for International Peace Studies at the University of Notre Dame, and while teaching in the Anthropology and Sociology Department at Spelman College. Jean Comaroff served as the adviser for my dissertation and was instrumental, and very patient, in helping me to develop it further. John Comaroff and Andrew Apter also served as advisers and offered a great deal of encouragement and constructive criticism. During my early stages of writing the dissertation, Brad Weiss, of the College of William and Mary, helped me think about maendeleo in terms of the experience of temporal movement when he offered a paper on development at a 2001 American Anthropological Association panel I organized entitled *Unanticipated Developments*. At the University of California, Davis, Donald Donham (Department of Anthropology) and Joe Dumit (Anthropology and Science and Technology Studies) closely read the book manuscript in its late stages and offered very insightful and supportive advice, which helped me develop the manuscript theoretically. Finally, I would like to thank the African Studies Workshop at the University of Chicago and the Chicago Center for Contemporary Theory, where I presented parts of this manuscript, and Jeff Mantz, Ralph Austen, Nancy Munn, Rosalind Hackett, Nancy Rose Hunt, Beth Buggenhagen, Rob Blunt, Hylton White, Daryl White, Antonia Jo Read, and Anne Marie Makhulu, who each individually offered criticism and advice on parts of this book. David Brent, my editor at the University of Chicago Press, has been instrumental in bringing this book to fruition; his patience and enthusiasm have been invaluable.

CHAPTER ONE

Bewitching Development: The Disintegration and Reinvention of Development in Kenya

The idea of development stands like a ruin on the intellectual landscape. . . . Above all, the hopes and desires which made the idea fly, are now exhausted: development has grown obsolete. —Wolfgang Sachs, *The Development Dictionary*

The problem with you Wataita is that you hate development! —Maji Marefu, a Tanzanian witch-hunter, to an impassioned crowd of spectators in the Taita Hills, upon extracting what appeared to be a human arm bone from near the foundation of a primary school, 1998

Discourse—the mere fact of speaking, of employing words, of using the words of others (even if it means returning them), words that the others understand and accept (and, possibly, return from their side)—this fact is in itself a force. Discourse is, with respect to the relation of forces, not merely a surface of inscription, but something that brings about effects. —Michel Foucault, "Society Must be Defended"

In this era of post-everythings, we are often told that development is dead, despite the fact that the business of international development continues—still largely with a view to reshaping the world in accordance to the "natural" logic of the liberated market. Indeed, the matrix of international institutions that provide interest-bearing loans and aid, such as the World Bank and the International Monetary Fund (IMF) (or, as Kenyans put it, the International Mother and Father), exercise unprecedented control over the legal and economic systems of nation-states in the global South. But the idea that the West (or these days, the East) can bring development to the rest, in terms of global equity or sustainable improvement of living conditions, has been largely abandoned by many of its former proponents (see also Leys 1996). As Andre Gunder Frank put it, "Most development for one group . . . comes at the expense of antidevelopment for others. . . . That is what real world development really means" (Frank 1991, 58–60). Moreover, such high modernist staples as rationalized scientific planning from "above" and the attendant ideology of unilinear progress are now widely understood to be philosophically and morally moribund instruments of imperial control (Mitchell 2002; Scott 1998; Escobar 1995; Ferguson 1994; etc.). Now that many have judged the idea of top-down economic development to have rested on a misplaced and false understanding of particular moments in European history (e.g., the idea of rapid industrial "takeoff"), development has become an intellectual embarrassment that bears the weight of all the criticism directed at high modernism in its totality (cf. Scott 1998). And unlikely players jump on board this critique: even former chief economist of the World Bank Joseph Stiglitz has argued that the guiding principle of the new world order—the market unfettered—is a chimerical product of the secular imagination (Stiglitz 2002).

Much more than a critique of states and global lending institutions is at stake in the deconstruction of development. In this postdialectical, neoliberal world (which Fukuyama [1992] famously referred to as "the end of history"), many have come to think of the idea of unilinear progress as an illusion. Baudrillard put it even more dramatically, arguing that history's spectacular self-realization exploded linear progression and put an end to history: "[History] has become its own dustbin, just as the planet has become its own dustbin" (Baudrillard 1992, 26). And so development, with its explicitly teleological trappings, is left standing awkwardly alone and out of fashion at an angry global rave party where the tempo goes nowhere in particular. But, in this moment of state transformation, high modernist retreat, and global interconnection, history—or better said, historicity (the concept of history and historical unfolding)—is a site of profound meaning making and political struggle throughout the world. And the concept and practice of development is particularly fecund ground for people trying to reinvent their future around changing understandings of their history.

But most discussion of the topic remains wedded to "the development apparatus" normatively conceived. As Marc Edelman and Angelique Haugerud (2005) argue in their introduction to *The Anthropology of Development and Globalization*, two understandings of development dominate anthropology today. The first is deconstructionist, for lack of a better term, and argues that development theory, as it emerged through economic thought and the history of colonial and postcolonial governance, is an ideological instrument that ultimately produces dependency on the West. The most well-known proponents of this idea have been Arturo Escobar (1988, 1995) and James Ferguson (1994),[1] who argued that "development" was never a real condition that existed somewhere, the rules for which could be imparted to "less developed" nations or people by economists, as both modernization theorists and Marxist-inspired dependency theorists in the post–World War II era implied (see also Grillo and Stirrat 1997; Arce and Long 2000). Rather, they have argued, development is an imaginary telos entrenched with ethnocentric cultural assumptions, such as the stage theory of historical progress and the notion that the sovereign Individual and the co-implicated sovereign Nation-State are the agents of this history. These assumptions are grist for a bureaucratic factory (the development apparatus) run by experts whose work allows the "First World" to believe it knows something about the "Third World," which lacks development by definition and is therefore characterized by the condition of needing something that experts may be capable of bestowing. In Africa in particular, development merges with a historically thick discourse about backwardness and savagery through which this continent, "the very figure of the strange," has come to be known, to the West, "under the sign of absence" (Mbembe 2001, 3–4).

Critics of the deconstructionist take on development from within anthropology have argued that the issues associated with development work and thought, such as increasing global inequality, widespread environmental crisis, the spread of virulent new (and old) diseases, and the transplantation of market logics and ideology into virtually every sphere (the "commodification of just about everything" [Graeber 2001]), are real and pressing, and should not be dismissed, especially by anthropologists (see Hoben 1982; Chambers 1983; Gledhill 2001; Rahnema 1997; Rao and Walton 2004; Edelman and Haugerud 2005; de Sardan 2005, to name but a few). These scholars argue persuasively that the world would benefit from ethnographic analyses of existing global development institutions, such as the World Bank and the IMF, as well as transnational social movements and global religious movements aimed at generating development (Bornstein 2005; Finnemore 1997; Fox 2003; Harper 2000). Part of their argument is that the deconstructionist critique that dominated anthropology in the 1980s and 1990s was aimed primarily at large state and international organizations and, tellingly, emerged at the same time as these institutions were being supplanted, from within and without, by transnational governing institutions and the dominant ideology of the free market. As if to prove the Marxian adage that humanity confronts only the social problems that it is capable of surmounting at any given historical moment, social theorists were subjecting centralized planning to critical deconstruction at the very moment when structural adjustment and economic deregulation were changing the rules of the game.[2] Moreover, in criticizing the state, celebrating the power of the indigenous, and viewing global transnational flows as liberating, the deconstructionists gave intellectual voice to neoliberal ideology while neglecting the fact that small institutions, such as grassroots nongovernmental organizations (NGOs), can be as destructive and imperious as large ones (Edelman and Haugerud 2005; Cooke and Kothari 2001).

In this book, I push the discussion of development in a new direction by decisively not defining development as "the sum total of the social processes induced by voluntaristic acts aimed at transforming a social milieu, instigated by institutions or actors who do not belong to the milieu in question, but who seek to mobilize the milieu" (de Sardan 2005, 27).[3] Rather, I trace Africans' actions on the ground as they work to transform the present, a process that also always involves envisioning and modeling the future based on conflicted and contradictory understandings of the past and of other places. Development is particularly interesting because it is a relational concept that entails comparing one's condition to an ideal representation of other places and times to explain and measure circumstances and actions. In particular, I focus on how development becomes a prism for reimagining order and progress when established mechanisms for achieving development—such as state patronage and formal employment—have been thrown asunder. In Swahili, development is translated as *maendeleo* and literally means moving forward toward a specific goal (from *kuenda*, to go, and *kuendelea*, to go on or continue), both in space (expansion over terrain and bringing back things from foreign places) and in time (progressing toward the future). I argue that, beyond this spatiotemporal reference, "maendeleo" is also the name that Kenyans have given to creative energy that manifests for the public good, and that this energy is being put to work in a variety of religious and secular registers with a view to fundamentally changing the world. These new understandings of development have erupted from the fissures of the patronage state, whose mostly simulacral rhetoric of development implied a sustainable future for youth who now reinvent development with themselves at the center (Diouf 2003). Focusing on the Taita Hills of southeastern Kenya, I examine some of the various manners in which development discourse has been used and implemented and how it becomes meaningful in contrast to witchcraft; how different discursive threads, both religious and secular, have merged to produce a distinctive "political imaginaire" (Bayart 2005); and the ways in which the location and directionality of development discourse and practice have changed. When I do refer to recognizable "development projects," I focus on how they have allowed particular groups of people to realize their ambitions in a new historical context, by appropriating things and procedures locally associated with withheld powers (such as that of the state bureaucracy) for themselves.

By writing about Kenyan understandings of development, I wish to demonstrate the power and pitfalls of hope in Kenyans' lives in an effort to palliate the Afro-fatalism that characterizes public, and much academic, discourse regarding the state of affairs on the continent. Rather than generalizing about ideal-typical kleptocratic states and necropolitical pseudostates, I assume that, in any specific African context, an intensity of moral debate and action exists, coupled by efforts to construct viable moral and social boundaries that can mitigate the impact of violence, greed, and death from within and without. I examine social history as well as the ethnographic present in a particular place, focusing on how people have lived on the ground, and how they have worked to make sense of and control the growth and decline of putatively rationalizing processes, such as state and market expansion. While these imaginative actions engage with national and global forces and idioms, they take local forms and are grounded in local practices. It is partly for this reason that I focus a great deal on witchcraft (see below); the concept of witchcraft locates badness in particular places, and in particular kinds of activities, and witchcraft beliefs always imply antiwitchcraft actions, or attempts to control witchcraft. In much of Kenya, ideas about witchcraft and development operate in tandem, as that which needs to be excluded for a particular idea of society and history to emerge is condensed in ideas about witchcraft, and in witchcraft accusations. Historically, these local ideas about witchcraft, grounded in localized social relations and understandings of the relations between means and ends, have been projected to the national level, just as the formerly expert discourse of development has come to permeate society, the two ideas coalescing to shape a distinctive social and political imaginary.

The Meanings of Development

In the West, people typically refer to development in three senses. The first is synonymous with progress and does not necessarily imply any intentional development intervention. The second posits and rationalizes a global status hierarchy, referring to the condition of possessing that which other people desire—that is, of being developed in relation to a developing world—or of lacking a certain set of things, and so being undeveloped or underdeveloped, and thus prompted by desire to acquire development. The third, related, usage, around which the entire development industry is built, refers to planned interventions aimed at generating improved standards of living in less developed parts of the world. Kenyans know about, and invoke, all of these meanings, in addition to a few others.

In Kenya, development is, as Ivan Karp has noted, "a fundamental feature of national and political discourse," which differs markedly from the "technocratic" discourse of development articulated by northern nation-states and international organizations (Karp 2002, 87). For example, Karp notes that the term can refer to the process of growing up (*umendelea vizuri!*, "you have developed well" in Swahili), and becoming a socially recognized adult. This usage has indigenous roots, but it also echoes the colonial regime's use of the word to imply that the entire African population was slowly "developing" into adult Europeans, and therefore still required careful tutelage (see below; see also Karp 2002). In this quotidian, intersubjective sense, the term has long had a masculine connotation, referring to a man developing or attaining development (*amepata maendeleo* in Swahili), a condition symbolized by a house of one's own, a wife and children, and perhaps a fattened physique. Because it implies spatial and temporal expansion, development runs parallel to witchcraft, which also allows for the extension and multiplication of the person—witches move rapidly from place to place unseen, through means that are secret and unknown. One major difference is that, in most understandings of the concept that I am familiar with, true maendeleo is supposed to harm no one and be open to public scrutiny and inspection; it is not supposed to be occult, or secret and remote, at least not for the people who imagine themselves to be included in the projected community envisioned in any specific use of the concept.

Linked to the idea of development as expansion is the notion that maendeleo consists in the adoption of innovations from other parts of the world. In a corollary sense, maendeleo implies inventiveness (potentially in anything from clothing to sex to cuisine to agriculture to electoral procedure) and the concomitant willingness to transgress social and political norms and mores (Wataita refer to such people as those who "love development"—*wanapenda maendeleo sana*); hence, something like progress. But central to the Kenyan idea of development is that, although people can realize this state through their actions—some more than others—there is, and probably will always be, more development elsewhere than in Kenya. Development, then, is imagined to exist in another place (another person, another village, another ethnic group, another country, another time), and African state officials have at times promised to give a taste of this thing development to the public as a gift in exchange for the equally enigmatic gift of loyalty. Thus it is that "maendeleo" can also refer to gifts that come unexpectedly, indeed seeming to drop from the sky, in much the same way that high-level witches bestow unexpected gifts in order to seduce desperate people into their cults (see chapter 3).

If development implies moving forward and appropriating new things along the way, Kenyans also invoke the term to refer to an inevitable, as opposed to constructed, future, which "backward" or "savage" people (be they powerful or powerless) resist at their own risk. This sense of the term has origins in the colonial encounter but is also informed by Kenyans' knowledge of things they believe exist in the present, in other parts of the world. This tension in local understandings of development—that it implies action as well as waiting for something withheld—comes to light in local debates about what development means and the kinds of attitudes that are most likely to generate this state. Finally, we will see that Kenyan understandings of development are related to competing understandings of temporal unfolding, and that different groups of people work to assert their control, or sovereignty, over this unfolding, and in the process try to insinuate themselves in history. Thus, when Kenyans debate the definition and nature of development, they also pose questions such as the following: is development always headed in a single direction (say, forward in time), and is it the case that the taken-for-granted means of achieving development are universally valid across time and space?

Development as an Act of Refusal

Each of development's different meanings has a history, or rather histories, yet none of them, either alone or in combination, can account for the fact that Kenyans continue to invoke the concept of development despite the fact that, as they are quick to admit, it has been abused so often that it often seems absurd and ridiculous. And certainly none of these meanings can begin to account for the passion with which many Kenyans engage the idea. To understand this passion, I argue, we have to recognize that development only makes sense for Kenyans in relation to an opposite that is being rejected. In Kenya that opposite is not necessarily tradition (the rhetorical opposite of modernity), for many have long seen tradition in largely positive, or at least ambivalent, terms, and as something not necessarily inimical to development. Rather, development is largely understood in contrast to witchcraft, or *uchawi*, which can be synonymous with either modernity or tradition, depending on the type of witchcraft that is being considered. This perceived tension between witchcraft and development is more or less national in scope and scale (although see below for exceptions) and is the outcome of a combination of distinct, coalescing, discursive threads: one of these is rooted in colonialism and the equation of African culture with witchcraft and Satanism; another thread is Christian and concerns the imagining of a time of redemption from evil and suffering; and yet another thread has roots in African understandings of work, virtue, and reconciliation, in which selfishness and greed are held to threaten public prosperity.

One of the most important aspects of the Kenyan concept of development is that it usually implies rejection of a status quo—whether in everyday life or in formal local or national politics—and so in everyday practice it can refer to the refusal of engaging in anything from petty family and neighborhood quarrels, to the practice of taking bribes, to obsequiousness in the face of powerful people, to adherence to senseless traditions, to blind submission to the false tokens of modernity (such as fancy cars, new suits, and cell phones). This oppositional capacity sometimes manifests in very dramatic and effective ways, as when the Nobel Prize winner Wangari Maathai successfully opposed the construction, by President Moi and his business associates, of what was to be the gigantic Kenya Times Media Complex in Nairobi's Uhuru Park in 1989. In the process, Maathai articulated a countervision of development that coimplicated womanhood, nature, and the development of horizontal sociopolitical alliances for and against an exploitative, elitist, and male-driven development that leeched economic and moral value from the nation. "Maendeleo" thus implies action in the sense Hannah Arendt employed to speak of original, inchoate activities whose outcomes are unknown, but that echo into the future: "it is in the nature of beginning that something new is started which cannot be expected from whatever happened before" (Arendt 1958, 46). More specifically, development can be defined as action that occurs because passions have been aroused against venal reality and toward utopia; this passion against injustices in the present mobilizes people to act in ways that are often not practical or effective, and that in retrospect do not always make sense, even to the actors involved (such as the witch hunt discussed in chapter 9). Nonetheless, these actions leave traces—a new word, a new expectation, a new committee—that are picked up by subsequent generations and become the staging grounds for later struggles.

Because development implies refusal, and therefore also sacrifice of self, it is also an invitation to enter into a dialectic that moves toward a desired goal and away from a reality that is represented as the antithesis of development. Saying "no" to the world as it is, which is implicit in all invocations of the concept of development (even if sometimes the utterance is in fact a ruse), is aided and abetted by the act of representing negative aspects of the social world in the most diabolical ways possible, naming abuses as a prelude to acting on them (Siegel 2006). In this way, standardized nightmares, in the sense that Monica Wilson (1951) used the term, are productive, because they involve representing aspects of everyday life in a way that evokes charged emotional reactions and widely shared cultural and political memories (or, more frequently, misremembered events or images). The productive dissembling of the world as it is, or as it is represented to be, is accomplished by making it appear mad and demonic, so the idea of development generates the idea of witchcraft, and vice versa. Development refers to creative action; witchcraft refers to socially destructive action; and society is the ultimate object envisioned, mapped out, and delimited in the national Kenyan discourses of development and witchcraft. As Erica Bornstein has put it in reference to the development discourse articulated by Christian NGOs in Zimbabwe, "Witchcraft interfered with development. . . . Embedded within the development discourse of ambivalent progress existed its inverse: the evil of Satan and witchcraft" (Bornstein 2005, 141).

Development, Tradition, and Modernity

Development thus also implies acquiring access to the universal, or something outside the experience of most Kenyans, the presence of which Kenyans are nonetheless aware and whose terms they have often mastered without fully realizing that they have done so. The idea of development, then, functions as a Sorelian myth promising universal belonging while always coming up against the constraints of local realities. This conflict between the universal ideal and the particular reality creates all kinds of paradoxes, such as the ethnic revival movement that tries to generate a universal Kenyan culture by converting everyone in this country of forty-plus ethnic groups to "Kikuyu religion." Typically, then, development implies modernity, but not in a simple and straightforward way, and the concept is more powerful than modernity, in part because as an act of rejection it precedes qualification, and so can be qualified in many ways. It can also be invoked by conservative forces that want to clamp down on creative change, but in the process these agents of conformity expose themselves to the most virulent critiques and risk being permanently unsettled.

Ideas about which actions might constitute witchcraft or development draw on understandings of tradition and modernity, which are themselves products of collective memory or mismemory, typically of events or practices that were never experienced by the actors involved. These memories are sifted through often ironic sources, such as the "common sense" of the European colonial period regarding African reciprocity, filtered through a Ngugi novel, come to life as a violent neotraditionalist movement in the city. Thus the images of development and witchcraft are typically debated through reference to the not-exactly-isomorphic concepts of tradition and modernity, which are in turn symbolized by things, places, and activities (a tree, a greeting, a particular boulder, a type of food, a shop, money, etc.). These things embody memories that speak to the future, almost always in a way that admonishes the present.

As concepts, development and witchcraft thus stand in relation to tradition and modernity as actions stand in relation to things, and as two different potentials of the uncanny. But the relationship between the terms "witchcraft" and "development" and the terms "tradition" and "modernity" is not, and probably never was, a stable one—and still less stable is the relationship between actual things and practices and all of the aforementioned conceptual categories. This instability is exaggerated in periodic moments of crisis, when old methods for generating development appear absurd and are sometimes represented as demonic—as in the case of the Satan rumors of the 1990s, in which the state and schools were portrayed as the primary mechanisms through which the nation was being sold to the devil through the machinations of an elite clique of devil worshippers. In general, development implies, for Kenyans, achieving control over both tradition and modernity, as well as all of the real things to which these concepts refer.

Development as the Appropriation of Other People's Characteristics

In practice, for Kenyans and Wataita, development typically involves the adoption of other people's practices, or practices embodied in objects, with a view to re-creating oneself or the society with which one identifies. This adoption can be interpreted as a kind of memory appropriation, for the things being diverted always have some local associations, even if they are new things, such as human rights discourse or a computer class. The location from which these practices are adopted and refabricated may be the West or China, but it may just as well be the local past, or a combination of both, and there need be no coherent or enduring position regarding from where, and from whom, one should appropriate. Despite this polysemy, symbols of order, power, and rationality figure prominently here as worthy objects of appropriation and domestication—bureaucracy in all of its forms, including the committee; the record book; the honorific; and powerful discourses of rights, law, and science. Often these things, such as record books and the practice of keeping minutes, have at some point been associated with the Kenyan state, and are appropriated at the same moment as the state is rejected as being backward and enmired in witchcraft and savagery. In fact, the act of appropriating these objects is typically synonymous with the condemnation and demonization of the other from which they were appropriated. Thus the public poaches ideas about democracy and the value of cultural heritage from the international world of NGOs, media, and international monetary institutions at the same moment as they reconceptualize those institutions as sinister and destructive. This practice of "structuring one's identity in opposition to the other by assimilating the latter's prestigious and efficacious cultural characteristics" tends to have enduring effects that may have nothing to do with the purpose for which the objects and practices were originally appropriated (Christophe Jaffrelot, quoted in Bayart 2005, 37).

Again, the idea of development is always invoked in relation to another place or time, in comparison to which Kenya is temporally and spatially "behind." For example, my unemployed, thirty-year-old friend Rasta was acutely aware of the power of other places, particularly the United States. He tried to acquire mastery over the power of those places and to uncover their mysteries from his inconvenient vantage in the Taita Hills, which he often perceived as a prison, preventing his access to better, more universally true things. Steeped in American films that he watched studiously on bootlegged videos at private video houses in his town's market, he often referenced them to make sense of, and act on, his own personal situation. One of countless instances occurred when we were walking up a steep incline: Rasta stopped, cast his hands about the air, and, quoting Sean Connery's ex-convict character when he introduces Nicholas Cage to Alcatraz in the film *The Rock*, intoned, "Gentlemen, welcome to the Rock!" Not only did Rasta thereby reference his familiarity with an American movie while equating his home with Alcatraz, but he also implied that he recognized his situation in relation to his understanding of how things were in another, more developed, place. That is to say, he understood himself and the Taita Hills relationally, and he felt in some important way more a part of that imagined, withheld culture than his own. The walls of his room, festooned with advertisements culled from eviscerated magazines, were testimony to the fact that, like all of his fellows, he was painfully aware of a parallel "economy of desired goods that are known, that may sometimes be seen, that one wants to enjoy, but to which one will never have material access"—a feeling that Achille Mbembe argues is fundamental to the contemporary African experience (Mbembe, quoted in Ferguson 2006, 192). And yet, as conceptually connected as he was to a society that he never visited, Rasta nonetheless inhabited recognizably Taita understandings of the world. In the very same conversation in which he referenced *The Rock*, I tried to shock him by telling him a story about 800-pound "shut-ins" in the United States who occasionally had to be rescued by the fire department. Rasta whistled to show that he was impressed and, reiterating the common Taita equation of fatness with health and well-being, wistfully intoned, "There sure are some healthy people in the world!"

To be sure, Rasta moved between two imagined worlds, and had largely mastered the terms of both. But rather than voluntaristically "merging" the indigenous and exogenous "to create modernities that are not reducible to either but superior to both" (Nyamnjoh 2001, 111–39), he felt the power of the local thrust inexorably upon him. In particular, though he spoke English better than most American undergraduates, he found his progress in life thwarted by the resentments, manifested as inherited curses, of his grandfather's dead co-wife, a person who had never left the hills (see chapter 4). Like many of his fellow youth, Rasta experienced locality and the past as synonymous, and both manifested in his life as irritation. His goal was, whenever possible, to bring the power of the past and modernity under his control. During my fieldwork in the Taita Hills, I discovered that most people living there seemed to feel that they had lost control over both "tradition" and "modernity"—that the local and the urban had turned against them and left them to fend for themselves. In the Taita Hills, *fighi* protector shrines embodied the irritating, even deadly, character of the past when, like machines gone mad, they killed the very people they were supposed to protect, either because they could not recognize contemporary Wataita as Wataita or because their senior male programmers (the ritual specialists) had forgotten how to command them correctly (see chapter 5).

The Respatialization and Retemporalization of Development in the Context of Decline

In order to understand development in Kenya and/or Taita, we need to know not only what development means but how the meanings change in relation to historical conditions, such as structural adjustment programs. As Mamadou Diouf has argued with respect to youth in urban Senegal, the exclusion of large groups of people (especially, but not only, youth) from the "bankrupt national development project" has underpinned the emergence of a new "geography of possible developments outside the conventional images of success," in spaces that escape state surveillance and administrative control (Diouf 2003, 5; see also Simone 2004). In the process, development has joined forces with the related concept of democracy to imply the popular rejection of an oppressive state, as well as the irrepressible democratic force that powerful leaders try, at their own peril, to quell. Thus, in the 1990s, the idea of progress was turned against the erstwhile bearers of development, such as former President Daniel arap Moi and his inner circle, by the Kenyan masses, who rejected his leadership as backward and his tempo as slow and old, in comparison with the youthful, progressive forces that surrounded him—such as the opposition political party FORD, whose name suggested the inventiveness of Henry Ford and modern capitalism. This active, transgressive meaning of development was best expressed in the phrase, common during the Moi years, "we want *maendo . . . leo*." Here development (maendeleo) was modified to refer to actions (maendo) performed today (leo), a usage that cut against the idea of a natural, slow development manifesting behind people's backs, for which citizens and politicians had to patiently wait (epitomized by Moi's *Nyayo*, or "footsteps," philosophy of development, which suggested painstaking following upon a fixed course) (Moi 1986). In the process of becoming disembedded from the state, the concept of development became linked to everyday practices such as getting married, and to the forging of new subjectivities through religious conversion. For example, it is now common for people to speak of the marriage process as a development project, and even to go about fund-raising for it by organizing an impromptu *harambee*—a term of official origin (coined by Jomo Kenyatta) referring to large public projects, such as schools and medical dispensaries (see below).

This shift in the concept of development implies a respatialization of the term as it becomes unhinged, both in thought and in practice, from a central location and former point of entry to the outside world (e.g., Nairobi, the State House, or the university). At the same time, the state is no longer understood as a vertical, all-encompassing entity operating from on high, as in the old days when President Moi was synonymous with the state—"*L'etat c'est Moi*," the educated joked, while his supporters greeted him by pointing their fingers to the sky and screaming, "Moi is up high!" (cf. Ferguson and Gupta 2002). Rather, the state and its agents are today perceived as being on the same level as the citizenry, with all of their vices and temptations. Sometimes they are even depicted as living underground, as in the rumors about devil worship, which depict subterranean states and cities. Meanwhile, as ideas about witchcraft are projected to the national level, their nature has changed, as the demons with which people bargain or do battle are now conceptualized as universal rather than local (as demons rather than ancestors).

This respatialization is coupled by a retemporalization, which is dependent on the collective feeling of decline—of being behind in relation to where one was before, and in relation to where others are imagined to be (Ferguson 1999, 2006). This sense of lagging behind implies jealousy of others, and even of one's former self. Specifically, in Kenya, time is no longer only experienced as future-oriented movement, as virtually all Western thought from Condorcet to Baudrillard has presumed, but as a fraught process that is sometimes moving forward, sometimes halted, and sometimes moving backward. Ordinary people experience this backward movement in their daily lives, in a way often synonymous with being "tied" (in Taita, a term also used to refer to bewitchment) at home, and compelled to depend on kin and neighbors (see also Ferguson 1999). In this context, progress can be conceptualized as a kind of backward movement, or rather retracing, as people fall back on collective memories to generate alternative paths to progress, some of which lie in received understandings of ethnic or regional tradition. While the subversion of forward movement reflects crisis, as Ferguson suggests in his critique of the liberal relativist notion of "alternative modernities," it also opens up new opportunities for thought and action, as well as new networks (such as connections between villagers and international patrons, mediated by NGOs) that bypass the state and whose emergence is already prefigured by the aforementioned transformations in thought. As Ferguson (2006, 191) admits, "Such new understandings of the temporal dynamics of social and economic well-being... may bring with them new strategies through which people seek to secure their own futures." One of these strategies, he points out, is escape, but others are available as well, such as Pentecostalism and autochthonous revivalism (Meyer 1998; Diouf 2003). While some may doubt the efficacy of such strategies, we cannot help but acknowledge that Kenyans as a whole are impassioned by the overwhelming fantasy of all that has not yet happened, but could happen. The future remains a great unknown, and it may be that positive transformation can come through unlikely means. As Colin Leys (quoted in Edelman and Haugerud 2005, 121), critiquing the economistic bias of Western development thought, has argued, "what about the effects of the passions aroused in religious movements, or the conservatism, loyalty, discipline, etc., embodied in cultural norms, or the reforming or revolutionary zeal generated by class or national feelings, all of which seem to have played no less crucial parts in determining economic performance at one time or another in history?"

Having laid out the thrust of this book regarding development, I want to discuss, briefly, where I am situating myself in relation to two major discourses, the first being the anthropological literature on witchcraft, and the second being the historical literature on Kenya. The second section, on Kenya, shows how development in Kenya has come, over time, to take on the particular implications that it has.

Witchcraft in Neoliberal Kenya

In his groundbreaking work on witchcraft and modernity, Peter Geschiere conveys the idea that witchcraft in Cameroon is a form of power. He describes the thrill his informant, Meke, experienced when he found himself stranded with Geschiere in a forest where invisible witches were believed to flourish. According to Geschiere, Meke was excited because he was close to power (Geschiere 1997; expanded upon by Siegel 2006). Like Meke, Wataita and many other Kenyans find the idea of witchcraft terribly exciting, and they describe the practice as an addiction that gradually hardens the practitioner, who eventually feels no remorse in killing people. Rather, with each murder the witch feels pride and a thrill at this testimony to his growing power. In the process of bewitching, then, the witch ultimately sacrifices his own humanity, but many innocent others are sacrificed along the way. This destructive sacrifice is present in all Taita understandings of witchcraft, and the equally ethereal concept of development is closer to the idea of productive sacrifice, a true gift in the sense that Derrida uses, contra Mauss, to refer to something bestowed without any expectation of return (cited in Siegel 2006, 5).

I use the term witchcraft (*uchawi* in Swahili, *βusaβi* in Kidabida) liberally in this book (as many Kenyans do) to refer to the destructive power of selfish desire, which sometimes causes fantastic things to happen. While Westerners tend to define witchcraft as a type of magic, the extraordinary nature of witchcraft beliefs were not what distinguished witchcraft from other kinds of action for Wataita, and for many Kenyans. In Taita, witchcraft implied secretive and destructive, and not necessarily magical, action that threatened and resisted the (imagined) peaceful and productive sovereignty of the group in question (see chapter 3). In turn, the symbolic elements that gave shape to any specific witchcraft belief or accusation condensed and communicated the substance of these perceived social threats. However, the extraordinary, supernatural aspects of witchcraft were commonly discussed, if only because people recognized that these actions and the emotions that underlay them were powerful, and powerfully tempting, and so had to be controlled for society to endure and prosper. In this book I am concerned with two major aspects of witchcraft. The first concerns how notions of witchcraft make sense of inscrutable social, political, and economic processes in culturally sensible ways—that is, the metaphoric and imaginative dimensions of witchcraft. The second concerns how people try to control and manage witchcraft, where their attempts to manage it lead them, where they locate it at different historical moments, and what conclusions they draw from perceived instances of it. Each of these lines of inquiry draws on long-held anthropological understandings of witchcraft—in particular, the idea that society is created and strengthened by people imagining and talking about what lies outside of it.

In a foundational gesture early in the history of modern anthropology, Evans-Pritchard argued in 1937 that witchcraft beliefs among the Azande people of the western Sudan were rational in two major senses, one epistemological and the other sociological (Evans-Pritchard 1993). On a conceptual level, Azande thought concerning witches provided a social explanation for misfortune, and thus went beyond Western philosophy without being inimical to it. The notion that the invisible actions of others could be responsible for one's misfortune was sensible, Evans-Pritchard argued, given a social context of conflict-ridden interdependence among kin and neighbors, and the manifold opportunities that Zande society afforded for offending people. Evans-Pritchard also argued that Azande witchcraft beliefs were rational in a sociological sense because they tended to foster social cohesion. Thus, witchcraft beliefs provided a model of antisocial behavior in the figure of the witch, as the desire to avoid being accused of being one encouraged the production of shared moral values and social habits in lieu of powerful regulating institutions such as states. Also, witchcraft beliefs, and accusations arising from them, allowed repressed social conflicts to rise to the surface, where they could be addressed through the Zande system of oracle divination. Finally, these beliefs functioned in the strict sociological sense that interested Evans-Pritchard (which is less relevant for my analysis) because they reaffirmed the power of the Zande princes, who controlled the oracles and who, in principle, could not be accused of witchcraft by commoners. Witchcraft and witch-finding, Evans-Pritchard argued, had to be understood in relation to one another, because witchcraft beliefs only made sense given the political apparatus through which these beliefs were enforced and systematized, and through which witches, and badness, were located.

Picking up on Evans-Pritchard's (1993) insight that witchcraft provides a social explanation for misfortune, a host of scholars have, over the years, extended his conception of the social to embrace the spectrum of social changes often referred to as "modernity," and have argued that witchcraft beliefs constitute a localized idiom for making sense of total social and economic crisis and change, while sometimes becoming a mechanism for acting on structural transformations (see, for example, Gluckman 1954; Comaroff and Comaroff 1993, 1999b; Geschiere 1997; Moore and Sanders 2001). Monica Wilson's concept of the "socially standardized nightmare" has been particularly productive: specifically, this concept suggests that witches and similar shared preoccupations with the horrific (such as vampires, alien abductors, child molesters, and terrorists) focus the collective imagination on a condensed, and exaggerated, visual representation of a particular society's fears at a specific moment in time (Wilson 1951). By examining these symbolic representations in their specificity—by asking why the spirit familiars that coastal Kenyans call *majini* bestow gifts of cash in exchange for the blood of livestock and children, for example (see chapter 3)—anthropologists derive a picture of what a society, or particular elements of it, are concerned about. They also develop a sense of where people are focusing their collective energies.

I take Wilson's concept one step further and argue that standardized nightmares are hieroglyphs that provoke action oriented toward the production of a positive future, which the nightmare illuminates by warning of the potential consequences of doing, or living surrounded by, evil. For example, during the 1990s, the national Kenyan discourse about secretive devil worship rituals and satanic business transactions, involving the sale of drugs, babies, and organs in the highest reaches of government, was one of the ways in which notions of public accountability and transparency became popularized through the media and churches and became desired by a wide swathe of the population. It was the figure of the human organ–stealing, land-grabbing devil worshipper who sold out national futures to international patrons that helped bring the Moi regime to an end, and that goaded the public into imagining a more democratic future (see also Blunt 2004). Witchcraft is thus one of the conceptual mechanisms through which development comes to be known for the public through negation.[4] This notion builds on the insight of a number of scholars who have stressed that witchcraft beliefs are not merely a commentary on events and processes, but a productive mechanism for influencing events, particularly at the level of national and regional politics (Geschiere 1997; Rowlands and Warnier 1988; Niehaus 2001).

Many have pointed out that African concepts of witchcraft are local idioms for making sense of inequality and extraction (Geschiere 1997; Comaroff and Comaroff 1993; Schmoll 1993; Auslander 1993; White 2000; Smith 2001), and that these ideas have long framed state-society interactions, as well as African understandings of capitalism. As James Ferguson (2006, 72) has put it, "Most generally, the production of wealth [in much of Africa] is understood to be inseparable from the production of social relations.... A common axis of contrast is an opposition between honest 'sweat,' which builds something shared and socially valued, and trickery or artifice through which one exploits or 'eats the sweat' of another." Geschiere (1997) has argued that witchcraft in Cameroon has an ambivalent relationship to capitalism: On the one hand, accusations can be leveled against elite expropriators, and thus can have an anticapitalist and a counterstate dimension. On the other hand, elites also deploy witchcraft accusations against jealous subordinates back home in rural areas and thus assert, idiomatically, that capitalist accumulation is morally acceptable and socially beneficial (see also Rowlands and Warnier 1988). Geschiere (1997) also describes witchcraft as a form of renegade power to which the state, through its efforts to control, ends up submitting itself. In this way, the Cameroonian state appropriates the discourse of witchcraft for itself, in the process becoming subject to local understandings of power and rationality. Thus, according to Geschiere, witchcraft beliefs reflect widespread social and political anxieties; have become the idiom through which political and economic conflicts are understood; and have a polarizing effect that parallels and feeds structural divisions in the society (the rural vs. the urban, the rich vs. the poor, the old vs. the young, men vs. women, etc.).

This polarization, reflected in and augmented by witchcraft beliefs and accusations, is especially acute in neoliberal times, as social classes and ideological perspectives have become ever more divided, and as the center of politics is increasingly difficult to discern, and thus open to speculation about occult manipulation (Comaroff and Comaroff 1999b; Ashforth 1999). Certainly, Geschiere's (1997) argument that witchcraft beliefs and practices flourish in a political environment characterized by secrecy is particularly applicable to the neoliberal moment, because there is great confusion among citizens as to what is happening to the structures they have known, if not always relied upon, for generations (see below). In Kenya, witchcraft discourse made sense of the national rupturing of signs and referents (for example, schooling and the good life, the state and the nation, work and prosperity, among many others), and in Taita this semiotic incoherence permeated family life. In particular, witchcraft discourse highlighted the stress placed upon families in times of crisis, and the "cracks," as Filip de Boeck has put it, in an idealized gift economy (2004, 172). As family members found themselves unable to provide for one another, and as men called on long-standing family debts to meet their other responsibilities, the family itself became a site of violence, exploitation, commodification, and paranoia. Some went so far as to accuse their own mothers of bewitching them by secretly administering poison through the food fed to them as gift (see chapter 4). Mothers were, in their view, committing a kind of sacrilege that made the image of women "as the generative force behind the social fabric" (De Boeck 2004, 172) appear as a quaint memory from a bygone era. In reaction, people like Rasta envisioned more "reasonable" ways of organizing family life and exchange through their efforts to control witchcraft (see chapter 4).

This book develops and extends these themes in important respects. First, building on Evans-Pritchard's (1993) understanding of witchcraft as a problem that points to its own solution and that allows people to publicly work through issues and trauma, I argue that witchcraft beliefs have a productive dimension. Witchcraft and development emerged as opposite potentials of the same moment, the same act, and the same idea, and notions of witchcraft gave meaning to the utopian vision of development. As Bornstein (2005, 167) has put it in reference to neoliberal Zimbabwe, "the evil of witchcraft was not produced by progress . . . it was its chorus, its counterpoint. Alongside the evil of witchcraft, the goodness of Christian business and development was articulated." Second, I argue that witchcraft discourse constitutes a field of knowledge that has been central to the work of governance in Kenya, and that it is therefore misleading to isolate it as an essentially African cosmology (see also Ciekawy 1992). This idea harmonizes with the new insight that, in much of Africa, witchcraft ideas emerged alongside colonialism, and they continue to embody memories of its violence (Shaw 2002).

In Kenya, the British colonial regime equated challenges to their rule, as well as to their modernist understanding of progress and history, with witchcraft: sometimes African backwardness itself was viewed as witchcraft, while, at other points, Europeans argued that the rupture of linear temporal unfolding was synonymous with and productive of new forms of African witchcraft (see "Some Historical Background to Development in Kenya" below, on Mau Mau, the 1950s African insurgency and civil war in Kenya). Colonial administrators implemented the first large-scale development projects, such as terracing schemes, with a view to this understanding, and their techniques for confronting threats to state sovereignty focused on combating the new forms of occultism (for example, they railed against their nightmarish vision of the mystically powerful Mau Mau "oaths," which, they argued, the detribalized African saboteurs of the modernist project used to conjure a counterfactual anticolonial sovereign order in the forest). Not that witchcraft ideas are somehow European rather than African; rather, the control of witchcraft has been central to governmentality throughout Kenyan history. The image of the witch is projected outside of emerging sovereign orders and is one of the mechanisms through which people work to make these orders real, and to interject themselves as central to forward-moving history (against repressed history, such as the history of the Mau Mau, which those doing the repressing identify as witchcraft). Conflicts over governance and social order are reflected in new ideas about where witchcraft is lacated, where it is coming from, and the forms that it takes.

Thus it is that this book has more to say about witch-finding than witchcraft, and this is particularly apt given the entrepreneurial and statelike functions of witch-finding in contemporary Kenya (see chapter 7 in particular). Evans-Pritchard's (1993) argument that witchcraft and witch-finding must be understood in relation to one another is a particularly important insight now, because African understandings of witchcraft are probably more susceptible to witch-finders, and the market logics that have produced new forms of witch-finders, than ever before. These days, witch-finders are in every village and urban neighborhood, and a multitude of different kinds have emerged (including a new wave of Pentecostal-inspired preachers), all of whom compete by trying to draw in as many customers, or congregants, as possible. Witch-finders work to spread the belief in witchcraft, and they are probably quite successful, because customers who visit them with a vague sense that they may be cursed invariably have their suspicions reaffirmed. Kenyans are well aware of this dynamic, and joke about it, and I have often heard that witch-finders are the primary mechanism through which people come to know about the specificities of what witches do, and to fear their power.

On the other hand, in the context of neoliberalism, witch-finders offer hope to many frustrated people, and Africans often interpret their work as a publicly accountable and proactive way for communities to establish order at a time when the social fabric seems fundamentally rotten. Witch-finders who engage in private consultations also introduce the consumer to an assortment of reliable patrons in the spirit world, whose loyalty and effectivity can be secured with gifts of cash, through which these spirits become fictive kin. Typically, witch-finders make this kin relationship explicit when they serve as intermediaries between the client and the spirits. One can easily see that, in a society where trust in others—including, but not limited to, state officials—is severely threatened, and in which those who have promised to be providers turn into expropriators, these spirit agents present a model of reliability based on strict rules and ethics, which "real" life has made all too chimerical (after all, there are usually things that the spirits refuse to do, out of principle). But when the stresses of the real world make payment difficult, these spirits can be unforgiving creditors.

One diviner in a Taita neighborhood in Mombasa was renowned for his skill at handling the police: he was particularly famous for using his occult powers to have a police officer who had seduced his client's wife relocated to another city. He also "persuaded" landlords to beg off their tenants and was adept at influencing public officials to provide business permits and other favors. When clients failed to pay him at the agreed-upon time, as they often did, he would appear at their homes with the police, who would end up accusing the client of some kind of crime—often an absurd one such as treason or organizing a secession movement. After spending a few nights in jail, the client would typically hand over a large sum of money to the police—not the witch-finder—out of fear, and the witch-finder would suddenly stop making demands. From an outsider's perspective—mine—it was clear that police and witch-finder were bedfellows, and that at least some of the latter's putative occult powers were derived from his connections with law enforcement. People in the neighborhood agreed that collusion was taking place, but this acknowledgment did nothing to assuage their certainty that the witch-finder was genuine, for his power was confirmed by the fact that he had worked for the police, and perhaps helped them to solve crimes or deal with personal matters. This connection implies that witch-finding can become a means of revenue collection for state officials in a time of crisis, and also that certain state functions have devolved to institutions that were formerly well outside of the state, such that witch-finders can be used for surveillance and information gathering, for example. At the same time, the widespread suspicion that the state was infiltrated by witchcraft—that state officials were using witchcraft or had sold themselves to sinister, secret forces or agents—came to be sensible through these low-level cases of outsourcing, which exposed the vulnerability as well as the reach of the state. Such dynamics give substance to the critique that the state may be involved in witchcraft, and render the accusation more than merely speculative or metaphorical.

Finally, Kenyan understandings of witchcraft and development reference spatiotemporal unfolding, reversal, and rupture. The dynamic conflict between the past and the future, the movement between the two, the fear of turning backward, and the irony that going backward (in the sense of a respect for tradition) may in fact be moving forward are all important aspects of Kenyan popular and official discussions of witchcraft and development. In Kenya, and in all of Kenya's different regions, the idea that the progressive exists in tension with the backward, and that national political life is constituted by their struggle, has a history, or histories. This struggle is constantly performed for the public, and often inverted, as if for dramatic effect: the neotraditionalist movement, Mungiki, attacks the modernist state for being backward and parochial, plagued by self-interest, and incapacitated by greed; the state responds and promises to bring Kenya reeling back into modernity by banning the "criminal" Mungiki and implying that its members are deranged sociopaths linked to international patrons/terrorists in the Middle East.

Sometimes people felt that modernity was being swallowed up by a demonic past—the dangers of moving backward, so poetically expressed in Wahome Muthai's (2000) story "Grazing Cows in the Lecture Theatre" (see below)—but they also felt that they could harness the past to protect themselves from the worst aspects of the present. When the rainmakers in the Taita town where I did much of my work could no longer rely on the support they had been receiving from state officials, they decided to stop tending the fighi forest shrines and to abandon the practice of making rain. They converted to Catholicism and declared that they now recognized their former ritual practices to be devilish. At the same time, formerly staunch Catholics in the town, who had long separated themselves from the "traditionalists," were growing critical of the church (it was infiltrated by elite witches who were "turning development back," *kurudisha maendeleo nyuma*) and suddenly argued that, in the past, when they remembered the ancestors and performed rituals for them, there was abundant rain and little disease. Seizing on the moral ambivalence of the categories "tradition" and "modernity," they changed their position and sought ways of returning to past practices, while making Taita ritual public and transparent. They even suggested changing the name of the local secondary school from the Christian name St. John's to Mvumu Secondary School, after a species of large tree that was once abundant where the school is now located; the tree is frequently used in non-Christian ritual and has deep roots symbolic of kinship. Even though people differed as to their value, held contradictory positions, or transitioned back and forth depending on the context, these symbols of the past constituted a shared mnemonic and were sources of commentary and critique that encouraged people to envision alternative futures.

Development and the Historical Imagination in Kenya

Cows in the Lecture Theatre

Sometime in 2000, I came across a humorous story by the late Kenyan essayist Wahome Muthai, known by the pen name Whispers. The narrative, called "Grazing Cows in the Lecture Theatre" (Muthai 2000), revolves around a parodic argument, delivered in jest: "[Since the street] lights have taken off [turned off for lack of funds] and cows taken over the city, I think Nairobi should never again be called the city of many lights [its local nickname]. It should be re-named the city of many cows." Whispers begins his meandering story by inviting the reader to imagine the world of his perhaps fictive uncle Jethro, whom Whispers tells us was a young man during World War II. He recalls Jethro's sense of wonder upon first witnessing Nairobi, "the city of lights," in 1939, after traveling there by truck from his rural home in the Rift Valley. Jethro was en route to a war that would send him all the way to Burma. This mythic experience of coming to Nairobi and witnessing a modern spectacle that completely transforms the person and his relationship to the world figures prominently in collective Kenyan memories of the historical and personal development of a kind of national self-consciousness—an awakening that went hand in hand with Kenyans' introduction to the constraining world of the Europeans (*wazungu*), and of colonialism itself. In Whispers's version, Jethro comes to believe—naively, from Muthai's point of view—that "the white man" is a friend of God, assuming that his magical ability to "turn night into day" comes from a higher power.

Whispers disrupts his recollection of the city of lights by suggesting that Kenya has been derailed from this sacred path and has in fact gone back in time (and, by implication, to the devil): "In 1939 there were more working lights in Nairobi than there are today" and, he augurs, "Pretty soon, herdsmen and hooligans will be running this city." From there, Whispers's narrative becomes a firsthand account of an increasingly common sighting at the University of Nairobi campus: a small group of Maasai herdsmen in traditional dress, displaced from their former grazing lands in this time of drought, are allowing their cows to feed on the campus grass and flower beds. What begins as a bit of Kikuyu-centric ethnic humor about the willfully antimodern Maasai becomes, for Whispers, a bitter warning about Kenya's retreat from the promises of development, the hopes that once flourished in and around the city of lights. Whispers presents the coeval copresence of incompatible essences and trajectories (the Maasai and the university, the past and the future, the parochial and the universal) as symptomatic of Kenya's decline, in much the same way as colonial administrators did fifty years ago, when the colonial order was coming undone (see below). In Whispers's story, the Maasai warriors stand scantily clad (one warrior inadvertently exposes himself to a campus professor), each precariously balanced on one leg and armed with a club. Yet at the same time, some yards away, a physics professor lectures on "the amount of aerodynamic resistance created by the concave spanning of a Boeing 707. . . ." The Boeing 707 becomes a symbol of speed, transcendence, upward movement, and escape—all central themes in popular Kenyan conceptions of modernizing development—but the professor's lecture has come to seem more absurd than the pastoralists on the campus lawn. Clearly, the narrative implies, it is ludicrous to educate unemployable university students about advanced flight when the countryside is swallowing up the city, when the only useful thing the once proud university can produce is grass for cows and nomadic pastoralists.

In 1939, the quasi-fictional Jethro traveled all the way to Burma to participate in a global conflict that epitomized the ideology of modern universalism. His passing through the showcase city of Nairobi was a personally transformative rite of passage, initiating him into a newly discovered world community. Ironically, at the onset of the twenty-first century, connectedness to the world seemed purely theoretical to Kenyans, akin to abstruse academic lectures about aerodynamics. The reality of the nation was potholed roads, decaying infrastructure, bankrupt treasuries, infinite debt peonage, and curtailed relationships with international patrons. The nation-state appeared to be losing ground to the aboriginal countryside (though the slums of Nairobi continue to account for nearly 90 percent of Kenya's population growth [Davis 2006, 18]), and the national identity, rooted in places like the University of Nairobi Fountain of Knowledge, appeared to be threatened by the proliferation of what Kenyans understood as more primal identities—perhaps something Maasai, but not something Kenyan.

There is, in Whispers's narrative, a sense of disconnection from a modernity symbolized by the city and the university, whose gates are being trampled by Kenya's own self-styled barbarians, the Maasai. At the same time, the narrative suggests that this modernity is being swallowed up by the global circulation of ideas and commodities, for the jocular narrative ends with the two underdressed Maasai herdsmen taking out their cell phones and alerting their comrades in the city about fresh grass on the campus lawn. There is also a symbolic disconnect between the institutions that have stood for development, progress, and the good life and the real futures that they are capable of producing. So the university is simply an edifice, a sign that indexes a more optimistic past, and Whispers implies that it is fitting, if also sad, that Kenya's impoverished and land-hungry citizens be allowed to devour what remains of the carcass of that dead postindependence dream (with the aid of wireless technology).

How did these concepts (tradition, modernity, and development) become so hegemonic for Kenyan consciousness, and how have they become unleashed from their former referents? To answer these questions, we need a brief overview of certain key aspects of Kenya's peculiar history, with a focus on development and witchcraft. I begin with the early history of the Kenyan idea of development, nurtured by a state whose managers imagined their creation to be on the verge of collapse—soon to be engulfed by irrational and violent forces that mocked methodical control.

Some Historical Background to Development in Kenya

Colonial authorities perceived themselves as developers even before that concept was explicitly used, and before it was linked to large-scale, state-managed, rural development projects after World War II (Cooper 1996; Cooper and Packard 1997). Africans were perceived as incomplete, and their psychological, moral, civilizational, and economic development could only be realized, it was felt, through controlled contact with more developed, and more adult, persons (Karp 2002). Missionaries in particular had been centrally concerned with inculcating these new dispositions and behaviors from the beginning of the colonial encounter (Comaroff and Comaroff 1991; Burke 1996). But the late colonial project of development was rooted in the legitimation crisis facing late colonial empires. As Frederick Cooper has put it, "What was new in the colonial world of the late 1930s and 1940s was that the concept of development became a framing device bringing together a range of interventionist policies and metropolitan finance with the explicit goal of raising colonial standards of living" (Cooper 1996, 7).

Thus, in late colonial Kenya, development became an official discourse, as well as a state-centered practice, that was principally concerned with the control of Africans' use of space and their movement through space. Mostly, this control was expressed as anxiety about overly rapid modernization and was operationalized in the form of development schemes designed to prevent unchecked modernity from destabilizing the political order. In particular, colonial authorities and settlers were concerned about the disenchanting effects of education, as well as the movement of rural men to the city and back again, where their rebellious attitudes undermined the social order on which colonial rule was predicated. But more than colonial instrumentality was at stake here, because African migrants were moving, it was felt, between epochs, and this rapid conflation allegedly produced a form of schizophrenia in those forced to embody it, resulting ultimately in perversions, such as the inhuman Mau Mau cult of cannibals, baby killers, and sodomites (cf. Carothers 1954). Colonial officials were especially worried about migrant laborers, because they recognized that these workers belonged fully to neither the traditional countryside nor the modern city and seemed to poach indiscriminately from both. Moreover, these migrant youth had developed an individualistic, entrepreneurial ethos, which was, by colonial definition, nontraditional. This new, dangerous sensibility not only cut against the grain of traditional egalitarianism but it threatened the delicate resource base with soil erosion and land pressure, which colonial officials blamed on illegal African cash-crop production and the acquisition of land by a "detribalized" African petite bourgeoisie (Furedi 1989; Throup 1985; Kitching 1980). The Kikuyu were seen as particularly problematic, for their proximity to Nairobi and European Kenyans forced them to personally experience the strain of these epochs pushing inexorably against one another.

During the 1940s and 1950s, the colonial government responded to growing anticolonial sentiments in the city and among allegedly detribalized entrepreneurs in the African reserves by constructing what were meant to be totally transformative, grand-scale, and labor-intensive agricultural development projects aimed at bringing Africans back to the countryside (Cooper 1996, 261–71). These projects developed alongside the rumor that Mau Mau was a disease caused by overly rapid modernization, and the corresponding government attempt to revitalize traditional authority structures, such as councils of elders (Lonsdale 1990; Berman 1991). From the colonial regime's paradoxical point of view, post–World War II development projects, like terracing schemes, were needed to curb modernization and to make the rural areas more productive so as to stem the flow of labor to cities. But terracing was hugely unpopular, because it required gangs of largely female laborers to dig tens of thousands of miles of terraces, causing rural families to lose land to drains, runoffs, and irrigation channels, while also neglecting their own fields. Many Kikuyu also believed that this land was to be alienated to white settlers, or that wealthier kinsmen would ultimately acquire ownership rights to newly terraced land. Colonial administrators regarded popular resistance to these schemes as antimodern, irrational, and even occult and thus, ironically, set the precedent for associating witchcraft with every thing that was outside the control of the state, a discourse that postcolonial leaders would later develop further.

The African insurgency and civil war that white Kenyans came to call Mau Mau was in fact a diversity of revolts, organizations, and movements in the country and the city that threatened colonial sovereignty. It has long been established that the phrase "Mau Mau" was probably meaningless in Kikuyu; it was certainly a neologism, expressing a new phenomenon for both European and African Kenyans (Lonsdale 1992, 426). And yet, for many Europeans, it evoked images of a violent and anarchic past; others, such as Louis Leakey (1953, 1954), argued that Mau Mau had been caused by anomie resulting from overly rapid modernization (in particular, the alienation of youth from villages and senior men and the emergence of a new spirit of individualism fostered by migrant labor and monetization). Thus, Europeans and some Africans (especially senior male Kikuyu) conceptualized Mau Mau as a temporal anomaly: the youths who "oathed" each other in the forest and committed violent acts were opposed to modernity by allegedly practicing witchcraft, attacking the "modern" state, and disavowing Christianity, but they were also not traditional in any simple way.[5] Thus, they vexed anthropologists wedded to a notion of stable tradition vested in elders, as much as they frightened colonial authorities and many senior African males, who depended on the notion of a stable tradition to govern through indirect rule (Lonsdale 1990; Leakey 1954). The Kenyan government commissioner, Frank Corfield (1960, 9), put it succinctly, if defensively, in his *Origins and Growth of Mau Mau*: "This rapid transition [modernization] has produced a schizophrenic tendency in the African mind—the extraordinary facility to live two separate lives with one foot in this century and the other in witchcraft and savagery. This has often been noticed, but Mau Mau revealed the almost inexplicable lengths to which it could go. A Kikuyu leading an apparently normal life would, in one moment, become a being that was barely human."

As the Mau Mau war continued, the Kenyan government reversed its earlier efforts to maintain a putatively traditional and egalitarian rural society, and instead actively sought to create an elite African middle class and to slowly transition Africans into a present that existed for Europeans in the same colony, but from which Africans had been excluded (Leys 1978). Reforms such as land consolidation, credit provision, and the introduction of cash crops formerly banned to Africans were designed to instill a competitive, forward-looking sensibility in African subjects, in the hopes that a vigorous few would emerge as a forward-looking elite vanguard (Kitching 1980).

Thus, from the colonial perspective that developed in the post–World War II era, development was a process at once psychological, cultural, and material and consisted in a movement from one absolute (tradition) to another (modernity). Development was also the work that was done under the management of the state to ensure that this process went smoothly for individuals and society—that it was *controlled*. The most dangerous threat to development was the temporal hybrid—the African who was neither fully modern nor traditional, and who thus had no values, being bound by neither custom nor contract (Lonsdale 1992). Semiofficial documents like Corfield's *Origins and Growth of Mau Mau* and J. C. Carothers's (1954) *Psychology of Mau Mau* were quite clear about how horrible it was that Africans were erupting out of their traditional confines in ways that were not recognizably sequential, according to their understanding of linear progress. They tried to account for the uniqueness and violence of Mau Mau oathing rituals by blaming them on the sinister plots of detribalized Africans; for example, they argued that the criminal (and future president) Jomo Kenyatta had learned about the devil's sabbat while in England and had combined its elements with Kikuyu ones to enslave a confused African public thirsty for leaders and purpose.[6] In this way, formerly quiescent Africans had become zombies whose drugged passivity and self-hate grotesquely caricatured the detribalized African male (Carothers 1954, 169; Leakey 1954, 79–84). In short, colonial development work was largely a struggle to retain the authenticity of absolutes against the threat of too-rapid mutation, so as to prevent chaos. And the late colonial war against Mau Mau was in part a war against ambiguity, at a time when everything was ambiguous. Development work, which we typically understand as being very practical, even banal, was therefore oriented toward the most grandiose and symbolic of objectives: it typified a new instantiation of colonial tempopolitics aimed at managing the flow and sequencing of time, and peoples' experience of time, in order to save the empire and the world.[7] Late colonial tempopolitics did not pretend to limit itself to micromanaging Africans' quotidian experience of time (by introducing new technologies for persuading people to be timely, for example), but, through subtly insidious and grandly invasive new technologies, state agents actually aspired to centrally manage the recurring drama of world history, and the reemergence of the Promethean individual, as these processes seemed to play themselves out, again, at out-of-control speed, in a critical place and time. In the process, they formalized and materialized a discourse of temporal (mis)management that would supply rhythm to the dance of postcolonial politics and resistance right up through the present day.

In the late colonial and early postcolonial periods, mission-educated Africans insinuated themselves in and transformed this tempopolitics by using the British colonial understanding of development as control over time and controlled temporal unfolding (entailing an explicit fear of rapid mutation and vanquished innocence) to argue for a gradual "independence," or paternally guided self-maturation. African nationalists like Jomo Kenyatta were able to establish themselves as interlocutors with the government by representing themselves as a civil alternative to the sociospatial and temporal chaos embodied in Mau Mau. The model of development that these nationalists presented to the Kenyan public and to the world community was one of cooperation and slow transformation—markedly different from the overly rapid modernization, combined with artificial delays, that had allegedly helped to create Mau Mau. At the same time, development implied national sovereignty and state encompassment of the nation through the exchange of "gifts." These nationalists expressed the desire to produce a successful fusion of the African and the European, epitomized by "harambee," or "pull together," which became the slogan of the Kenyatta regime and the official development ideology of the early Kenyan state (Kenyatta 1964). But if harambee at one point epitomized the project of natural indigenous progress achieved through the mediation of the state, over time it became symbolic of the corruption of these original ideals by private interests. For over time, harambee drives became competitive potlatches through which politicians attempted to secure the loyalty of the electorate by demonstrating their expansive power and generosity, supplemented by smaller offerings from citizens. Often the money that elites offered as personal gifts was already earmarked for the region by the government, sometimes money collected from the public went to other regions entirely, and sometimes politicians simply absconded with it, never to return.[8]

During the first decades of the postcolonial era, in much of Kenya "development" became a byword for "rain," or patronage flowing from the state; in this sense it did not imply state sovereignty so much as regional and personal self-realization through the mediation of the state. As Angelique Haugerud has shown, this state-centered conception of development was rooted in the realities of daily life: prior to IMF-imposed structural adjustment, the state was Kenya's primary employer, and its patronage spending on development in the form of roads, schools, electricity, and medical dispensaries were the primary mechanism for establishing control over the population (Haugerud 1995). The Kenyan African National Union (KANU) and its member politicians established and entrenched their political authority over disparate geographical areas by donating funds to community development programs, and a unified single party state was created in the 1960s through the distribution of state resources and development projects to Kenyans who fell outside of KANU's Kikuyu-based power bloc (Gertzel 1970; Wallis 1982; Throup and Hornsby 1998). Beyond Kenya and Africa, development also became the shared idiom of connection between a world defined as "third" and a potential benefactor known as "first": the concept of development gave international donor agencies and Third World states alike a raison d'être grounded in the social and economic improvement of the world's poor (Cowen and Shenton 1997). Development as state-engineered gift giving thus fueled national unification around the sovereign state, to which the concept development also referred.

Thus, "development," by this time transformed by the Kenyan state into the Swahili "maendeleo," became, and continues to be, the ultimate rationale of government (the witchcraft of jealousy was one factor that threatened its existence). Importantly, the related concept of democracy came to be associated, for the public, with the equitable distribution of state resources between ethnic and regional groups, in contrast to the more individualistic one person, one vote idea. Moreover, development and the state became indigenized through state rituals like harambee and patron-client exchanges that were equated with fictive kinship, while rural communities came to be progressively integrated with, and dependent on, the assistance of politicians and other state officials (cf. Barkan 1979). This was a period of dense articulation between the state and development, when the ideology and apparatus of development helped to forge patron-client relationships at all levels of the social hierarchy. But from the beginning, many felt that development had a dirty secret—underneath the surface good intentions lay something sinister, something more like witchcraft. For very early on, Kenya's development policy marginalized the poor by redistributing land and opportunities to elites who could afford to purchase their own property, while neglecting the forgotten Mau Mau insurgents whose image state officials simultaneously appropriated in the name of development (Leys 1978).

Like the colonial regime that preceded it, the postcolonial Kenyan state's developmental rhetoric conceptually ensconced the majority of citizens and their rural communities in a backward and contentious past, while also encompassing the past's virtue and authenticity—as when politicians visited the countryside from Nairobi and admired the "tribal" dances, thus signaling the state's superiority and rationality in relation to these purely aesthetic demonstrations, which it contained within itself. State officials also accounted for resistance to state policies or individual politicians by invoking the universal struggle of modernity over parochial tradition and chaos. As Haugerud (1995, 81) has put it, "In short, when colonial and post-colonial state authorities addressed citizens in the countryside they struck a hazardous moral bargain. The state would protect citizens from civil disorder or 'chaos.'... To reward citizens' compliance and obedience the state would bring the material benefits of 'progress' and 'development.' To the extent that state officials succeeded in equating themselves and the state with development, they made themselves more vulnerable to public critique and contempt, for the failure of development to flow outward to communities appeared to rest on their shoulders. After an abortive coup in 1982, President Daniel arap Moi staged a government crackdown on all forms of perceived protest and opposition, and drew on colonial and African idioms and memories (such as the repressive laws of the 1952–1959 State of Emergency, when the Kenyan government conducted mass detentions of Kikuyu) to create a paranoid political culture where state development was contrasted to society's witchcraft. Moi accused his critics—especially the Kikuyu, who had come to feel increasingly marginalized under his rule—of oathing in the forest again, and thus drew on a combination of colonial-era terror about the Kikuyu Mau Mau insurgents and widespread Kenyan understanding about witches' destructive, nocturnal rituals. He also implied that Africans' witchlike natures (contentiousness and jealousy) made them unready for democracy. Government officials, in their visits to rural areas, reinforced the theme by explicitly blaming "backwardness" (or poverty) on witchcraft, which was also synonymous with resentfulness, and hence opposition to those in power.

While Moi rhetorically equated development with modernity and science, the concept became all the more theological in its ideal, a noumenon that, according to Moi, citizens could only approach through loyalty to the state. At the same time, it became a joke, but like the failed priest who declares his divine love through blasphemy, the fact that development became an object of ridicule only sacralized it all the more. For example, during the years of Moi's presidency, the public was repeatedly reminded, at public gatherings called *barazas*, that they could only develop by following Nyayo, or footsteps, which came to mean the upward path taken by the president and his friends, deviation from which would lead to chaos, violence, and poverty (Haugerud 1995).[9] When politicians came to speak, rural audiences collectively raised their arms to the sky, extending a single index finger upward, in a symbol of unity, as if to the place where development existed, while shouting "Moi Juu" (something like "Moi is high," but not exactly) enthusiastically. At the same time, in an oblique reference to the opportunism of elites, the public came to use the term euphemistically to refer to selfish accumulation, as in the phrase, "I have got a little development" (*nimepata maendeleo*), meaning some wealth, property, a commercial enterprise, a car, or an opportunity of any kind (Weiss 2001).

Beginning in the 1980s and accelerating in the 1990s, the nature of Kenyan society changed fundamentally, as the state appeared to be imploding, while a new global network of institutions was clearly controlling the nation's fate in the name of a vision of development based on the ideology of the free market. In Kenya, the progressive unraveling of the state was widely understood as a retreat from modernity itself, and it also threw the value of formerly all-important structures, such as schools and mainstream churches, into question for many Kenyans.[10] By way of a brief background, in the early 1980s, under President Moi, Kenya began taking structural adjustment loans, all of which were tied to conditionalities; by 1992, annual debt repayments were equivalent to 40 percent of export earnings (U.S. Department of State 1995). After the fall of the Soviet Union in 1989, aid throughout Africa was increasingly linked to "good governance" and democratic reform. Between 1990 and 1992, half of Kenya's foreign aid funding was cut in an effort to pressure Moi to allow for multiparty "democracy" (Haugerud 1995, 202). In 1991, Moi was forced by Western donors to repeal the constitutional amendment outlawing opposition parties and to make way for the first multiparty election since 1965. As in other African nations, such as Rwanda, the Kenyan state, under KANU, tried to hold onto power in the wake of intense political competition; dwindling state resources; and an increasingly critical, activated, and impoverished public. During the first multiparty elections in 1992, President Moi's KANU party diverted money from the treasury and organized the printing and distribution of millions of shillings that were never registered with the central bank—all for purchasing public support for an election that nearly everyone expected the incumbent to lose. According to some estimates, the monetary supply increased by 40 percent during that year, causing an unprecedented fiscal crisis; in the following year, inflation hit 100 percent (Barkan 1993, 94).

Moi thus invited the *wananchi* (citizens) to devour the state, while asserting with force that KANU stood for maendeleo, or development, for and against the disruptive and disgruntled politics of the fragmented opposition, which Moi's government helped to fragment (see Throup and Hornsby 1998). In short, his regime hastened the process through which the sign development was unleashed from its referents and came to appear simulacral. Then, in 1993, members of Kenya's political opposition informed the newspapers of a major corruption scandal that remains at the center of Kenyan politics. Beginning in the early 1990s, government officials and prominent politicians had siphoned over a half-billion U.S. dollars from the treasury, apparently diverting it to Goldenberg International, owned by the Kenyan Indian Kamlesh Pattni. The company was illegally subsidized to export gold and diamonds that turned out to have never existed, despite the fact that official, signed documents declared that these minerals had entered and left the country. State officials were thus outwitted by their own bureaucratic mechanisms and procedures (one could also say fetishes). The Moi regime, and the Nyayo "philosophy" of development, was now widely equated with theft and counterfeiting, as well as the illegal plundering and redistribution of state resources. Meanwhile, international and local NGOs took on many of the development responsibilities that citizens had formerly expected from the state, despite the fact that nearly half of the registered NGOs were apparently fronts for KANU, created so that the party could import duty-free cars (Tom Wolfe, pers. comm.).

After the fiscal crisis in 1993, Musalia Mudavadi, the minister of Finance, initiated what was perhaps the most rapid and total deregulation of an African economy ever seen: Kenya eliminated import licensing and price controls, floated the Kenyan shilling, removed restrictions on the repatriation of profits, dramatically cut public spending and reduced the number of civil servants, and began privatizing a broad range of companies. Then, in 1997, the year I began conducting fieldwork in Taita, the IMF withheld a $220 million aid package, citing widespread corruption, with a particular focus on the Goldenberg diamond and gold importation scandal (Barkan and Ng'ethe 1998). Aid was not resumed until 2000, and was again withheld the following year, apparently because of delays in privatizing the Kenyan telecommunications and power companies. During this time, the period of my fieldwork, Nairobi was literally plunged into darkness, as electricity went out, roads turned into quagmires, and the nation's dependence on foreigners became increasingly obvious and humiliating to all Kenyans. The government responded to the 1997 aid withdrawal by cutting public spending by more than 20 percent and eliminating 60,000 civil service positions (Devarajan, Dollar, and Holmgren 2001; Olowu 1999). During the 1997 elections, as in the 1992 elections, KANU and its member politicians tried to maintain their position by promoting violence against the Kikuyu in the Rift Valley, fragmenting opposition parties, purchasing the services of youth militia to intimidate voters, and buying voters off with money and gifts.

By the end of the 1990s, Moi's concept of a development rooted in national sovereignty seemed less parochial and backward looking than it had ten years earlier, and formerly outspoken critics of the government echoed him by challenging the moral and economic sensibility of neoliberal reforms and by defending state institutions. In a *Kenya Daily Nation* newspaper article entitled, "Welcome to Kenya, the IMF's little colony," Mutuma Mathiu, formerly a vitriolic Moi critic, argued against those who brokered neoliberalism from within, chastising Attorney General Amos Wako for submitting draft anticorruption laws to a "faceless cabal of foreign bureaucrats" at the IMF "before the Cabinet and Parliament had a chance to see them" (Mathiu 2001). Many interpreted the decline of national sovereignty as one aspect of a global conspiracy, and they seized upon the historically entrenched understanding of development as a sacred ideal, arguing that international development institutions were rendering this goal impossible, and were therefore incarnations of evil. In this widespread view, the World Bank and the IMF were false fronts for the transnational corporation known as the Satanic Church, which many Kenyans held was a global organization dedicated to undermining national economies through the importation of drugs, condoms, and used clothing and the exportation of human organs and children (see also Blunt 2004). Consider the following paraphrasal of the remarks of Archbishop Nicodemus Kirima, chairman of the state's official Commission to Investigate Devil Worship, who counseled Africans to "ask themselves why the Western countries are using so much money to bring changes in our society" (*KDN* 1999, 1–2):

> Devil worship has been introduced into Kenya by the international community as part of their campaign to drain Africa of her resources, Nyeri Catholic

> Archbishop Nicodemus Kirima claimed yesterday. The cult, the prelate said, had been brought into the country in a gradual process under the guise of the New World Order "which has completely changed our system to suit the needs of the devil." The Archbishop continued, "In the New World Order, the Western countries first brought capitalism, which came with poverty. Then today we have liberalization and computerization which have left our nations poorer and a clique owning the state." Archbishop Kirima asserted that "these impositions have forced Africa to privatise her public enterprises, which are being bought by a minority rich." This has left a big part of the population living in perpetual poverty, "and therefore they find it hard to resist the devil.... You will try to look for money by all means available as you will find it hard to survive in the liberalized economy."

While this interpretation might seem far-fetched, it bears much in common with the insights of some of the most eminent economists in the world, though it be couched in a different idiom. As Stiglitz (2001, 40) wrote in the *Atlantic Monthly* around the same time, "Because so many of its decisions are reached behind closed doors, the IMF leaves itself open to suspicions that power politics, special interests, or other agendas unrelated to its stated purposes are at play."

The Moi regime appropriated the discourse of devil worship, blaming the failure of the national development project on Satanism, which it in turn equated with transnational crime syndicates, new religious movements, and global youth culture. Schools were cited, by the government and popular rumor alike, as the new factories in which products of the global Satanic Church were processed. To quote from the government's report, "The Kenyan Government Development Plans have, over the years, consistently stated the major educational objective as that of producing properly trained, disciplined and patriotic youth.... However, in the recent past, there has been hue and cry in the country that some evil practices, such as those associated with devil worship, have infiltrated the learning institutions ... and, if not checked, will derail us from accomplishing our educational and national objectives" (Presidential Commission of Inquiry 1995, 90).

The national story about devil worship drew attention to the possession of modernity's vehicles (such as schooling) and caused people to dwell on these threatened sites as places that needed to be either transcended or repossessed by activated society. This concern was related to the fact that structural adjustment had nearly put an end to government-subsidized education. In this era when teachers went without pay for many months at a time (often relying on illegal forms of business for money in the interim), rumors abound of teachers selling drug to students and corrupting the productive promise of young girls (and their bridewealth) by impregnating them. A new cadre of preachers claimed that, when they were students, their teachers used sexual temptation as a recruitment strategy for the Satanic Church (Presidential Commission of Inquiry 1995, 25). These Satanic recruiters offered gifts of illusory value in exchange for enduring futures: they gave their student recruits a poison that "tastes sweet but has the smell of blood," and later came looking for the organs of the student's loved ones (Presidential Commission of Inquiry 1995, 59; later reported on by Njau 1999a). When several girls' schools were set on fire in the late 1990s, many speculated that devil worshippers had offered the girls, who embodied a potential national future, up as a sacrifice. As one newspaper editorial put it in 1999, "Time has proved the assurances from the President [about the existence of devil worship in schools]...as today students torch their colleagues in dormitories with abandon and the nation hurtles painfully over Bombolulu, St. Kizito [school arson cases that resulted in the loss of many lives], and other horrid kaleidoscopes of disaster which people link to devil worship" (Njau 1999b).

Conclusion: Some Cases of Popular Kenyan Development in Action

And each time is like a miracle when after such a shallow, fading period all at once there comes a small upward surge.... This illusion, embodied in the magical date of the turn of the century, was so powerful that it made some people hurl themselves with zeal at the new, still unused century, while others chose one last quick fling in the old one, as one runs riot in a house one absolutely has to move out of, without anyone feeling much of a difference between these two attitudes.—Robert Musil, *The Man without Qualities*

We can extrapolate a few major points about the meanings and uses of development for Kenyans from this brief national history. For colonial authorities, development was a powerful rhetorical device that sacralized domination in a secular idiom, and was thus a state-centered continuation of the explicitly religious idiom of conversion and salvation deployed by missionaries. Late colonial development practice was overshadowed by the attitude of emergency and the shared trauma of the Mau Mau period, and the concept acquired its life or death connotations and its immediacy from this period of crisis and collapse and from the sense of optimism and possibility that soon followed. Despite its religious connotations, late colonial development was synonymous with the modern and the future; it implied the victory of reason over primitivism, superstition, and magic (all of which defied governance). But for Africans, development was something withheld, something spectral, and so too were the objects and institutions that were synonymous with reason and secularism for Europeans (Smith 1998). The idea of development came to embody the overarching desire to break free from the constraints imposed by colonial and, later, postcolonial authority, and also became synonymous with the vehicles of modernity (such as schooling), because they contained and allowed for this transcendent power. Rather than referring to a known telos synonymous with civility and modernity, development became synonymous with the impossible and the absolute, and was permeated by religion and religious imagery of redemption and salvation. Thus, the concept of development, and the means for achieving it, always had the quality of magic, and gaining access to development's fruits in turn often seemed to require recourse to magical powers.

But in recent years, the sign development has become unhinged, and freed, from its referents in two major senses. First, as stated above, it has become dislocated from the state, as communities try to acquire control over the meaning of the concept, and the objects of their desire, while in the process defining themselves as communities. Second, the concept has become increasingly disconnected from the categories of tradition and modernity, each of which seems increasingly beyond the control of any person or community. Kenyan development efforts consist, then, in attempts to acquire control over the future by drawing on memories of the past, and these efforts suggest the emergence of complex relationships with the state, the main originator and former conduit of the concept. Before concluding this chapter and moving on to the Taita Hills, I offer three vignettes that reveal Kenyans in different regions of the country as they attempt to manufacture and envision a localized development by conjuring up memories—or, more to the point, creating memories—of once bountiful hope, vanquished innocence, and all-too-real violence and humiliation. Each occurred at moments of some small hope during the period of democratization and multipartyism that seemed to reach an apex, ultimately, in the elections of 2002, in which Moi's twenty-four-year reign came to a peaceful end.

Mungiki, or The Return of the Repressed

Beginning in the mid-1990s, a neotraditionalist Kikuyu religious movement called Mungiki (the exact meaning of which is debated, but whose best translation in Kikuyu is something like "the activated public/totality") became popular and powerful in the city of Nairobi and some large Kikuyu towns in the Rift Valley. It was composed primarily of impoverished young urban men, and had complicated origins. The desire to pinpoint these origins has dominated Kenyans' discussion of the movement: Who is really behind it, and what do they really want? Is the movement autonomous, or is it controlled by invisible state and international figures? Like the1950s Mau Mau movement, which its members emulate, Mungiki has never been a uniform social movement, although there have been central figures behind it, or behind factions of it, throughout. Nonetheless, many who identify as Mungiki have fabricated a cohesive and strict set of behavioral practices rooted in received understandings of traditional Kikuyu religious beliefs and practices in their effort to purify the national consciousness from the bottom up (Wamue 2001, 2004). Members have claimed to be the inheritors of Mau Mau practice and ideology, and at times they have verbally attacked the government for its enslavement to foreign interests, specifically naming the World Bank. They have mocked the government's, and middle-class Kenya's, commitment to Christian rectitude and have argued that the Christian elite have corrupted Kenya by making the foreign values of individualism part of the common sense of the nation. In 2000, these urban youth famously marched on the president's house and the Masonic church (President Moi had long been rumored to be a member) and threatened to expose the links among national elites, foreign financial backers, and secretive religious cults. Their self-avowed leader, Ndura Waruinge, echoed a national sentiment when he declared that, "Kenya today is controlled by the International Monetary Fund, the World Bank, the Americans, the British, and the Freemasons. It can't initiate its own development and has sold all its properties to Westerners in the name of liberalization" (Mwai 2000).

Mungiki leaders vowed to convert the entire nation to their religion, regardless of ethnicity—a very strange claim, given that the religion was based on Kikuyu cultural practices garnered mostly from ethnographic and literary texts, and so Mungiki was widely understood to be vowing to make everyone Kikuyu, at the same time as they struggled with other Kikuyu over the meaning of this cultural identity. One of their major innovations was that, at least in theory, Mungiki practitioners turned ethnicity into a church/religion into which they could convert people and which non-Kikuyu could choose to inhabit. But the group's vision of Kikuyu and Mau Mau tradition came to be perceived by many as activist attempts to "return the country backwards" to tribalism. In particular, they became infamous for forcefully excising women's clitorises and for attacking urban women dressed in slacks. Moreover, powerful patrons seemed to be deploying these activated youth for their own purposes, such as mobilizing people to vote for particular political candidates. At the same time, Mungiki gangs seemed to become a parallel shadow government (perhaps augmenting the state, in William Reno's [1998] sense of the term, or perhaps sapping its power, depending on the rumor). The group came to dominate the *matatu* (privately owned passenger minivan) transport trade in parts of Nairobi and many large towns, collecting tax and engaging in running battles with the police and matatu operators over the control of matatu platforms (Anderson 2002). This control of transport was widely read as an attempt to capture the public sphere and the currencies of national articulation, and led to volatile speculation about what the Kenyan media now called a "mafia."

By 2002, the media, government, and much of the public converged to blame Mungiki for most gangster activities in Nairobi's slums, where some Mungiki pitted themselves against rival ethnic gangs, raided police stations to free captive members, and controlled access to electricity. The majority of citizens were appalled by Mungiki members' apparent efforts to return the country to the "dark" past, and they wondered aloud whether this group was engineered by powerful politicians (perhaps President Moi himself) to create chaos and confusion. Many held that Mungiki members were a new type of witch: in 2003, people in Nairobi told me that you could easily tell the difference between a Rastafarian and a Mungiki adherent by closely examining their dreadlocks (Mungiki's were frayed) and their eyes (Mungiki had insane eyes, it was said, for they were possessed by demons). Police reports explicitly invoked colonial government studies of the "cult" of Mau Mau from the early 1950s when they described such pornographic Mungiki atrocities as "organ theft, drinking human urine, eating a human being's umbilical chord, sniffing tobacco and burning scents" (Kwamboka 2004). After Moi stepped down, the new government, presided over by the Kikuyu Mwai Kibaki, attempted to demonstrate that the days of unscrupulous and mysterious politics, as well as the era of moving backward, were over by declaring war on the backward-looking Mungiki and jailing many adherents. By extension, the government was also declaring an end to the mobilization of youth gangs, which politicians had used to enforce order and loyalty under Moi. In jailing Mungiki, the government consciously repeated the State of Emergency–era war on Mau Mau's irrationality as farce, while conflating the Moi era with a mythic, savage past.

If for a time Kenyans seemed to have succeeded in defining Mungiki as backward by putting it behind them, Mungiki never actually went away, and this brand name, appropriated by some and thrust onto others, continued to resist any total definition. Moreover, Mungiki adherents appropriated key elements of the Kenyan development vision for themselves, consistently asserting (like Mau Mau before them) that their powerful organization was everywhere, and that it was therefore more capable of generating development than was the state government. In the context of burgeoning street violence and parallel taxing regimes in Nairobi and its environs, Mungiki became a larger-than-life fetish, and independent media helped fuel fantastic rumors about its statelike power. For example, a Mungiki "budget plan" apparently leaked to a minor Kenyan newspaper called *The Spectator* in April 2007 asserted (one imagines, absurdly, but who knows?) that Mungiki possessed 4 billion shillings in disposable income. The alleged "development plan," reprinted in *The Spectator*, directly invoked Kenyan government documents of the same type—though perhaps fictive, readers could not help but wonder how much more so than the government's official plan. In the plan, anonymous Mungiki authors revealed some of their many development projects, including plans to use their own engineers to build high-rise buildings in Laikipia and the implementation of a "youth enterprise fund" and a "women's fund" for which individuals could write funding proposals. The anonymous *Spectator* journalist reporting on the plan seems to gush with a combination of envy, disgust, and respect when he reveals that "Secretariat staff in Mungiki headquarters draw fat paychecks.... Sources of money include matatu routes, rent fees and land leasing, electricity and water diversions, security provisions and special contracts—described as hiring activities."

Exorcising Scotland's Devils

In 2004, St. Andrews Church in Nairobi, the oldest Kenyan Presbyterian church, was either desecrated or cleansed, depending on one's point of view, by high-ranking Presbyterian officials who declared that the country's early Scottish missionaries were "probably devil worshippers" (*Daily Telegraph* 2004). They reached this conclusion from the icons in the church, including the stained-glass windows, which depict snakes and wild animals and which bear symbols allegedly resembling those used by Freemasons. Reverend David Githii declared that now that the church was rid of this "satanic power" the "people have been revived and they are singing much more vigorously," and he encouraged churches in Scotland to take heed and follow Kenya's lead (*Daily Telegraph* 2004). Since the 1990s, Kenyans, inspired in part by Pentecostal literature and teachings, have viewed the Masonic church as the semipublic face of the international Satanic Church. They have linked both to unscrupulous Kenyan elites, who are widely believed to have attempted to turn the nation over to the devil by institutionalizing conflict and deceit (in particular, by creating ethnic and class conflict and institutionalizing corruption). However, these iconoclasts went further by arguing that national modernity had been corrupted by foreign agents from the very beginning of the colonial encounter. According to Githii and others, this semantic incoherence—the confusion of damnation for salvation since the beginning of colonialism—had made the production of peace and prosperity impossible, because people had been doing and saying the wrong thing for time immemorial. But not everyone in Kenya agreed with Reverend Githii. Reverend Timothy Njoya, a well-known multiparty activist in the early 1990s, criticized the group for condemning one set of transnational connections in favor of another, all in the name of returning to African culture: "What they are trying to do is cleanse Britain out of our history. . . . They say they want us to dance in the African way, but all they are doing is dancing like backward Texans" (*Daily Telegraph* 2004).

Snake-Driven Development

In 2003, a python that appears at times of great portent for Luo people returned to the comparatively poor and marginal village of Wasare in Nyakach, western Kenya, just after the historic election that brought President Kibaki to power. Many Luo believed the python to be the incarnation of a woman named Omieri, who allegedly lived in the nineteenth century and who now returns as a serpent, bringing fertility to communities and to the individual women to whom she appears. The python is a local symbol of mutation, change, and ambivalent power, and has also come to stand for local history as well as the uncertain but promising potential of the future. A grassroots NGO composed of educated Luo elites, called the Sondu Miriu Nam Awach Development Organization (SOMNADO), tried to acquire funding from the government and the international community in order to protect Omieri, which they now referred to as their cultural and ecological heritage. The NGO's effort to build a snake park to hold Omieri forever, so that the village would not have to depend on the python's capricious whims, was in part an effort to fix that future and to expunge it of ambiguity (Smith 2006). Their efforts were partly informed by their desire to protect and promote local ecology, which was threatened by the ongoing construction of a hydroelectric dam that promised to divert local rivers and thereby endanger the local human and animal populations. The NGO received some support from the national government, which no doubt felt challenged to prove that it was more democratic and respectful of Luo culture than the Moi regime had been: in 1987, the Kenya Wildlife Service had created a national incident by taking Omieri to the National Museum, perhaps precipitating the python's subsequent death (many Luo argued that the death had been engineered by their ethnic enemies, the Kikuyu, who wished to sabotage Luo harvests and futures) (Cohen and Odhiambo 1992, 105).

The national and international media picked up on the story of this community that treated a snake like a person, and made a great deal of the eternal conflict between traditionalists and Christians on the one hand and traditionalists and scientists on the other. Soon, tourists came from around the region, and even the world, to see the serpentine visitor and the people who were said to worship it, and a thriving local business developed, as locals sold soda, samosas, and doughnuts to the tourists. Many claimed that this tourism was indeed the rain that Omieri's visit presaged, and thus argued that there was continuity between the development strategies of the present and cultural values and heritage. Yet others wondered aloud if Omieri should be incarcerated in this way, because this meant that she could not bring fortune to the community as she pleased. They worried that the community would be cursed for commercializing the python and trying to control its movements, and they also debated aloud about the effects of tourism on the region's already high rate of prostitution and AIDS. The local state administration granted Benta, the woman whose child found the python, authority to charge money to see the snake, but many accused her of expropriating the funds that were supposed to be used for Omieri—a secretive, slippery act that was sure to turn Omieri against the public, bringing untold misfortune. As they saw her household grow richer, they accused Benta, first quietly and then publicly, of practicing witchcraft.

The event stimulated local conflict about the value of tradition and the past: staunch Luo Christians, including the Anglican archbishop, insisted that the python was an incarnation of Satan and that Benta was a devil worshipper. He threatened to burn the snake alive, and SOMNADO insisted that if the church leaders did so, they would be attacked. Luo and Kikuyu state employees in the Kenya Wildlife Service deployed a scientific, secularist idiom to make claims about the python and the public's proper disposition toward it. Backed by a Luo herpetologist at the Kisumu Museum, they pleaded to the public, reminding them that "It is not the python that has appeared to you, but you who have appeared to the python." They thereby referenced the gradual incursion of these marginalized people into their wetlands environment, and challenged the idea that they were chosen, and thus makers of their own history. Some locals, especially the NGO leaders who wanted to promote the region nationally, countered that Omieri was their religious heritage, and that recognizing her was their constitutional right. They argued for a localized development, built around local beliefs and values, and contraposed this vision to the false, foreign development embodied in the potentially destructive dam project, which could electrify the nation at the expense of Wasare. But the capricious forces that the villagers sought to control ultimately eluded them: as if to prove the secularists right, Omieri eventually laid its eggs and disappeared, and the villagers have yet to build a snake park.

These three examples were all dramatic public events, but the tensions and aspirations that they reveal are central to popular and political culture, and they emerge as well in quotidian domains. I now draw attention to some of the major themes: First, all three incidents took the form of an intervention, a popular attempt to reverse a perceived downward trend that has a history. In the cases of Mungiki and the Presbyterian deconstructionists, the downward spiral is located in colonialism, while the Luo celebrants of Omieri the python were more concerned about injustices that had begun under Jomo Kenyatta. All three incidents were attempts to change society *in toto* and sought to revolutionize all of the interconnected aspects of that totality (the religious, economic, political, etc.). In addition, all three examples consisted in a reinterpretation of established authority structures, as well as modernist conceptions of progress, and an inversion of their normative value: Mungiki attacked the modernist state and the legacy of Christianity while appropriating some of their key elements for themselves; the Presbyterians seized upon the concept of progressive modernity but argued that the church had been corrupted from the beginning; the Luo community counterposed the power of locality and heritage against the crumbling, but potentially salvageable, authority of the state and against the idea that marginal communities should be sacrificed for the national interest (the dam). Each intervention ended up assuming a very different trajectory than originally intended, either because of the way it was received by others or because the realities of daily life in contemporary Africa—such as the desire among political patrons to encourage disorder so as to forge bonds of dependency with their clients (Chabal and Daloz 1999)—transformed the nature of the intervention.

Importantly, each of these interventions implied that contemporary social reality is complicated and pervaded by inscrutable forces and motivations that have to be decoded before they can be acted upon. Deciphering the hieroglyphs that comprise contemporary Kenyan society and culture requires Kenyans to first locate a pristine and external analytical and discursive space from which to do so. However, locating this space turns out to be highly fraught, if not impossible, because the social reality of the present is always pushing up against one's efforts. Thus, Mungiki located truth in an imagined past, and their efforts to force it upon the present ended up exposing the absurdity of the project and drawing attention to its own internal contradictions (such as the conflict between elite leadership and marginalized urban youth; see Wamue 2004). The Presbyterians attempted to locate a space that was at once Christian and not colonized by protecting the church from its own relics, but in the process revealed that they had been unwittingly colonized by "backward" Americans from Texas—that they were, ironically, moving backward when they thought they were moving forward. The Omieri supporters projected the ambiguity of the moment following an election onto a python and located their pure space in local heritage, culture, and ecology, while attempting to expunge the python of ambiguity; by doing so, they fed local conflict over a range of issues—especially the conflict between private interests and the public good.

All three interventions were attempts to change the future by turning to the past, and they reflected a concern with origins. That concern was an aspect of the desire to establish coherent social and cultural boundaries, so that individual interests and desires might be monitored and controlled. This desire turned out, in each case, to be difficult to achieve because of conflicting interpretations of what history entailed, competing visions of the future emerging from the multiple subject positions that exist in the present, and the conflicted nature of actual history—the fact that Mau Mau divided African Kenyans more than it united them; the fact that the Omieri mythology always expressed conflict between social groups, such as men and women; and the fact that the Presbyterian community, and the Christian community, was never a homogeneous thing. In addition, all of these events were mediated spectacles that presented Kenyan dilemmas to Kenyans by universalizing highly particular phenomena: Kikuyu culture and the Mau Mau insurrection, Omieri the python from the village of Wasare, and an old church in Nairobi. In this way, they were acts of reification (of culture, the past, a group of people, an institution) that transformed complex processes into signs in order to better act on them, but in doing so they wandered further and further from reality as lived by most Kenyans, and so came to be perceived as evidence of absurdity, particularity, and even chaos, rather than universality and enlightenment. Thus, ironically, all three interventions came to be perceived as instances of backwardness for others, against which the nation constructed itself as possessing a shared cultural matrix. These cultural activists thus ended up doing, in part, what they intended to do, by becoming negative symbols for others through an act that appeared, in the end, as a kind of sacrifice. Thus, for example, Mungiki became a scapegoat for the Kibaki regime and was temporarily defeated after a mass-mediated war so that Kenya might have modernity again.

Finally, all of these actors engaged directly with global institutions and attempted to control their influence and power, at times reasserting national sovereignty in the face of globalization. Mungiki rejected the World Bank and called for what used to be referred to as "delinking," then tried to establish itself as a countergovernment by controlling transport. The Omieri enthusiasts sought support from global institutions, but attempted to control the terms of globalization by governing the inflow of aid and tourism, and using it to regenerate heritage. The Presbyterians tried to cleanse themselves from an earlier phase of globalization, and did so by establishing networks with institutions located in another place (the United States) in the present. They then offered to be an agent of globalization by teaching the world what they had discovered. In the act of defending sovereignty, these groups mobilized powerful regional and national images while rejecting foreign ones. Thus, Mungiki chastised the government for forsaking national security and protested against the world government symbolized by the IMF and the World Bank, while the angry Presbyterians destroyed images that they deemed un-African and searched for an authentic Africanity in an American religious tradition. In protecting the national, these groups also often ended up doing violence to those who represented it, particularly women, for "the protection of the nation in these circumstances always also requires the intensification of control and violence directed against women as signifiers of the nation—through motherhood and the reproduction of future generations" (Parker 2004, 19 paraphrasing Slavoj Zizek).

In any case, each of these interventions was an act of cultural and territorial production that used violence, or the possibility of violence, to establish a fraught order. Not simply struggles for position, these were attempts to locate an unambiguous truth around which to build community, and they suggest that development is an imaginative project that manifests in the construction of social boundaries in a context defined by crisis and flux. They also suggest that all struggles to construct social order through a policy of containment and boundary construction must confront the challenges of fragmentation and economic pressure, which in turn incite new utopian imaginings.

Plan of the Book

In this chapter, I have provided a historical and theoretical introduction to development and witchcraft, in Kenya and in anthropological thought. In subsequent chapters, I move from the national to the regional, focusing on the Kenyan development imagination as it comes to life in the Taita Hills. In particular, I focus on different levels at which people work to construct viable boundaries and sovereign social orders, focusing on the household, cultural heritage and space, political and associational life, and even subjective personalities and emotions. At each level, people find that these protected spheres are already cut through with internal divisions and jealousies, which resist any simple attempt at boundary construction or sovereignty; these threats to homogenous order are often conceptualized in terms of witchcraft. In chapter 2, I explore crucial aspects of Taita history, political economy, and sociospatial geography, showing how Wataita's experience of this backdrop informs their changing understandings of development and witchcraft. Chapter 3 considers Taita understandings of witchcraft, or the epitome of that which Wataita feel must be excluded for development to emerge, and focuses on changing Taita perceptions of a particular type of witchcraft associated with cities, commercialization, and the eradication of traditional Taita-ness.

In chapters 4 through 7, I shift attention to specific cases, focusing on actual events that were also efforts to create development—most of which also came to be perceived as witchcraft by those who were excluded by them, or suffered because of them. In chapter 4, I examine the domestic sphere and various efforts to transform relations within it. Specifically, I follow a family's attempts to become developed by seeking employment opportunities while simultaneously avoiding, appeasing, and counteracting the witchcraft of their jealous neighbors; this chapter also explores the social and moral implications of household architecture in some detail, focusing on issues of generation and gender. In chapters 5 and 6, I move away from the household and focus on public attempts to change the present by acquiring control over the forces that acted on Wataita; chapter 5 discusses forces associated with the Taita past, while chapter 6 deals with international NGOs and the fragmentation of the masculinist state. The discussion in chapter 5 focuses on rainmaking, fighi shrines, and ideas about ancestors. In chapter 6, I move to an emerging public sphere, examining the reorganization of political life and the multiplication of governing bodies, and the concomitant appropriation of ideas of governance by different social groups. I analyze an NGO that was widely accused of being a vehicle for the Satanic Church, in part because it seemed to be commercializing children and transferring their inherent rights to unknown foreigners from the United States and Europe. The NGO ended up having to address the accusation that they were complicit in a new form of sorcery by handing over authority to elected local leaders. In chapter 7, I move beyond formal politics to examine the penetration and public revelation of secrets associated with witchcraft, arguing that public efforts to manage witchcraft were aimed at changing people's intentions and dispositions outside the realm of formal politics as a precondition for democracy and development. Specifically, I examine the politics and controversy surrounding the hiring of a transnational witch-hunter and the social consequences of his actions.

CHAPTER TWO

I Still Exist! Taita Historicity

I Still Exist!—A reminder painted on the back of a privately owned passenger vehicle in large, red block letters in the Taita Hills

Off the Beaten Track?

The Taita Hills in southeastern Kenya is a place easily missed by visitors, Kenyan and foreign alike. Yet most people who have visited Kenya for any length of time have passed near them, for the hills lie close to the main road that links the capital city of Nairobi, in central Kenya, with the coastal city of Mombasa, 150 kilometers to the east. Tourists are likely to confront the moniker "Taita Hills" without having actually entered into them: Hilton Hotels Inc. owns the Taita Hills Safari Lodge near the base of the hills. The hotel lies in Tsavo National Park: roughly the size of Israel, Tsavo is the biggest national park in Kenya and one of the world's largest game sanctuaries, famous for its herds of elephants and for its sizable black rhinoceros population, among numerous other animal and plant species. Divided into Tsavo East and Tsavo West for administrative purposes, the hills lie roughly in the middle of the national park, and the people, who number approximately 250,000, are sequestered from the wilderness below—at first by their choice and now by the force of state and international law. Textual references to the region, on the Internet and in tourist brochures, rarely mention the Taita people (though they refer to the hills in which they reside), preferring to dwell on the "heroic" and "fearless" Waliangulu hunters, who lived in the region and served as game trackers for white hunters before the park was gazetted in 1948.

Wataita are often defined, by visitors and state officials, as "sedentary agriculturalists," because they practice agriculture (their landholdings are very small) and have a sophisticated and socially complex irrigation system of which they tend to be proud. Yet, far from being sedentary, Wataita are a people of diverse origins with a history of long-distance trade networks dating back as long as oral and written testimonies record (Bravman 1998). Interestingly, "Taita" is actually a Swahili word for the hills that Wataita occupy; the local language word for the people is *βadabida*, which many Wataita translate as "those who are passing," from *daβida*, meaning "in transit." Though "in passing" may not actually be the origin of the ethnic label "daβida" (which is also the name of a hill), Wataita often reference this translation when they speak about themselves as people who are constantly on the move and who occupy a perceived cultural borderland between "the coast" (hot, Swahili speaking, historically mercantile, and partly Islamic) and "up country" (fertile, cool, agricultural, politically connected, and strongly Christian). Moreover, Wataita are far from being purely agriculturalists: because of small holdings and increasingly uncertain rainfall (probably due to rapid deforestation), they are compelled to purchase about 75 percent of the foods they eat, a percentage far greater than the national average (Ministry of Planning and National Development 1998, 33). These days, most households receive some food aid from the government, in cooperation with international nongovernmental organizations (NGOs), such as the Danish International Development Agency and CARE. Because of their long history of dependence on income earned outside Taita, Wataita have long traveled the road from the historically Swahili port city of Mombasa. From the 1920s, and especially from the 1940s, many adult Wataita men have lived in Mombasa and other cities their entire working lives, only occasionally visiting home. Because of the out-migration of males, Taita has long had among the highest percentages of female-headed households in the country, with adult male household heads being somewhere in the background, their interests with respect to land and politics typically articulated, sporadically, by their female and senior male relatives. Government reports indicate that the number of female-headed households is around 40 percent, but my own household surveys suggest that de facto matricentric households are closer to 75–80 percent of Taita homes, as most of these families seem to receive little or nothing in the way of income from migrant male laborers (Ministry of Planning and National Development 1998, 2).

Their allegedly sedentary culture, combined with their outwardly "modern" ways; their high levels of education; and their ambivalent, even somewhat ashamed, attitude about "tradition" (although this attitude is rapidly changing), makes Wataita rather uninteresting to outsiders, except perhaps missionaries, so they are not at all marketable. As a result, it is mostly Taita people who come to the Taita Hills, although the main towns around it are often visited by non-Taita Africans interested in the mostly illegal mineral trade that thrives around the lowland towns of Mwatate and Voi (various types of garnet and rubies are found there, among other precious stones). When they return home to Taita, Wataita must pass through the rapidly growing dust bowl town of Voi, one of the main entrances to Tsavo East National Park. Voi is a dry, unattractive railway depot where Wataita compete with the more prosperous and connected Kikuyu, Kenyan Indians, and Swahili for a stake in the commercial and mining wealth of this region. Although most Wataita believe that the area around Voi belongs to them, they do not have much stake in its most productive industries: tourism in Tsavo National Park, gemstone mining, and sisal production. Though many highlands Wataita come to Voi for shopping, court cases, and romantic liaisons in hotels away from the watchful eyes of neighbors, they dislike staying there for long periods, and they have long seen work in the sisal plantations that surround Voi as a form of slavery.

Typically, Wataita traveling home to the Taita Hills from other parts of Kenya via Voi will board a *matatu*, or privately owned passenger minivan—perhaps one emblazoned with the plaintive yet thankful reminder quoted in the epigraph at the beginning of the chapter. As the matatu slowly climbs up from the Taru desert, people's language shifts to Kidabida, and talking becomes more animated, cutting across social class and categories to include men and women, old and young, relatively poor and relatively well off alike. They may talk about the changing weather, about who owns what building, about how family members are doing, or about the unprecedented number of people who are dying, and often one gleans that they are talking about the same thing: decline and loss. Sometimes the talk becomes heated and controversial, touching on politics and "land grabbing" by the rich. Some older travelers may take the opportunity to gently chastise the youthful matatu conductor for his Rastafarian dress or for smoking marijuana, which they will assume he does. One can gradually feel the weight of what could be called Taita's socializing power, but which could also be the many historical layers that Taita people feel thrust upon themselves when they are here. Taita people recognize, and talk about, the behavioral shifts that take place on these journeys: they often say that they become more "moist" (*kinsyoshi*), meaning their behavior becomes soft and pliable, in comparison with that of the "hotter" people who live in the plains and on the coast.

From the gradually rising plains one can now see the Taita Hills jutting up steeply and implausibly, a fortress of undulating slopes whose highest peak is 7,500 feet above sea level. For centuries this dramatic bulwark has attracted waves of migrants seeking refuge and protection from enemies, including Arab slave traders and Maasai cattle raiders. From this outside perspective, the hills appear small and compact, as if very few people could live there, but once one has entered into them it becomes clear that, like a coiled-up intestine which, if unfolded, would stretch out for miles, the Taita Hills contains a whole world, deceptively appearing as if it exists unto itself. In fact, Wataita deploy this anatomical image themselves, and senior men use outstretched goat intestines to diagnose social ills and cleanse (*kuora*) the land, where the intestines stand for the Taita social and geographical landscape in its totality. As the vehicle continues its ascent, the land becomes more fertile and moist, with banana, pine, and avocado trees gradually replacing the coconut palms. It is cool and wet here, at night positively cold, and there is often fog. Nonetheless, water is a constant problem for this rapidly growing population confined to a very limited area, and much politics and strife surround its flow: kin and neighbors regularly struggle with one another over blocked irrigation channels, people complain that those with means build pipes directly to the few remaining springs that exist, and lowlanders climb up the hills to confront their highland neighbors in arguments about blocked water that often become violent, and sometimes lead to death. Importantly, Taita idioms and language regularly invoke the idea that liquid "flow" is synonymous with individual and social well-being, while blockage or obstruction is synonymous with violence, discord, disease, and witchcraft. While it is easy to think of this idea as an aspect of traditional Taita thought or cosmology, it is clearly a rhetorical rendering of a concrete, historical situation underwritten by law and the nation-state.

The passenger unlucky enough to be pressed against the window of the overcrowded matatu can see the plains several thousand feet below, as well as Tsavo National Park, where elephants abound. Above, water cascades over sheer rocky cliffs and, to the side, rivulets snake their way downward through plots of maize, beans, and fruits. Along the side of the road one sees the occasional kiosk or drinking establishment: the Maendeleo (Development) Bar, the Florida 2000 kiosk (named after a popular Nairobi nightclub), the Treetops Bar (named after a famous tourist hotel in Tsavo National Park). Wataita know about these places, and work to re-create and appropriate their magic, if only in name. Other popular business names include "Jasho" (Sweat), and "Tabu" (Trouble): they indicate that the owners have worked for what they possess and that whatever prosperity they have is not the outcome of witchcraft, as many people assume. One has reached the highlands now, where the moist Taita heart is supposed to hold sway over the hot, contentious, and selfish ways that many Wataita believe characterize the rest of Kenya. Here people greet each other with pet names, regardless of whether or not they know each other: "Aβongo" (person of brain) between adult men, "Apesa" (person of money), or "Anguo" (person of clothes) between members of the opposite sex. These were originally names for blood brothers and affinal kin, respectively, referencing the successful exchange of gifts and the resultant cementing of social ties, but they have become generalized terms through which a kinlike relationship is suggested and transplanted onto all situations.[1]

The drive from the plains up to the hills takes the traveler past more than one invisible barrier, or zone, radiating out from ritually protected indigenous forests. These forests are called *fighi*, meaning barrier, and they are highly contested physical markers. Most people do not know exactly where they are, or if they are really there at all, and how far their power extends, and there is great disagreement about fighi's potency and current usefulness. But, in general, Wataita believe that these small parcels of ritually treated indigenous forests were created long ago and tended, now insufficiently and often without proper knowledge, by senior men who sacrificed (people often disagree about what was sacrificed, and the form that sacrifice took, or takes) to ancestors. They argue that these forests once protected people from the cattle-raiding Maasai by preventing these outsiders from leading stolen social resources beyond specific boundaries (the fighi made the livestock stubbornly immobile). In contemporary times, fighi are said to act like living embodiments of deceased ancestors' desires and attitudes. When they work—for many say that the "batteries," as they put it, have died—they strive to ensure cultural distinctiveness and pure Taita moral values. Fighi are generally represented as scarcely understood and inadequately controlled cultural resources that ensure the continuation of traditional Taita values, with varying degrees of success, regardless of what Taita people want or do. But the means through which these shrines "choose" to protect Taita often turn out to be harmful to Taita people, because fighi's understanding of tradition is widely seen as unsuited to present-day realities. Like an immune system mistaking allergens for dangerous pathogens, fighi violently assert themselves against benign foreign practices that they consider dangerous, often killing the human perpetrators.

Taita interest in fighi partly reflects people's growing concerns about the vanishing forests, which Taita proverbs declare were "finished" by "silence" (*kituri chemeriyee msidu*). A mere fifty years ago, much of this land was temperate rain forest, and though patches of this forest still exist (about 1 percent of the total land area), almost all of the land is under cultivation, and one finds terraced plots at the most unlikely of elevations and inclines. Most land is privately owned (a situation that dates back to the state's "land consolidation" programs of the early postcolonial period, of which see below), so the few parcels of forest that exist have only remained because they are small, are difficult to reach, and cannot be irrigated. These humid cloud forests are home to an unknown number of indigenous species, including the Taita thrush, Classen's Aloe, and African violets, so the Taita Hills has of late become an internationally recognized ecological emergency area.

If my description of the hills thus far has made the place seem somewhat secluded, and if many Kenyans (including Wataita) affirm this, Wataita are very quick to point out that they are the most modern of their neighbors, sometimes using the term "developed" to describe this condition (*daeendelee sana*, "we have developed," or "we have come/traveled far"). What they tend to mean by this is that they have incorporated formerly foreign things into their world, and these things have come to shape who they are: they speak Swahili, the language of commerce and the city, and often English, the language of governance and global trade; they are familiar with the Internet (as of 2004, every post office in the Taita Hills had an Internet connection), and many of the self-professed "dot com" generation (generally, those under the age of about fifty-five) download the same things, for better or worse, as Americans do; they play host to numerous international NGOs; and they can watch, on bootlegged videos in the smallest of villages, American movies before these films hit the big screens in Nairobi. They have a long history of Christianity (originally Anglican and Catholic, but these days variations of Pentecostalism are growing rapidly throughout the region) and are the most educated people in Coast province, their levels of schooling rivaling those of much more prosperous regions, such as the Kikuyu-dominated Central province. Today, it is estimated that 50 percent of Taita's male population, and 30 percent of its female population, has completed secondary school. And yet, despite all of this self-professed modernity, Wataita are quick to point out that they grow poorer with each passing year. There are simply very few jobs anymore, and most men and women now drift back and forth between the country and the city, finding odd ways to survive, barely, in either place. In the absence of sustainable formal employment following upon the structural adjustment programs of the 1980s and 1990s, most Wataita today argue that the only way to make money is either from business or by acquiring support from outsiders who would be willing to help Taita, if they knew about its existence (read: an NGO).

The same people who argue that Taita is too traditional will often assert, with the same breath, that Taita is not traditional enough, because its people have been uprooted from traditional values that sustained them, and they see themselves retreating further from an idealized past with each passing day. Indeed, Wataita who live in Taita are compelled to confront destruction every morning when they awake and look outside at what they consider to be a landscape that has grown increasingly inhospitable (dry and devoid of trees), due in part to the severe impact of a growing population on the environment. One constantly hears the sound of chain saws, and Wataita of all ages complain that the old men have lost their power to curtail this wanton destruction, although it is really unavoidable, because these trees lie on privately owned land and are the only source of fuel. At the same time, they decry the rapid spread of the eucalyptus tree, which, along with grevilla, has almost completely replaced indigenous tree species (indeed, some people identify places as fighi simply because they contain indigenous trees). Wataita claim that this fast-growing foreign tree (eucalyptus was introduced by the British to make wet areas suitable for agriculture, and for timber and fuel) extracts water from the ground, precisely because it grows so quickly. Its accelerated growth, leading to desiccation, heat, and contraction, has become a metaphor for Wataita, as well as being one of many prisms through which they have conceptualized historical change (cash crops and money, for example, are widely associated with heat, and people say that Wataita dispositions have become hotter and less moist with time, mostly because of financial pressures). Many Wataita blame eucalyptus for the fact that rivers, streams, and ponds have dried up, and their growing concerns about this tree partly reflect the desire to protect autochthonous values and resources against foreign threat and encroachment (see also Comaroff and Comaroff 2000). Wataita often speak of dispositions and ecological environments as dialectically intertwined: bad habits and deeds register on the landscape (partly because God or the ancestors "turn away," and partly because of the direct ecological consequences of unregulated selfish action), and, in turn, an infertile and inhospitable landscape hardens people's hearts and inclines them toward selfish acts, the epitome of which is witchcraft.

In general, Wataita are nostalgic about Taita's verdant beauty in the not-so-distant past (say, thirty years ago), and many adults claim that the landscape and weather have changed so much in their lifetimes that, as they put it, they are confused and do not know where they are or how to act. During my fieldwork, they regularly counted off the names of birds, animals, and edible plants that were now gone, due mainly to deforestation and the uncontrolled use of the pesticide DDT. Poisoning of the groundwater, which has affected everyone in the area, also underpinned growing class inequalities in the 1970s and 1980s, as DDT allowed those with means (who alone were able to grow "European" vegetables for sale) to deliver as much product as possible to local and regional markets. While this selfish destruction of the area fed into local thought about the witchcraft of elites, many nonelites were also quick to blame themselves for participating in this destruction. For example, one middle-age man claimed that DDT had become widely used in the 1980s because, as wealth differences became more obvious, people of different socioeconomic backgrounds stopped wanting to depend on each other for help: they feared being bewitched with poison when they visited their neighbors. Thus, instead of staying overnight at a neighbor's house when safari ants invaded their home, they decided to use DDT to kill the pests to avoid interacting with potentially antagonistic neighbors ("safari ants used to really bring us together," he said).

A main idea here is that Taita appears to be a place of extremes: one is immediately confronted with a sense of alterity and even islandlike isolation in relation to the rest of Kenya, which seems at first to be a feature of geography, but turns out to be directly related to a politics of exclusion that victimizes Taita people in the name of development. For, again, the Taita Hills are hemmed in by the park, an area that abounds with natural resources (including water that could be harnessed for energy) from which Wataita receive no direct benefit and into which they cannot enter without a costly permit. On the other hand, Wataita recognize themselves as modern, Christian, and developed. They are well aware of life in more prosperous far-flung places, and many of them speak English better than the vast majority of Americans—in fact, Taita below the age of forty rarely speak Kidabida among themselves, preferring to move between Swahili and English as a sign of cosmopolitanism. But increasingly this idiomatic modernity has become more of a liability than a boon because many are coming to believe that the past is a potentially beneficial resource from which they have been alienated, at the same time as their education and familiarity with the city have ceased to benefit them in concrete ways.

The physical confinement of Wataita within the hills has long defined local thought about what development means—mainly, an end to this confinement, one that would allow Wataita to use the resources of the park or share in the profits generated by park fees. Probably for this reason, Taita understandings of development have tended to rely heavily on themes of escape and travel, while their historical narratives focus on the dual processes of restriction and increased mobility. Historically, elites have been able to extend their networks beyond Taita, establish second homes in the city, and send remittances home, so the issue of the park has been less pressing for them. However, these days all Wataita are forced to consider more local approaches for getting ahead and getting by. Of course, the sovereignty of Tsavo is backed up by a transnational ecological discourse, as well as an international institutional apparatus of aid organizations and regulatory bodies that contribute to park development and that urge the Kenyan government to protect the area against poachers. Thus, one sees an immediate conflict between Taita development, in the sense that most Wataita would use the word, and the transnational, neoliberal discourse and practice of development, with its focus on the management and protection of the natural environment. As an "opposition" politician campaigning for Taita inclusion in the management, and profits, of Tsavo put it to a crowd of listeners in the late 1990s:

> True development is when everybody has a hold on something his own. If few have wealth and many don't then that is not development at all! Taita has enough land for its people because God did not create many people so they can't get land. But what is being seen in Taita? The portion that is left to animals is bigger than that left to people so they can grow food. That which remains was divided again [by the colonial government] and the bigger portion of it is for growing sisal [grown in large lowland plantations, most of which are still owned by a single European settler]. That small portion for humans to grow food and doing other things of development, they share with big ravines

> that scare and rocky plateaus that have no end and clumps of mountains and hills! We endure this situation, why? Because we feel we must be Gentlemen [in English]. Because we are too proud. And meanwhile less proud people are stealing everything that is ours!

The Origin of the World System

Consider this Taita story about the origin of the world system, narrated to me by Mighanyo, a retired civil servant:

A long time ago, an African, an Indian, and a European went to sleep in their respective homes. While they slept, God visited each of them in separate dreams. God said that they should go to a nearby mountain. There, on a path, they would find something new. God told each of them that, once they found it, they should take it to the top of the mountain and await further instruction. The next day the African woke up and immediately set off for the mountain on foot. The Indian also made his way to the mountain, but riding a motorbike. The European awoke and drove toward the mountain in his Land Rover. For good reason, the European expected to arrive first, but the African knew a shortcut up the mountain, and he passed the Indian and the European, who were both stuck in the mud. Eventually, the African came upon something that was indeed new, the name for which he did not know: a book—in fact, the Bible. When he saw it, he was amazed and a bit afraid, having never seen such a marvelous thing. For a while, he sat there, examining this book, wondering who could have made such strange markings. After some time, the European reached the African on foot, huffing and panting, having left his Land Rover behind. In the spirit of friendship, the African showed him the book he had found, inviting him to share in the wonder. The European, though, knew exactly what to do: "It's a book," he said matter of factly, "Give it to me." And so he took it up the mountain, and when he reached the top he met God. Suddenly, God's voice boomed from above: "Listen to me!" He demanded. "This European is the only one who has obeyed my commands. From now on, he will rule over the both of you (African and Indian), and no matter how hard you work, you will never surpass him. You, African, will remain forever behind, because you had the word and you did not listen. The Indian will always despise you, because you are such a fool, and he will treat you cruelly." And so it came to pass.

Mighanyo's story concerns Taita's impoverishment and humiliation before an expanding global regime, and it pinpoints the origin of World History in an act of expropriation. It thus comments on the cruel origins of Kenya's peculiar modernity, based on a tripartite system of racial and economic segregation. But a lot of meaning is found in this story, and it is worthwhile for us to unpack it. First, there is its spatial setting: a mountain that the competitors (who do not know they are competitors) have to travel up, presumably with great difficulty, the goal being to temporarily abandon the lower elevations, where people live, in order to acquire something new and probably momentous that exists in the clouds, and can only be imagined. This mountain has side trails that are more familiar to the African than they are to the European; perhaps the place is the Taita Hills or somewhere near the Taita Hills, or perhaps not. The European and the Indian would seem to already be rich—they have motorbikes and cars—and possess greater mobility than the African, who nonetheless acquires some benefit from being close to the ground. Each group has, in short, certain advantages over the other, but at the beginning of the "game" none of these are particularly important because historical time has not yet begun, and these different people begin their separate journeys from a place that is outside of time. This prehistorical timelessness is underscored by the story's radical, but unremarkable, anachronisms and the absence of chronology prior to expropriation (cars and motorbikes at the origin of the world system, prior to the introduction of literacy and Christianity).

These chosen people are apparently unknown to one another and exhibit qualities that mark them as separate (different attitudes toward the book and toward reciprocity, for example), but they are drawn together by an exogenous force that reifies and systematizes their relationship to one another, while also making total change improbable, due to God's fiat. At first, the experience for each individual is somewhat unreal (it begins as a dream) and highly personal, as each, we imagine, experiences a sense of Something Amazing About to Happen without realizing that the main objective, in the end, is something mundane in comparison: governance, and the development of a world political and economic system that shames the African. There is, in short, an intervention by a spectral force that first invades their subconscious minds as an incitement to curiosity and discovery, but which turns out to have the capacity to rearrange the material world and the experience of time in a way that is embarrassing: from here on in, the European and the Indian will be able to progress and to have a history (which exists at this point in the future), while the African will be denied a future history and will have to satisfy himself with whatever falls from the tables of those who rule and despise him. Rather than depicting progress as a natural process, this story implies that at least two interconnected spatiotemporal experiences are at work in the world system: stasis, which is synonymous with spatial restriction and servitude, and positive transformation over time, which is synonymous with spatial encompassment. It is worth pointing out, in this vein, that the Swahili and Taita word for European, *Mzungu*, is probably related to the verb *kuzunguka*, to move about from place to place.

Again, God is present at the highest peak of the mountain, and what becomes a race for development begins as a race to reach God, who turns out to be embodied in the Bible and seems to be angered at having been treated carelessly (although it is implied that God misrecognized the fact that He was actually being treated with the noninstrumental awe He deserved). Thus development turns out to be a sacred, religious venture—and a religious venture turns out to be about development—and the journey is taken with an attitude of submission to a higher authority that is other, and unknown. This is significant because Wataita typically speak of colonialism as having begun with an exchange of gifts between missionarics and the Taita population, through which Wataita were seduced into abandoning their religious traditions and their autonomy, and into submitting themselves to colonial governance (the government's system of chiefs, which did not exist before). Midway through the story, and halfway up the mountain, we are confronted with a difference in response to a happening. The African makes an attempt to exchange information with the European, but the European is not interested in exchanging things or ideas with the African, partly because the European already has some sense of what is at stake. It would not be going too far to say that the African offers a gift to the European, who refuses it in favor of carrying out the directions of a higher authority, who turns out to be a very strict master. The African ultimately chooses friendship, and reciprocal give and take, over a capricious command from a superior authority. He tarries, hoping to figure things out with the help of other mere mortals like himself, and, like Adam and Eve in a tellingly similar story, his insolent desire to assert some small control over the course of events costs him the world.

In contrast, the European sees the book as a thing and merely a thing ("It is a book"), and not as the pretext for developing a relationship with another human being. It is something that can and should be possessed by an individual ("Give it to me"), but this attitude on the part of the European appears to be new to the African. The African does not resist him, or try to fight, when the European absconds with the book, perhaps because he wants to give it away, in the hopes of developing a relationship later on. Unfortunately for the African, before any of this had taken place, a new political, economic, and religious order had been hatching in the Mind of God. Suddenly a new system of gift giving is imposed on everyone, apparently out of spite, and the African will hitherto be removed from a greater, global network of gift distribution, compelled to remain "behind" in these hills that he knows so well, because of the arbitrary command of a legalistic bureaucrat (God).

Zooming in on the thwarted gift exchange in the middle of the story allows us to access something about Taita understandings of themselves and the past that is significant. Most Wataita, as I mentioned above, have an ambivalent attitude about the past (for example, many Wataita, old and young, said that their ancestors were "thieves" because they stole cattle). These days most tend to see the past as something detached and alienated, a lot like a commodity, partly because they feel foreign in relationship to their understanding of it, and partly because many would like to make use of it to improve their lot. Some traditions are good, they often say, and others are bad, and people need to choose which ones to let in and expand, and which ones to abandon altogether. But because they are compelled to live in the hills and are constantly butting up against an only dimly understood history in their efforts to survive, they rarely see themselves as having the luxury of choosing these things, because the past controls them, capriciously, rather than them controlling it (this is especially evident in local fears about fighi, of which see chapter 5). Regardless of their feelings about specific Taita cultural practices, most Wataita, old and young, male and female, hold that a spirit of reciprocity was alive in the past, and that even today this spirit continues to exert itself on the present by tormenting people who refuse to recognize the obligation to give, either to each other or to the past embodied in ancestors and fighi. Thus, an alternative notion of development, and an alternative temporality and model of community, is implicit in the actions of the African, who opts for close attention to locality and a commitment to reciprocity against the Will of God. So we have in this story a layered argument about the nature of development: There is a global development that eludes Taita (or Africans) because they were unwilling to immediately follow orders administered from on high. One could say that they felt compelled to act with respect to a habit that defined them. But their willingness to share is a moral virtue (at least it was described as such by the storyteller), and the European's refusal to share results in inequality and poverty, and sets in motion the train of History, which leaves Taita stranded and vulnerable.

It should hardly need to be said that this Taita vision of a harmonious past has little to do with what the past was actually like—a great deal of inequality existed even in the precolonial past. However, this widespread belief in a reciprocal African nature is deployed, by many Wataita of all ages, classes, and sexes, to make sense of the real expansion and reification of inequality over time; the belief in an egalitarian and "generous" past also suggests the possibility, for Wataita, of transcending their current situation by accessing this potential that lies in the past, which is also embodied in places. It bears mentioning now that witches embody the opposite of this ideal of reciprocity: they acquire power by trading in the futures of people they should love, and whom they are connected to through numerous acts of exchange, to demonic agents, who in turn give them individualized power and wealth. This happens, typically, under the cover of generative gift exchange: the witch slips poison into the food or drink of the person hc or she wants to control.

Sources of Taita Understandings of Development

Taita understandings of development have arisen from a few concrete, shared historical experiences. First, divergent understandings of development emerged from conflicts with the colonial state and with missionaries over local ways of organizing the production of social life and the future (land tenure practices, household architecture, treatment of ancestors, beer brewing, etc.), where Taita ways were first castigated as being backward and primitive, and later came to actually appear backward because they were retained by (or in many cases relegated to) the uneducated poor. Often, these marginalized people came to be perceived as witches by the more prosperous, as did their ritual practices (Kidabida, also called *βutasi*). In contrast, those excluded from respectable ways of making a living often held that these Christian elites were false pretenders to virtue, and thus were the real witches.[9] This Manichean opposition between the backward and the progressive, and the shifting moral category of the witch, became the prism through which political argument and moral debate were filtered and through which socioeconomic inequality was widely understood. Conflicts with the state over development continued in the postcolonial period (particularly over land consolidation and forest management), but state interventions were by this time supported by an influential educated Taita elite with strong connections to Nairobi and Mombasa. Thus, what began as a conflict between Africans and colonial experts became, very quickly, a conflict among Africans, where issues of class were articulated in the idiom of the backward versus the progressive, the parochial versus the global, and witchcraft versus development.

The second major influence on Taita understandings of development was the experience, shared by all Wataita to some degree, of being closed in, in terms of territory and options, and the consequent feeling that development was synonymous with mobility and escape—especially for young men who wished to make a name for themselves outside of the control of their seniors. This telos was not realizable over the longue duree by the vast majority, partly because of colonial restrictions on urban residence and low wages, and so the desire was tampered by the general understanding that the tactic of escape was neither sustainable nor desirable. Escape also led to the emergence of a cadre of what older Wataita often refer to as "lost" people (*βalegheriya*), who cease to be of assistance to their progenitors and often become a threat to their survival (as in the case of mostly absent, politically connected, land-grabbing elites). This concern about those who are lost has fed into a simultaneous concern with protection, and with the preservation of local ways against foreign threat, or from insiders who have lost their way (this concern is epitomized by fighi).

A third major influence on Taita understandings of development, and one of the factors that gives the concept and the means of enacting it so much complexity, is the conflict arising from the sedimentation of different, imagined historical epochs, in which Wataita hold that different value systems, based on different modes of generating wealth, power, prestige, and virtue, predominated. These different modes are often only vaguely understood by the living (who recall, for example, that their fathers were blood brothers who ate cow brain together) and are alternately romanticized and demonized, a by-product of their being highly abstracted. It is often difficult to know whether the different temporalities to which Wataita refer reflect actual historical transformations, people's present concerns, or both. However, there were critical historical junctures, which we could refer to, somewhat problematically, as the precolonial period, the colonial and early late colonial period, and the neoliberal period. Each of these periods introduced changes, creating crisis and opportunity and allowing the "old way of life" to be objectified and to appear in "the present" as a model of either development or antidevelopment (the latter widely understood in terms of witchcraft), depending on circumstance and one's shifting position. But this periodization is faulty because these different temporalities coexist in the present and draw attention to themselves through concrete symbolic representations, such as a dramatic rock from which morally self-confident seniors once cast bound witches into the lake below, or a big tree where old men used to drink beer but which now is on an absent civil servant's private property, or a cave containing the now vandalized skulls of the dead, or a half-completed building that once had ambitions of being a store or a school, or an old thatch house dwarfed by a mansion, or a young NGO employee's motorcycle speeding past all of these things.

Spatiotemporal markers like fighi ensure that the past is never truly past, because even if a neighborhood no longer exists, and the conflicts between neighborhoods that had once existed are now irrelevant (because the people are no longer there, and the space is arranged completely differently), the fighi, or some remnant of the fighi forest, is very often still there, and its anger is perceived as unpredictable and eternal, even if it is also inconsistent. In practice, this presence means that when people talk about development they draw on their understandings of the value systems of different time periods, often striving to create the appearance of historical continuity (such as when a politician implies that his fatness is generative of social well-being), and it is at these moments that the conflict between historical epochs becomes discernible and real for consciousness (as when a critical interlocutor argues that fatness is sinful because it is old-fashioned and backward). Contemporary development initiatives (such as a witch hunt or a cooperative banking project) are both forward looking, in that they strive for newness, and backward looking, in that they are also always engaging with the past, resuscitating dead or dying institutions (such as schools, fighi, or the neighborhood collectivity), and trying to recuperate an idealized moment in time (or minimizing the capacity of a demonized past to regain momentum and send society back into the time of darkness—whether that be the 1890s or the 1980s).

The fourth major influence is the notion of the project (*miraadi* in Swahili) on Taita thought and practice since the end of the colonial period. It has a history, one pivotal moment of which was certainly land consolidation, of which see below. Debates about who should be in control of the project or some aspect of the project, where the value generated from the project should go, how long the project should take to yield rewards, whether the benefactors are genuine or not, who really stands to benefit from a project and who is doing the work, and why certain areas get projects while others do not generate a great deal of excited interest, cynical speculation, and resentment in rural areas. They are also cut through with local speculation about culture, temporality, history, power, and the invisible. Furthermore, the very idea that there will be a project, which will be the culmination of the work of locals and typically the affection, or love, of others (such as politicians or NGOs and other international patrons), and that afterward there will be a qualitative shift in the way things are, has become a hegemonic idea, despite the failure of so many projects.

The mystique of the project is perpetuated by an array of institutions competing to bring development (and often to acquire a small percentage from locals) and is sustained by local ritual and productive labor organized toward attracting NGOs (dance groups and song, public feasts prepared by local women for the NGO representatives, contributions of labor and materials, etc.). Some Wataita argue that the expectation of the project is the real force behind kinyoshi, or Taita moistness, as this disposition results from their long history of trying to acquire the favor of powerful guests—for a guest is rain, as they say. Often these visitations turn out to be destructive—yesterday's saviors regularly reveal themselves as sinister, expropriating funds for themselves, and leaving locals with very little recourse. But so powerful is the concept of the project that one cannot really appreciate so many of the other things that people want to do (the power of religious movements, rainmaking rituals, or witch hunts, for example) without it, because these various actions retain the mystique of the project, displacing it from the state and from high modernist science.

Some Aspects of Taita History and Some Taita Understandings of History

It should come as no surprise that, when Wataita speak of the past, they refer to different times and different things, and the difference is of course partly dependent on the age of the person. But two degrees of "past" appear to be particularly significant: One is "a long time ago" (*ko kala*, or, in Swahili, *zamani kabisa*), which usually means, for most people, a time before the 1950s or 1960s. The second, "some time ago" (*kitambo* in Swahili), refers to a socially significant period of time past. This definition depends on context, but for most adults most of the time kitambo seems to refer to the period from the 1960s through the mid-1980s—a time generally remembered as one of relative hope and prosperity following the acquisition of independence. When most Wataita speak about the former time (zamani or ko kala), they refer to a state of being that is very general and even stereotypical. For example, they often imagine a people who were extremely healthy, who indeed lived for centuries, and they speak about a spirit of peace and reciprocity that was enforced by just senior men (definitively not the senior men of today). But they are also just as likely to speak about ignorance, dirt, and backwardness. For the most part, they imagine a homogeneity that tells us far more about Taita people today than Taita people in the past. This distant past is important for most Wataita, particularly insofar as they recognize in it a potentially different and valuable disposition, which at times makes itself felt through now weakened institutions, such as the capricious fighi. But it is this more recent past—for people under forty, the past of their parents—that young people in particular measure themselves and their opportunities against, developing new understandings of development in the process.

Wataita of all ages represent the past in terms of radical break, but tend to differ about when to place the break and what aspects of that past to emphasize. For example, middle-age and senior men often refer ambivalently to the decision, made by the generations that preceded them, to sell off their lineages' livestock in order to pay for their children's schooling. These children became the established senior elites of today, sometimes emerging as powerful politicians and civil servants. Again, these elites are often held to have "lost their way": their "hearts" are "hot" and "hard" because they are disconnected from Taita, typically by virtue of having spent long periods of time away, in Nairobi or Mombasa. One dominant version has it that these elites are rapacious because they seek to regain the herds that their parents sold to pay for their education. They are, from this generous local perspective, sad and adrift, and so these land grabbers cannibalize their home in an effort to become part of it again.

The simultaneously promising and dangerous capacities of mobility and expansion were central to Taita reflections on the history of schooling.

Many seniors narrated origin stories of schooling that highlighted seduction and erotically exciting individuation, and their histories of schooling were also often histories of witchcraft. According to many middle-age and senior men, schooling was introduced to Taita through a Faustian bargain with missionaries that transformed senior producers of sugarcane and sugarcane beer into consumers of refined sugar whose educated children would grow up to despise their unclean and uncouth practices as witchcraft. Their standardized stories about these early missionary efforts to seduce Taita fathers with sugar suggested that schooling opened people, and Taita, to the world in ways that were at once promising and dangerous. As Sebastian, a retired dockworker, put it, "In those days, white men carried sugar everywhere they went. Now, the first whites who came here, they saw they had to teach us. They tried to convince the old men to send their children to school, but the old men said, 'Eh? This one is for digging, this one is for herding. What do you give to me if I give you my son?' And so now this white father, he would do something very clever, he would reach into his pocket and pull out a handful of this sweet white stuff."

Sebastian described an old man's first taste of sugar as a divine experience: "Old men used sugar cane for their beer, but this was something totally different!" Pretending to be a man tasting refined sugar for the first time, he licked the tips of his fingers. His eyes widened in amazement, as his expression became soft and agreeable: he became, in a word, open, and his new disposition in turn opened Taita to new transformations. "OK, you can have my boy," came Sebastian's reply to the imaginary missionary: "Then, after some time, the same teacher would return, and ask for something from the old man. Something small, like an egg or a piece of sugar cane. He didn't need those things, but he wanted people to learn that schooling had value, and had to be paid for."

These short-term desires for prestige and pleasure on the part of senior men permanently cost them their rights to their son's labor and respect, while also leading to the demise of sugarcane (a male crop) and everything that was associated with it (including the fabled peaceful domestic beer drinks of a bygone patriarchal era). In these men's stories, schooling was the principal site of alienation from the past, epitomized by the fact that it produced incest by destroying kinship: students in the 1990s continued to acquire curses from ancestors because they met in school and had sex without realizing that they were related to each other in ways that were once understood to be socially significant. Importantly, youth and women also often deployed a notion of reified tradition against the present, but often accused seniors of disavowing the past, and the ancestors, by converting to Christianity. As one man in his thirties put it to me, "The youth today are joining criminal gangs because they don't know what else to do, and they are frustrated because there is no avenue for them. Their parents don't understand. They think that their own [deceased] parents are punishing them [from the grave] because they have turned away from the traditional religion."

This is an appropriate point to pose the question, what exactly was Taita like in the past? The classic ethnographic record, a mirror of senior male ideology and nostalgia, suggests a bounded system in which persons of rank developed themselves by transcending, with the help of masculine ancestral spirits, social and territorial boundaries that were ordinarily widely desired and guarded. According to Grace Harris (1978, 56), the Taita social landscape in the early 1950s was defined by discrete, nonexogamous neighborhoods (*izanga*) whose members were bound by complex affinal, patrilineal, and matrilateral exchange and loan networks, including but not limited to bridewealth transactions. Senior men acquired exchange partners and wealth by extending themselves beyond the neighborhood and venturing into foreign lands protected by fighi—a feat that required recourse to magical protection (see also Bravman 1998, 125). Fighi forests marked the boundaries of neighborhoods, and the vast majority of marriages were of people who shared affiliation in a neighborhood, which "strongly resisted the sale or even the loan of a plot to a resident of another neighborhood" (Harris 1978, 11). Yet despite this apparently bounded territorialism, households were fairly mobile, as people took up residence in new locations to plant on other land owned by the household head, cultivate borrowed land, or open up new lands to cultivation. Indeed, mobility was crucial, for the steep and differentiated Taita topography encouraged people to acquire diverse holdings, in terms of size and soil type, in differentiated agroeconomic zones (Fleuret 1985). Moreover, groups of younger Wataita migrated back and forth regularly, throughout the region, into contemporary Tanzania, and to the coastal Swahili towns, to engage in long-distance trade with other peoples.

Men's public authority was based on the idea that they produced social wealth; this authority ran counter to the fact that women performed most of the agricultural work. Men's claims found legitimacy in a ritual system in which ascending males acquired access, over time, to spiritually animated lineage shrines, which authorized, or "called," them to develop in life and acquire greater political and social authority. The senior men of the early 1950s argued, like their counterparts in the present, that their success in life was mandated by spiritual agents (in this case, deceased representatives of their respective lineages) who compelled them to progress by making them sick, thus drawing them into the system of divination, through which they learned what they were compelled to do. In principle, these shrines enabled and forced men to marry, acquire wealth, sit with the councils of elders, and extend their exchange networks over space and into time (Harris 1978, 49–77). The shrines, or *milimu*, were evocative everyday objects of ascending power and importance bestowed, according to the ethnographer Grace Harris, in the following order: cowbell, medicine bag, and sitting stool. They enabled seniors' control over land and people, generated and symbolized by livestock (cowbell), ritual knowledge (medicine bag), and a seat on the council of elders (stool).[2] These days, these very objects, when discovered by younger people, are often held to be "proof" of witchcraft.

Despite contemporary Taita assertions that life in the past was relatively egalitarian, evidence points to a great deal of inequality, even prior to the colonial period. In particular, debts could cause men to lose their herds, and, with the loss of his herd, a senior man also lost customary rights to grazing land, which often meant that his descendants lost the right to use land formerly held by him. In addition to inequalities in wealth, Wataita also recognized a great deal of social and cultural difference among themselves, despite the fact that, over the course of the colonial period, they increasingly came to identify as Wataita.[3] Even today, internal Taita diversity continues to be recognized through the divination system, which, in non-Christian ritual, is the first step toward identifying the social causes of private and public misfortune. This system, called βutasi, identifies people according to their imagined origins, while also attempting to unify them through a shared set of religious terms and practices. In reference to the practice of divination, through which people were identified using a numerical system, Harris (1978, 9) gives an instructive picture of the contested nature, and the fluidity, of colonial-era Taita identity, as expressed in non-Christian ritual:

> The Four people dominant in Teri valley on Sagala mountain were considered to be of fairly remote Giriama origins, but the Four people of other parts of the Hills were sometimes spoken of as being (even more remotely) of Kamba descent. Some of the latter denied the claim, countering that they and the

Six-people were the "real" Taita autochthones while Three-people and the alleged Ten-people were of foreign origin. Some of the Three people in central Dabida claimed to be "from the side of" the Masaii, while others posited ultimate descent "from the side of" the Sambara.

Wataita participated in, and had thrust upon them, many fundamental changes throughout the twentieth century, including migrant wage labor and monetization; the progressive conversion of livestock herds into cash; the increasing importance of schooling for money and respectability; the introduction of cash crops and the gradual demise of sugarcane; and the establishment of the system of administrative chiefs, which enabled young appointed men to usurp and surpass the authority of their seniors (Bravman 1998). It would be too unwieldy to focus in depth on any one of these changes, but it is worth pointing out that today, those who came into their own in the early postcolonial period and who are today's seniors reflect upon the 1960s in terms of a moving away from the ways of their parents and of leaving tradition behind, despite the fact that by the 1960s most Wataita had been exposed to the practices and institutions that Wataita now identify as modern for at least fifty years. Many of the most educated among them acquired positions in the new, independent government and felt it was their personal duty to expunge tradition, which they associated with backwardness and resistance to Christianity.

For example, the state-sponsored library in Wundanyi town was built, in the late 1960s, directly on top of a fighi forest shrine, at the base of a steep incline leading to a peak that became "Government Hill," where one finds all of the governmental and administrative offices of the district. It was Taita people in the Ministry of Lands who organized this allotment after securing the support of younger, mission-educated "progressives" in the area. Their message was straightforward: education and reason were to replace the earlier traditional knowledge, which had protected, and thereby also secluded, Wataita from outside forces. As one now senior male who had worked in the Ministry of Lands at the time put it, "We wanted to get these people to see that a new era was here. That Taita was now open to the world, and that we didn't need to be afraid of things. Even fighi. We felt that fighi was scaring people, so they couldn't develop." Elites of this same generation had also tried to convince people to think of new practices and institutions, such as schooling, as forms of fighi, which would protect and enrich Wataita without pulling them backward. The first Taita-based "nationalist" organization, formed in the 1950s, had called itself the Taita Fighi Union, and it tried to extend the idea of fighi while arguing for a Taita cultural sovereignty guaranteed by institutions that allowed for the appropriation of non-Taita things. As documented in the organization's minutes to its first meeting on November 11, 1950, its members declared, "Fighi reigned over all the people of Taita and the country of Taita [!] before the rule of the Europeans arrived. . . . If we want to uphold the respect of our heritage it behooves us to join together . . . to search for new means of defense, such as education and similar useful things" (Bravman 1998, 247). By building a library over fighi, educated Wataita suggested that tradition was backward and destructive—indeed, that it was witchcraft. But in positing that tradition was witchcraft, they opened themselves up, ironically, to the counteraccusation that their particular brand of modernity was actually a form of witchcraft, because it had subverted socially beneficial traditional practices and boundaries.

Land consolidation, a major reform carried out in Taita at the behest of these Taita progressives during the early postcolonial period, is worth commenting on at length, because, for these Wataita, it was perceived as the material culmination of the new values associated with Christianity and commerce, in the form of a project. In Taita, land consolidation was initiated on a large scale in the 1960s and was still ongoing in parts of the hills in the 1990s. In general, the process involved the transference of rights in land to a single, title-holding individual, typically male, who was then in a legal position to secure loans from banks (at least in theory). At the height of the project (the late 1960s and 1970s), the process typically entailed the consolidation of all of a household's scattered plots into one single, ideally larger, plot, often with a view to making intensive cash-crop production possible. While the late colonial Kenyan government strongly supported land consolidation in Kikuyuland in response to the Mau Mau insurgency, in Taita land consolidation was primarily pushed by educated local elites in the early postcolonial period.[4] They were supported by Kikuyu civil servants, many of whom felt that individual land tenure was a necessary precondition for creating a habit of competitive individualism in landowners so as to break the bonds of dependency created by kinship.

But the steep and rocky topography of the hills was ill-suited for the project: an independent British commission visiting Kenya three years after independence, in 1966, concluded that consolidation would never succeed in Taita, as holdings were so small and so climactically and geologically diverse that it would be impossible to provide people with single pieces of land of the same character or quality as their former holdings (Tom Wolfe, pers. comm.). It was wealthy Wataita who benefited from consolidation, as those who had made an investment in their land by planting coffee and vegetables for sale were given priority in the relocation process, and were allowed to combine their holdings around their most productive cash crop–dedicated plot (Fleuret 1985). Those displaced from prime (*ipara*) land were invariably dissatisfied with their new allotments, which were often located on rocky or steep parcels.

In practice, land consolidation also involved the fragmentation of villages occupied by generations of brothers, who typically lived adjacent to one another and held land in diverse areas (which they often still do). My own limited experience[5] suggests that land consolidation helped put an end to the circular villages composed of agnatically related households, for the new system placed individually owned plots adjacent to one another. Brothers who inherited land tended to follow suit by building their homes next to, but at some distance removed from, one another, usually in a line rather than a circle. In the villages where it was carried out, the process generated a highly charged debate about the nature of the new society Wataita were creating. The process seems to have always been contentious, and very often violent. Wataita said that some people lost all of their land, while others had their new homes burned to the ground by angry kin and neighbors.

People who remember those days—most of whom are now seniors themselves—often state that corruption existed at the level of the local adjudicating committees of village elders, who tended to rule in favor of the claims of members of dominant lineages within a neighborhood composed of several lineages (see also Fleuret 1985; Mkangi 1983). Often they depict land consolidation as a coup carried out by powerful witches, who became even more powerful after consolidation, because they were freed from the social control of their kin and erstwhile neighbors. During my fieldwork, I heard many argue that "modern witchcraft" had emerged with land consolidation, because individuals with occult knowledge that was formerly managed within particular neighborhoods now found themselves in "alien territory," where they felt no qualms about using their skills to terrorize others, and thereby enrich themselves.

A young Taita civil servant who worked in the Ministry of Development once explained to me the link between government development interventions and witchcraft, underscoring the notion that powerful knowledge had become unleashed from kinship, and thus commodified (see also Comaroff and Comaroff 1993, 1999b; Geschiere 1997). He informed me that he understood his work as undoing the terror and inequities that those witches had engendered by establishing development projects (such as a vegetable cooperative) in communities that had been abused or sidelined by witches. In his words, spoken in English:

> Do you know why the witches of today are so terribly strong? It all happened because of money and land consolidation. You know, witchcraft runs in families, but the witchcraft families of today were not always so. Before land consolidation, these families were defenders of villages. They prepared the medicines[6] which were used to make fighi and *mbenge*. They protected us from Maasai and the few witches we had. The old men guarded this information jealously, for our good. They would never allow the knowledge to go to a bad person. But when land consolidation came, everybody was on his own. You may find someone relocated far across the hills, in another region entirely! He is not under anyone's control! Now these men, alone in alien territory, started using their powers to make money. Who was there to tell them they couldn't? They sold their power to others for money! They used their power to grab land and cows and to ruin people!

Those who supported land consolidation also invoked the image of witchcraft against an idea of spatially compressed and polluted conviviality glossed as backward. The idea of "putting people on their own" appealed to many Wataita, especially mission-educated Christians, who associated circular villages, and the central fora (*βaza*) at their center, with the backward tyranny of senior men. As one government chief put it to me in 1998, "The beauty of land consolidation is that it puts every person on his own, and opens him up to real education. When they're together, they learn all kinds of nasty things, like how to bewitch one another."

Land consolidation was an extreme instance of a more general process of simultaneous spatiotemporal expansion and contraction at work in Taita history, and in Taita perceptions of history. While new forms of land tenure engendered positive liberation for some, they relegated others to places where the scope of possible action was severely curtailed, such as rocky cliffs. In addition, while some people acquired a certain autonomy with respect to land tenure and residence, the mobility of the larger population was significantly decreased, as the vast majority of "common" and reserve land disappeared during this period, and formerly public (or, perhaps better said, transcendent) fighi came to be placed on private land.

Yet most Wataita depict these transformations as more sudden and dramatic than they actually were, and this is why it is difficult not to slip between Taita representations of the past and the past as it actually was when writing about Taita history. For example, one young man described land consolidation in terms of interplanetary travel: "You found yourself on Mars!" he declared, in English. In reality, this was probably not the case as, in most villages, people were not relocated beyond their villages (although in some, especially the administrative center of Wundanyi, they were taken quite a distance away), and in most cases new lineages formed around the households that had been relocated.

A Model of Mid-Twentieth Century Masculine Development

The men of the generation that is now senior forged an idealized system that few people actually managed very successfully but whose mastery, they argued, generated development (*maendeleo*), despite the fact that women continued to perform most of the agricultural work. The system ideally involved going to school, which also meant, ipso facto, being Christian: either Catholic, if one was from one side of the hills, or Anglican, if one was from the other side. With education invariably came work. Taita men of all ages say that, up until the 1980s, it was easy for someone with a primary school education to acquire work in Mombasa or elsewhere and, though they certainly exaggerate when they say that employment was close to 100 percent, it seems that most people with education managed to secure jobs. As a councilor put it to me, "In the 1960s, you didn't actually have to look for work if you had been to school. A relative would come from the city and pick you up and say 'let's go! I have something for you.'"

These people who worked in Mombasa often spent their entire working lives there, the most successful working in the hotel and tourist industry, construction, transportation (particularly bus companies), or government, including the police and customs agencies. In reality, wages were rarely enough to allow one to move with one's family and live permanently in the city, even if that was desired. People depended, therefore, on their lands and kin networks in the rural areas, and elites built up homes to secure their connections to these places, even if they almost never visited, which was often the case. At the same time, the wealth of wage laborers placed them in conflict with their fathers as, for many years, senior men claimed that money wages were like livestock, and so belonged to them. Much of this male intergenerational conflict was displaced onto women as, from the 1920s, men increasingly gave their remittances to their wives, who lived in the homes of their husbands' parents (Bravman 1998, 206–28). Moreover, men and women struggled over the control of money earned from cash crops such as vegetables and coffee: throughout the hills, men claimed to be the "owners" of cash crops throughout most of the twentieth century and worked to limit women's contact with these crops, though their efforts were never entirely successful.

For those who did not move away but who depended on those who did, there seems to have always been a sense that those who had left (the lost) were mingling with forces at once promising and dangerous, whose intrusion had to be managed (see, for example, the section titled "Engendering Spirit Possession" in chapter 3 for a description of *saka* possession). Fighi, for example, came to be conceptualized as protecting Taita-ness in general, and so a kind of ideal system emerged through which Taita people were able to survive, if not prosper, by appropriating outside wealth without being changed by values that were perceived as destructive. As Grace Harris put it, in reference to her fieldwork in the early 1950s, "A great *Figi* protecting the plains lying in the direction of Kamba country especially 'disliked' persons wearing traditional Kamba clothing or acting like Kamba. Taita, including [especially?] those suspected to be of ultimate Kamba descent, had to avoid being mistaken by the *Figi* for Kamba; they had to behave and look like Taita for their own safety" (Harris 1978, 9). These beleaguered forests came to symbolize a waning and erratic public sovereignty whose power and legitimacy came from outside the state and the market, and challenged their increasing predominance (see chapter 5). This interpretation is strengthened by the fact, that during this period, Wataita began to be concerned about a new form of witchcraft that fighi were allegedly battling, with minimal effectiveness, in an invisible realm. This form of witchcraft, called herding *majini*, entails feeding household livestock and children to purchased demonic agents (majini) that resemble the commodity form, and whose hunger for blood invokes the imagined shift from an idealized agricultural, kin-based system of production and circulation to one based on cash and markets (see chapter 3). According to Taita stories, these majini appeared to migrant men as apparitions and curses on their way to the city, came under their partial control when they bought them in the city, and moved out of their control when the majini were brought back to the countryside. There, the majini threatened innocents at the same time as they sustained families with occasional cash when their earning males were away from home.

In the early postcolonial period, the wage labor system was propped up by a state patronage system through which politicians, acting as fictive husbands, purported to support Taita families when their male members were away. In turn, Taita migrants were expected to eventually return home and contribute their earnings to development there, typically through state-sanctioned *harambees.* When these men returned home, they did so as Christians, and often spent their retirement days on the church councils, where they achieved maximum respectability (*ishima*), wielded political influence, and managed development projects that came under the auspices of the church; often, these positions opened up opportunities for earning money. Others chose to spend their retirement years working for the "other" church by fulfilling the function of traditional practitioners. They became *wakireti,* or men of the wilderness (see chapter 5), and thus came to embody tradition and its discontents for others. This circular movement from country to city to country again, carried out over the course of a life and interpenetrated by an array of political and mystical forces (the state, demons, fighi, etc.), implied a particular relationship between tradition and modernity in which the two became linked to the country and the city, respectively and, ideally, sustained one another. It is possible to sketch this idealized, phenomenological model of development, which became reified in the mid- to late twentieth century, as in figure 1.

Such a model is of course a fiction, and exists so concretely in people's minds because the current decline of formal opportunities makes it appear more normative and generative to Wataita in the present than it actually was for Wataita in the past. Men were never the only people to work in the city, although fathers, husbands, and in-laws of both sexes did try to limit women's migration. Until recently many women tried to conceal their knowledge of Swahili for fear of being marked as polluted or promiscuous, but they often became prominent social and political figures at home, in their husbands' absence. Moreover, this was not the only mechanism for succeeding during the mid-twentieth century; some fabulously wealthy Wataita never went to school (for example, many men became very rich from game poaching, from the colonial period through the 1970s). Nonetheless, this model secured itself as the one that was most likely to lead to respectability and Taita social welfare, and it is the one

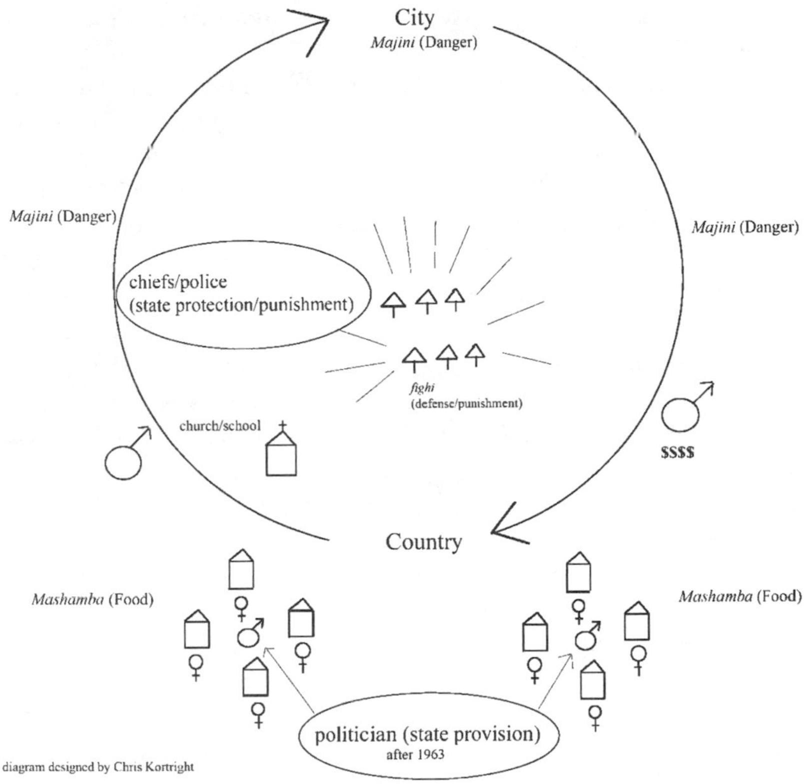

FIGURE 1. A male-centric model of mid-twentieth-century devlopment.

that became most closely associated with progress for Wataita. Wataita often perceive the decline of this ideal network of spatiocultural articulations in temporal terms, as "turning backward."

The life history of the family of Rasta, discussed in some detail in chapter 4, provides an example of the major transformations in Taita ways of making a living. Briefly, Rasta's mother's father, born in the late nineteenth century, was successful in the system that dominated at that time (roughly precolonial and early colonial): he owned, according to Rasta and his father, "countless cows," and he used these cows to develop relationships with senior men in far-flung areas. He had many blood brothers, and he acquired ritual power through the acquisition of lineage shrines and a seat on the council of elders. The next generation of Taita people—to which Rasta's parents belonged—widely considered him to be a witch, largely because his wealth was dependent upon spiritual forces that were excluded from the church.

Rasta's grandfather parlayed his success within that particular model of and for development into success for the subsequent generation of Christian "readers" (*βashomi*, people who can/do read, those who are "literate") when he sold off all of his cattle to pay for the education of Rasta's mother and his mother's brothers. All of these children became the most successful people in Rasta's village, just as their progenitor had formerly been the richest and most respected according to the earlier system, which came to be known as *βutasi* (pejoratively, the practice of spraying beer out of one's mouth). These people used their education to acquire employment in the city. The most successful son acquired a management job in a Mombasa hotel, where he started working in the 1960s. The daughter, Sarah, married Rasta's father, and later became an influential local political figure through her connections with the Catholic and, later, Pentecostal churches. Thus, precolonial elites were able to convert their position into success for the subsequent generation, who came to see themselves as being in opposition to the former system and its values, despite the fact that their lives were the outcome of their elders' success within that system. Rasta's father's father provides an interesting countercase: he was a successful poacher/hunter beginning in the 1940s, and was later employed as an undercover agent by the colonial police, helping them to catch other illegal (read: African) hunters, at first in Tsavo, and then throughout British East Africa. Later in life, he spent most of his time in Tanzania, and rarely returned home. While he often had money and was one of the first people in Taita with a car, he was never quite as respected, nor as feared, as Rasta's mother's father was. Rasta's father used the money earned by his own father, the game poacher, to acquire a substantial education, which helped him to acquire a managerial position in the East African Breweries.

Born in the late 1960s, Rasta had a much harder time securing employment and position than his own parents had, and despite his exceptional English, he remained unemployed and unmarried on his parents' farm when I knew him in the late 1990s. At that time, his entire family, once among the most successful, rich, and religiously devout in that town, was as poor as any other. As Rasta put it, "In the 1970s, when my father worked for the brewery, and we built this house, there was no house like that. We were high/the tops [*juu kabisa* in Swahili]! Now it is a shell. Jealous people outside have no idea about the suffering inside." This formerly elite family responded to their radical downswing in many ways, economic and noneconomic, but the most notable, for others, was their rapid shift in religious denomination: from being one of the most respected Catholic families in the region, they quickly became its first Pentecostals, also known as the "saved" (*kuokokwa* in Swahili).

Neoliberalism and the Dismantling and Reinvention of Development in the Taita Hills

When I was conducting fieldwork in the hills in the 1990s, Wataita were coming to terms with social phenomena that seemed to be simultaneously eroding opposite ends of the idealized modernity that had been constituted over the course of the last century. On the one hand, they felt cut off from the institutions and practices that had long fostered success and respectability. They simply could not find work in an economy where nearly everyone was unemployed[7]—certainly not in a state civil service gutted by structural adjustment programs, or a tourism industry decimated by global anxiety about Kenya's escalating ethnic violence and spiraling crime rate. In this context, every aspect of schooling seemed to have lost value, and Wataita were especially critical of teachers, whom they saw as amoral alcoholics and womanizers, having abandoned the upstanding moral rectitude that had been such a central part of mission education.

One Taita primary school teacher explained that schools were shells of their former selves and depicted backward temporal movement in terms of lost universal knowledge: "Every year, [the colonial overseers of the Kenya African Preliminary Examination] asked us to explain tea. What is tea? We would write A, B, C, D. Later, they would ask, What is a torch [flashlight]? A torch is A, B, C, D. But these days you'll find a student has reached university and cannot explain to you what a torch is. He'll say it is some metal with a light inside. But to really understand what a torch is, inside, that inside secret of a torch, that is very difficult." Most people claimed not to understand why schooling no longer guaranteed access to employment, and often developed occult explanations for this crisis. They claimed that jealous Wataita wanted to "destroy education," and many asserted that schools were bewitched. As one man put it to me, "Wataita have a lot of education! Our people have studied! And yet we don't have jobs. This is because of witchcraft!" Despite their declining value, schools continued to foster a destructive competitive atmosphere in an economy of diminished returns. Students bewitched each other by stealing their colleagues' pens and papers; their parents then "worked" on these stolen objects until their high-achieving owners turned into imbeciles. Moreover, teachers were mostly well-traveled foreigners with access to virulent new forms of witchcraft, which they used to get ahead, sacrificing students along the way.

Youth seemed to feel that history had cheated them out of the opportunities that their parents had. To me, they seemed to be shamed by their parents' relative success, at the same time as they felt vindicated by their relative worldliness, especially with respect to the English language, computer technology, and the Internet (and all of the wonders that are available for viewing on the Internet). Some of these youth, especially the males, at times referred to themselves as the "dot com" generation, or simply "dot com" and they tended to think of cooperative entrepreneurial commerce and religious revival and transformation as the only means available to them for achieving some modicum of success. They were very fond of Swahili rap music, a hybrid musical form that focused on personal improvement, romance independent of family influence, the difficult struggle to achieve development, and the related threat and temptation of witchcraft (Weiss 2002). Youth were well aware, also, of the retreat of the state, and felt that this affected them personally. One young man, when asked how his generation was different from the former, quipped that "those people would get invited to State House [the president's house] to dance, but these days that is all over."

This severance of the articulations that had long connected Taita to the world beyond the hills was combined with a seemingly opposed sensation: mainly, that the autonomy and integrity of Taita locality was being subverted by foreign forces. This sentiment was most evident in the widespread belief that the fighi had "dead batteries," and that this was somehow related to the fact that they were not being cared for or believed in. The liberalization and globalization of the Kenyan economy also profoundly affected people's ability to maintain households through local agricultural production. For example, the liberalization of the East African maize market had encouraged well-connected Taita elites to flood the local market with cheap, imported maize, sold at prices far below what area farmers were able to charge. Additionally, the deregulation of the market in seeds, fertilizers, and pesticides had caused the prices for these commodities to treble in a few short years. Many people found that this inflation, combined with unpredictable and inadequate rainfall (itself widely interpreted as the result of a failure in local morality and the atrophy of Taita identity), made agricultural production more costly and risky than purchasing ground maize for household consumption. The decline of the household as a mechanism for organizing production was matched by the decline of the household as a node of socializing and network formation, realized through the distribution of gifts (mostly food). The fusion of production and distribution, and of the household with Taita society and resources (the world over which Taita was sovereign) had long been expressed in the phrase "a guest is rain"—a comment that linked reciprocity with productivity and the household with society. Now the demise of the household as productive and distributive body was culminating, many Wataita argued, in diminished rains.

Economic deregulation was one among a host of processes that seemed to threaten the viability and integrity of local culture and territory. Men of all ages complained that they had lost control of women and had become dependent on them, and young men accused their parents of pimping their daughters. This attitude reflected the spiraling price of bridewealth, as well as the fact that young women were leaving Taita to trade and manufacture clothes in Chinese-managed export processing zones in Mombasa, where their labor was in higher demand than that of their male counterparts (Taylor 2005). In these unregulated nonunion zones, which employed 40,000 Kenyans in 2004, women (some of them pregnant) were known to collapse from fatigue and sickness, but their wages were highly desired by their families back home (KHRC 2004). This diminished control over women and their reproductive potential came to light in widespread rumors about the scourge of foreign majini, which afflicted the bodies of young women whose education prepared them to leave Taita or to be bound at home, in marriage (see chapter 3).

Local concern and hope about foreign forces was augmented by the unmonitored movement of entrepreneurs and NGO employees across regional and national boundaries, a process that progressively ethnicized local commercial competition and undermined the power of local state authorities (the chiefs). Also at play was the proliferation of commodities associated with a global youth culture, from condoms and rap music to imported "mystery" liquors made from unknown chemicals, which many seniors viewed as strengthening the autonomy and depravity of youth. New forms of transregional trade (in used clothing, for example) took men and women to distant, and mystically powerful, border towns, where they risked polluting themselves, and Taita, with the underbelly of global capitalism—alcohol, prostitution, and AIDS (see also Hansen 2000). Perhaps more than anything, Wataita were perturbed by the rapid increase in violent crime and death, social facts that directly contravened the image of their region as a place of serenity and moist-heartedness. Suddenly, small shops, medical dispensaries, and the homes of comparatively wealthy people were targeted for robbery by gangs of male youth armed with machetes. There was a spate of car and minivan thefts, from individuals as well as schools and government offices, and some automobiles were eventually located in towns as far away as Dar es Salaam, Tanzania.

Most locals with whom I spoke believed that this criminal activity was engineered by powerful Wataita with political influence in both Kenya and Tanzania. For them, this conspiracy theory accounted for the profound incompetence of the police, for when the police acted at all (typically they had to be paid first), they responded in broad-scale sweeps, often arresting innocent youth from out of town at rural video houses and bars. The apparent indolence of the police fueled a grassroots response to crime. Suspected maize thieves were pursued, captured, and set on fire by ad hoc vigilante groups. Their numerous defenders claimed that "corruption" in the police force had forced those wronged to take matters into their own hands. In 1999 and 2000, the provincial commissioner toured the region to beseech communities to desist from taking initiative in such matters; however, a few local chiefs privately lauded the vigilantism, admitting that the state's officers were incapable of protecting the citizenry. At the same time, some criminal youth became heroes of the young, and were bestowed names of global notoriety, like Saddam Hussein. True to his name, Hussein embodied the idea of Taita autonomy with respect to governing authorities: he was said to have lived for months in a cave on a cliffside above the government town of Wundanyi; when he was not stealing from the wealthy or from non-Taita Kenyans in Taita (most of them government bureaucrats), he was allegedly visiting his poor neighbors with gifts of food and money. Hussein held off three contingents of police from Voi for two days in August 1999, was eventually shot, and fell to his death firing into the air a weapon that observers claimed was an AK-47. Local rumor had it that Hussein had used majini to render himself invisible and that the police had to rely on magicians of their own to locate him.

In addition to public concern over crime, much of it from outside the Taita Hills, local commentators complained that death had become an increasingly common fact of life. Many claimed that, in earlier times, people had walked great distances to attend infrequent funerals, often remaining and being fed for a week at a time—some said that their forebears, happily unaware of sugar, canned lard, and mystery liquors, had lived for eons. Now funerals were so numerous that it was financially and physically impossible to attend all of them, and households had to divide their personnel and material support among burials. And so death had caused communities to contract at the very moment when they should have been uniting against the various foreign threats.

But there was cause for hope. As mentioned, NGOs were a major catalyst for the imagination, not only because they were potential sources of income. Many people appropriated their neoliberal vision of sacred humanity, democratic transparency, and reasonable communication to challenge historically entrenched power brokers: in particular, the Catholic and Anglican churches, and the devout Christians, who tended also to have once been successful wage laborers. To make their concerns known to these NGOs, these people formed communities of like-minded individuals and appealed to the shared experience of their frustrated and worldly generation. At the same time, they developed their sense of individual responsibility and worth in the religious sphere by becoming saved Christians (*waokokwa*), and so invulnerable to petty local antagonisms manifested in witchcraft. The more established churches—particularly the Catholic Church, which had formerly been the only source of religious authority in many of the towns and villages where I conducted most of my research—were clearly concerned by what they sometimes referred to as a "revolt," and devout Catholics sought to reestablish their control over key social resources, as well as the concept and practice of development.

Although there are many sociological differences between the mainline churches and the Pentecostals (somewhat more youth and women in the latter than in the former, in particular), the most notable difference in the social composition of these churches is the types of work in which their member are engaged, or have been engaged in the past. In particular, mainline churchgoers tend to be people who have had formal employment for most of their lives, or who hail from families that have depended on male migrant laborers. In contrast, Pentecostals tend to be entrepreneurs of some kind, though not necessarily successful ones. As one, admittedly biased, young Pentecostal man put it, in English, "Saved people are looking for something new, a miracle. They are experimental, and they are not so focused on trying to find work in Mombasa. We know that development can happen wherever we are." Interestingly, many people seem to convert to Pentecostalism after losing their jobs—people who once had very good jobs often segue directly into becoming pastors. One could be cynical about this trend and say that, in Pentecostalism, conversion often translates into commercial opportunity; all people who declare themselves saved can become pastors and need rely only on their wits and oratory skills to acquire tithe money from their followers (regular tithes being a major aspect of Pentecostalism). But Pentecostalism also provides an ideological, and deeply felt, support for being on one's own, and for not depending on higher authorities for jobs and patronage.

The message of Pentecostalism is particularly appealing to anyone who wants to break free from the structures that have dominated social life and economy in Taita, and there is also an interdigitation of Pentecostal thought and the neoliberal subject: Pentecostalism in Taita involves, in brief, individual faith and responsibility; the development of relationships with powerful spiritual figures who try to solve converts' life problems; and the concomitant belief that God is immanent and interested in mundane issues, rather than being transcendent and aloof, or downright abusive, like the colonial bureaucrat-God depicted in the world system origin story above. Pentecostalism, or becoming saved, also implies the rapid accumulation of wealth (the health and wealth ideology) following a break with outmoded ways of doing things (both traditional Taita religion and more modern practices, such as taking bribes and competitive beer drinking), and the total transformation of the self through a process of divinely inspired individuation (Meyer 1998). The convert also physically inhabits secrets that were formerly withheld and were powerful enough to make a person insane. For example, converts like to point out that older Catholics still refuse to read the Bible, for fear that they will go mad, an idea that has often been tacitly encouraged by African priests. Pentecostalism offers a new life, and a form of citizenship that is not prescribed and proscribed by writing and bureaucracy, as Catholicism, with its dependence on withheld texts and hierarchical authority, suggests. Yet Pentecostalism implies that people are almost never free, because demons pervade everything, whether people realize it or not, and any kind of economic progress, individual or social, requires that they be expunged.

Many of these aspects of Pentecostalism are contradictory. For example, the stress on individual faith comes into conflict with the prevailing social dynamic through which searching individuals submit themselves to powerful patrons who wield power over them. So too the elaboration of new forms of secrecy, such as possession and speaking in tongues, conflicts with the overall ideology of transparency. In short, Pentecostalism is far from being the end of history, if only because the religion, in practice, is driven by dialectics that cause most individuals who enter into it to go through certain kinds of experiences. For example, Rasta, whose experience is described in some detail in chapter 4, came groping to Pentecostalism for answers after failing to secure employment and losing faith in the Catholic Church (he was at one point a seminarian). He liked the message of individual salvation, but eventually grew skeptical of the rituals that his patron-preacher compelled him to undergo, ultimately coming to believe that he was being duped, even bewitched. He retained the idea of demonic influence that is so central to Pentecostal thought, but argued that it was in fact the preachers who were demonic. In this way Rasta continued to carry the trace of Pentecostal thought and teaching even after he left the church, and declared himself a secularist with an interest in traditional religion.

The groups that seek assistance from NGOs inhabit an idea of the person, and of social action, that fits well with Pentecostalism and the neoliberal ideology promoted by NGOs, as well as the decline of the state. They are mostly youth groups, and they are in a perpetual incipient stage: their members speak in a charismatic way, redolent of the Pentecostal church, and bandy about ideas ranging from writing a Taita dictionary, to cultivating African violets, to developing small-scale tourism, to selling bootlegged videos, to using the Internet to promote awareness about conditions in the hills to the world community. These groups combine a neoliberal concern with law, order, and office—uprooted from the state, but in some ways containing the state within itself—with at least a tacit interest in imagined traditional forms of solidarity, such as those arising from and embodied in fighi.

Conclusion: Debating Development

To give a sense of the parameters of public discourse concerning development, I reproduce part of one typical conversation that occurred among four men of ages ranging from about fifteen to about sixty-five in 2006. The conversation took place in the home of Rasta, and in this conversation Rasta's father, Zablon, a former quality control inspector for East African Breweries, served as wise and supportive moderator. The pretext for this particular discussion was the proposed formation of a youth group that would begin to implement new ideas about development. The intervention began with an attempt, by several unemployed and critical young men in their twenties, to find a place to meet. In doing so, these youth came up against the fact that the town social hall, which was being managed by senior members of the Catholic Church council, demanded that they pay dues. The prospective organizers felt that they should not have to pay, because the hall had actually been built by an NGO, Plan International, whose funds had been generated by Taita children who were sponsored by American and European families abroad (see chapter 6). These now grown youth claimed that they had once been those very children, whose bare life had paid for the hall; now that they had grown up, they were ready to seize control of their legacy. They also claimed that Taita's backward superstition had enabled the Catholic Church to illegally seize public resources.

In the course of this discussion, those present began talking about ways to develop Taita through business. These ideas were presented in opposition to those of the elected councilor, Christopher Nyange, who was not present, but who had recently presented a speech at a local *baraza*. Nyange was a fifty-something-year-old political figure who had worked in a Mombasa hotel before turning to politics (he had been fired for his union activities when an African managerial staff took over the hotel from its formerly British management in the 1980s). Nyange's main project has always been the reconceptualization of Tsavo National Park: Nyange asserts that the animal and water resources in the park should belong to Wataita because they fall within Taita/Taveta District. Nyange likes to say that Taita is currently "imprisoned" in Tsavo, which has become "a different world created within the district." He wants to bring that world under Taita sovereignty by compelling the government to allow for settlement in the park; confining the animals to large "zoos" that will be managed by the Taita public; and transferring the wealth generated by park fees into a Taita community development fund that Wataita control. Of late, Nyange had been speaking publicly about Taita's mineral wealth, and how unjust it was that mining contracts went to a small political elite from outside Taita. He had informed the local public that the Indian Kamlesh Pattni was one of a handful of Kenyans with legal mining contracts in Taita (see chapter 1 on Kamlesh Pattni's Goldenberg International company).

Nyange has also supported the rejection of President Mwai Kibaki's new constitution, which, he argues, fails to take into account the "existence" of Taita people. (The constitution, proposed in 2005, claimed that water and mineral resources fell under the jurisdiction of the central government. Many Kenyans see this assertion of state sovereignty as a thinly veiled attempt to give Kikuyu people control over the nation's wealth.)

Patrick, who was hoping to become the chairman of the incipient youth group, brought up Nyange in a negative light by invoking the Taita idea of reckless mobility and contraposing this idea to genuine development: "All Nyange knows is what he sees when he's driving through Taita in his car. Notice that only the path to his house has marram [meaning the path has been carpeted with soil and stone with a view to future tarmacking]!" Patrick argued that Nyange's politics were disingenuous and outdated, because the government had no intention of ceding that land, or the revenues generated from it, to Taita people, and Nyange knew this. Moreover, Nyange's message appealed mostly to "old men" who wanted to use that land so that they could "plant maize and beans." According to Patrick, Nyange was trying to retain the primary concepts in the older model of development—wage labor and land/agriculture—but development could no longer be conceptualized in terms of territory. After all, Patrick intoned, "The rains no longer fall anyway!" Patrick claimed that young people wanted to try something else, like forging connections with international donors, and he argued that a practical education might facilitate entrepreneurship and allow individuals to improve themselves: "What we need is to build a polytechnic in Mgange town. Werugha has a polytechnic, Lushongonyi has a polytechnic. Why not Mgange?"

Zablon, the eldest man present, did not think that Patrick's reasoning about the polytechnic was apt, and seemed to see in it the trace of a backward, and essentially Taita, cast of mind—particularly, the blind commitment to education, regardless of opportunities. He introduced the subject of "planning," a word that has been much in vogue in Taita, especially since the NGO Plan International has left the region, and Wataita have taken the concept of planning up for themselves. Planning (or *kupanga mpango* in Swahili) is also an activity that senior men think they do better than anyone else. Invoking concepts such as population and management, Zablon explained, "If everyone decides to enter into one thing, there will be no development. You have to look for what is not there already. Look at this town: how many butcheries are there here? Three! This is more than is needed, when you compare with the population that is here. And how many people are doing laundry? None! So now everyone entering into the butchery business has turned development back, because now there is no profit there." Simon, a young man, agreed, and blamed the lack of development on the Taita "inheritance" of fearful passivity: "You know, there is a particular idea inside the heads of people here. It is like an inheritance. People wait, because they are afraid. They think that they cannot do anything on their own. But then they see someone prospering and they say, 'My goodness, there is development there,' and now everyone begins to follow. We need to teach people that they need to be very creative!"

Rasta chimed in, linking fear to obedience, while declaring that development, which concerns the public as a whole, should be freed from religion, which is a matter of individual choice and faith. He told a story to drive home his point:

> Did you hear about [name of a local Catholic priest]? Two year ago, he hired a secretary to draft letters and keep accounts. He warned her when he hired her that, if she told anyone what she saw, he would destroy her with the power of God. You know what he did? He was writing proposals for funding from America, and he got lots of money, but he just kept all that money for himself! This secretary, she helped him write false reports back to the NGO! She knew what she was doing was wrong, but she feared the priest would curse her and she would die. That priest became very rich, and then he left us. And he took the motorcycle that people had bought for him.

Patrick continued the theme of abusive power, and added that faith in self is the key to development, and therefore development can occur in any place. His argument clearly drew upon the emerging idea that religious worship, and communication with God, can take place outside the context of the church and the clergy: "We have to finally recognize that there is no particular place where we have to be to get development. We have the capacity in ourselves, wherever we are." Simon seized upon this implicit focus on the generative power of locality, and argued that secret, local knowledge could become a powerful instrument of development if it were democratized, and so separated from secret "witchcraft": "Do you remember when the caterpillars came last year, and the people in the Ministry of Veterinary Science could do nothing? Our old men drove back the caterpillars with their medicine, and later these scientists said that our elders had defeated them [the scientists]! These old men are good [effective]! But they have no concept of *society* [in English], and mostly behave like witches!" Zablon, the elder, seemed to feel that the problem was not, strictly speaking, generational, but more diffuse. There needed to be a general respect for what he called "office," which he argued should be distinct from, and above, individual people, interests, and places: "There is a problem of office. People don't know what it means to lead. We have chiefs entering into bars, and drinking illegal beer! If there is a case evolving from the drinking, how can they be expected to be fair, if they were in fact bought beer by someone there?"

Perhaps the most interesting aspect of this conversation, which ended, ironically, when Rasta's sister brought us food, is that it is possible at all. A set of terms and perspectives that were at one time limited to governing authorities and NGOs have become so widespread that it is possible for five ordinary people—admittedly, all of them men—to have a conversation about them without questioning any of the key terms. First, they deploy the concept of a population, or society, which should come together and plan for a shared future, and development is seen as both the outcome and the precondition for this cooperation. One consequence of this concept of society seems to be that people are responsible for managing and improving it: development is thus the responsibility of the people, or "society," whose coming together is an end in itself. Second is the notion that state authorities should be removed from petty conflicts and exchanges, and should be above society at large; in a sense, the state is understood as deserving to govern insofar as it stands as a rational exception to the unfairness that inevitably emerges from close social contacts. The third major concept, redolent of state and more recent NGO-driven neoliberal discourse on heritage, is that culture has potential utility and is "good" when it can be deployed and rationalized for the benefit of the public, which is defined in vague terms (to be sure, this understanding of heritage as an ambivalent instrument extends back to the colonial period). In order to be of value, the past must first be rationally cognized and weighed against other alternatives, an act that already presumes the development of a detached relationship to the past: more like that of a consumer. Finally, dispositions and states of mind are held to be the main factors that influence whether things are moving forward, moving backward, or going nowhere, and individual persons are thus held to be ultimately responsible for the continuation of abusive practices and institutions.

The group's reaction to Nyange's ideas was particularly suggestive. Nyange's concepts were explicitly political in that they were directed against abusive state practices and structures, but they were criticized because they came across as disingenuous and unrealistic: blaming all their troubles on Tsavo and giving people a false hope about owning Tsavo was, the group felt, Nyange's way of being reelected councilor, and so securing a salary from the people. The alternatives to Nyange's views frankly depoliticized politics, and so harmonized with neoliberal ideology by foregrounding individual responsibility, awareness of market logics, and self-transformation. All of these themes have a long history in Taita discourse and understandings, and so are not intrinsically neoliberal (they have, for example, African and Christian equivalents), but the erosion and retreat of established structures opens up a new space for such musings and makes them seem all the more vital. This shift in understandings of development is partly related to the history of political abuse in Taita, and the conflict and poverty that has come from depending on, and becoming indebted to, politicians and chiefs. It also suggests that Wataita are adapting to the demands of contemporary capitalism, by opening themselves up to new social and economic flows, while also harnessing a potentially marketable autochthony grounded in loosely conceptualized traditional values (chapter 4; see also Geschiere and Nyamnjoh 2001; Comaroff and Comaroff 2001).

Pedagogy, once directed at Wataita by institutions like the state and NGOs, is now generalized, and "reasonable" people feel the imperative to use that reason to convince other people about how to leave their indolence, fear, and backwardness behind. While this interest in teaching is also not exactly new, and dates back at least to the early days of mission Christianity, what is new is the direction that pedagogy takes: in particular, toward creativity and invention in response to the perceived inadequacy of structures. Thus, the conversation above reflects a general uncertainty about how development might be created and an urge to search for alternatives to development as usual, grounding those alternatives in a self whose actions and attitudes cause opportunities and futures to emerge. Thinking about development in terms of dispositions and personalities, as opposed to structures, dovetails with the idea that witchcraft turns development back, because witchcraft is caused by certain emotions and attitudes (such as jealousy and indolence) that people can be taught not to have.

In chapter 3, I examine Taita ideas about the opposite of development—witchcraft—focusing on witchcraft as a form of badness that, many Wataita felt, had to be excluded for development to emerge. Examining witchcraft beliefs also allows us to understand how Wataita conceptualized social boundaries, where they understood threats to order and the good life to emanate from, and how they sought to shore up boundaries against malicious forces. Subsequent chapters explore Taita attempts to transform witchcraft into development in various spheres: the family (chapter 4), the past (chapter 5), politics (chapter 6), and subjective intentions (chapter 7).

CHAPTER THREE

Development's Other: Witchcraft as Development through the Looking Glass

In this chapter, I examine Taita understandings of witchcraft (*βusaβi*), dwelling on the ambivalent and relative nature of power and the perceived importance of creating and maintaining spatial and temporal boundaries that were also selectively permeable. For Wataita, witchcraft was the shadow of development—and development was the shadow of witchcraft, for neither was more real than the other—and witchcraft represented the dark antithesis of everything that Wataita felt modernity should be. After providing a brief description of different types of witchcraft, and the social dangers they referenced and represented, I analyze Taita concerns about *majini*—shape-shifting spirits from the urban coast that have long made up for the inconsistencies of men's wage labor, and that are now said to have gone berserk, attacking schools and young women on the verge of productive promise. The narrative revolves around a group of young women who felt themselves to be possessed by majini, and focuses on public understandings of this event, which were partly rooted in the gutting of the civil service under International Monetary Fund (IMF)–mandated austerity programs.

Witchcraft as a Synonym for Breached Social Boundaries

The Ambivalence of Power, and the Need for Boundaries

Rasta and I sat with my aged friend Marki, drinking palm wine from a plastic container that Marki's son had recently brought from Mombasa.

It was several days old and had turned quite sour, and strong. Marki was convinced that this was the best way to serve palm wine. Rasta liked visiting Marki for the stories, but disliked eating the food that we were served at his home. He felt that Marki's place and his ways were filthy, and perhaps he had a point. Marki was in his nineties and had begun his working life as a cook for German soldiers in neighboring Tanzania during World War I. He was, many would say, an agent of Taita modernity, for he had owned one of the first butcheries in the area, was one of the first Catholics in his town, and had introduced his area to a number of commodities that were new at the time, which he had purchased during his travels. But in his town Marki was known for his stories of life long ago, and for his skill at *βula* divination, and so he was considered one of the last surviving bastions of authentic Taita tradition.

Marki claimed to know exactly how much various items had cost at different points in his life, and he was able to give a history of inflation that reflected, in part, his understanding of the ebbing and flowing power of particular sovereigns, whose faces were imprinted on the currency. Queen Elizabeth's country was powerful and, most importantly, people's faith in her was strong, and colonial Kenyan money reflected this. During Jomo Kenyatta's time, the money remained strong but lost some of its value, because his actions and antagonistic disposition had offended foreigners. Under President Daniel arap Moi, money had become almost worthless, and its size had also diminished: the twenty shilling note, which was once able to purchase a cow, now could not even purchase a soda, and was reduced to a cheap coin that could be hollowed out and turned into the kind of rings young men give to girls. Unlike that of most other Wataita, Marki's view of the past was neither dark nor rose colored: there were always rich and poor in Taita, the wars with the Maasai were violent and terrible, and witchcraft had always been a problem. Under British rule, ferocious chiefs made up for the insecurity of their position by creating a culture of fear based on torture and plunder. Indeed, Marki had once been repeatedly submerged in water for hours, and nearly drowned, for impregnating a woman that he later refused to marry.

This time, Marki was explaining the origins of local retail commerce, with a focus on the market town near where he lived. He explained that, when he was young, what is now the market was a clearing surrounded by forest. When the young men of that time finally convinced their elders that "money was a good thing," the old men agreed to have an animal sacrifice, plant herbs in the ground, and perform a collective blessing (*kutasa*), all of which was aimed at bringing them customers. Afterward, people sang and danced for three days, and soon others began coming to the market from faraway places. The implication of Marki's story seemed to be that commerce, peace, and the successful appropriation of foreign value (potentially antagonistic outsiders and their goods and money) were so difficult to achieve that they required occult action, and that this positive power emerged ultimately from a collective unity of purpose and sentiment. Marki was clearly convinced that the market's extraordinary energy was proof that something miraculous had happened there: "You have been all over the world. But have you ever seen a market like that one, where the people are thick like leaves?" Marki demanded. He continued, explaining between sips of palm wine that the ancestral spirits in the forest had paid attention to the community's prayers, but that their power was weakening now because, ironically, the forests had vanished because of the growth of the market. In other words, unchecked commercial capitalism (the growth of the market) had threatened its own foundation by destroying social unity rooted in history and embodied in the forest. Familiar with this idea, discussed in more detail in the following chapters, I pursued another that had been bothering me for some time: Was this founding ritual witchcraft (βusaβi) because it involved accessing occult powers? Similarly, was Elizabeth a witch because her power was contagious, and followed her image? Marki seemed taken aback and adamant: "Witchcraft (βusaβi)?! Eh, no! A witch is a person who hates others. Those old men brought [the town of] *Mgange* up! They brought development!"

Later, when Rasta and I were walking home from Marki's place, he expressed his dissatisfaction with Marki's answer. Rather than seeing his history of the market as an ironic joke, as I was inclined, Rasta had taken Marki at his word: "How can that old man say that what they did is not witchcraft? To think that the reason our town has this market is because of some crazy old men years ago planting dirty things in the ground and talking with demons. It's embarrassing, *bwana* [man, mister, dude, etc.]! Let's be fair with each other, please. Do you really think that God has time for some old men digging around in the ground and spitting beer out of their mouths? Any money made there is coming from Satan." Rasta disagreed when I suggested that those men's expectations did not differ greatly from his, for he also anticipated great results from prayer: "But the difference is that it is secret. They were speaking in a demonic language.

How can anyone repeat what they have done, if they wanted to? And besides, that guy is dirty bwana."

The conversation with Marki and Rasta revealed a significant point about the idea of witchcraft, against which different groups of people imagine different types of righteous social order: mainly, few agree as to what, in fact, witchcraft is, aside from the fact that it is destructive, and this disagreement reflects the great diversity of opinions about the value of specific practices, places, and times. Thus the lack of consensus about what witchcraft was drew attention to the lines of social and ideological cleavage in Taita society, and also suggested alternative visions of the future. In principle, most Wataita asserted that some people had access to incredible, invisible forces, and the use of these forces was not necessarily witchcraft (or βusaβi). But in practice, any kind of occultism was likely to be perceived as witchcraft by those who differentiated themselves from, or felt themselves excluded by, those practicing the magic.

That witchcraft was best defined as destructive, rather than mystical, action was strengthened by the fact that many people told stories about "witchcraft" that had little to do with occultism. Once, walking through the market with a friend of mine, we were greeted by a young man who seemed somewhat confused and distant. "That man," my companion informed me after he left, "is being tied by someone," a common euphemism for being bewitched. When I offered that this young man might merely be "high" from smoking marijuana, which is readily available in the area, my companion retorted that these states resulted from the same kind of action: "If I give you something that does harm to you, and I make money from your turning backward, then what I am doing is witchcraft." Another friend told me of his close call with devil worshippers, practitioners of an advanced, transnational form of witchcraft. While riding on a bus to Nairobi, he had met two affable businessmen. When the bus stopped midway, my friend happily accepted the well-dressed travelers' invitation to a short feast of roast goat and beer, and again they boarded the bus for Nairobi together. When my friend awoke half-dead the next day, shorn of his wallet in the middle of a Nairobi street, he knew that he had been poisoned and mugged by devil worshippers: their dress and apparent affluence was the proof ("Devil worshippers love money!" he insisted). Still another friend informed me that one of the most traumatic events in his life was catching his mother's brother, the man who he considered, and who should have been, his strongest supporter and closest friend, trying to bewitch him. As he narrated the story, it emerged that very little irrigation water had been entering into his plot, and he suspected someone was diverting its course. One night, he followed the water canals from his compound up the hill and found his mother's brother in the process of rerouting them. "*Uchawi*!" he moaned, recollecting his disappointment.

In disputes at the chief's office, the idea of witchcraft was invoked to account for all kinds of secretive, destructive acts, including a woman who allegedly trampled her neighbor's maize fields at night, and another who was accused of keeping her husband in a state of constant inebriation so she could take over his bar business and divert the profits to her natal family. Even being involved in many cases at the chief's office often led to the rumor that one was in fact a witch, and such evidence was its own proof. In part, the use of the term witchcraft was a rhetorical device, in that it served to convince others that something was inherently wrong with the person in question, and that his or her very existence threatened everyone. But this simultaneously broad (in its practical aspect) and limited (in its moral aspect) understanding of witchcraft is important to keep in mind because it emphasizes the drawing of threatened social and moral boundaries, rather than extraordinary, supernatural feats in and of themselves. Power, in this definition, always tends toward being occult, but it is only immoral, and hence witchcraft, when it resists domestication by a community that defines itself as such. Of course, stories of pedestrian witchcraft were not those that dominated public discourse, focused as it was on the spectacular tales of the particularly powerful witches, or on speculations about virulent new forms of witchcraft.

Thus power was itself ambivalent, as Geschiere (1997) has also argued with respect to witchcraft in Cameroon, and Wataita made sense of this ambivalence in their jokes about substances that seemed to contain both witchcraft and development within them. Feces were a recurring example. When used as an instrumental tool, feces were always destructive: witches used shit to bewitch people, and their inability to contain their bodies was part and parcel of their occult power. They chewed with their mouths open, neglected to wash their hands, left their feces on the floor of the pit latrine, and sometimes wrote their names, in shit, on the walls. But when properly controlled, shit was positive: abundant feces indicated health and prosperity—a regular flow of value into and out of the body. Appropriately contained feces symbolized productive social order and figured in senior male ideology, where they referenced the importance of retention over dissipation and escape. In male-governed divination rituals, abundant feces in the large intestine of a goat meant that Wataita would hold onto their harvests. When senior men drank together, they sprayed beer out of their mouths, intoning what they understood to be an ironic and amusing blessing: "May your house overflow with shit!" (*muzi ghwako ghuchuo vichinga!*). Similarly, older people often reminded others of the value of their inherited cultural legacy by declaring, "If your child shits on your thigh you will not cut it off" (*Mwana ukakunyea ndambi ndekuichwa*), for social and historical attachments determined the meanings of actions and their products. Furthermore, when Taita males declared the virtues of hard work and deference, they said that "he who is loyal to an elder shits a big stool" (*mdumuβa βanyaa kichinga kibaa*). As embodied power, shit referenced the successful outcome of relationships but, according to senior males, only upright men could ensure that that which tended toward being harmful was beneficial. After all, only an old bull, or wise old man, knows how to hide his shit, or painful secrets, under his tail (*Njau mbaa yadavisa kichinga ghake na kizeri chake*).

The viscerally repugnant substance shit, then, was also, like fat, one of the signs through which Wataita reflected upon the violence of witchcraft, but it also embodied Taita understandings of moral relativity and social boundaries that, many felt, had the capacity to transform something negative into something positive. And it was not only senior men who argued for the importance of containment, focusing on shit as a symbol of power that needed to be controlled. The fat public official, or chief, who drank so much that he shat himself in a pub, the witch who left shit on his victim's door, and the society that allowed its shit to overflow from public pit latrines were ultimately the same in that they each epitomized the dangers of unregulated action and breached boundaries. Here uncontrolled shit indexed political abuse and misappropriation, and the extent to which their shit was contained was, by many accounts, the measure of Taita's health and development.

Tellingly, many stories about the existential struggle between witchcraft and development centered on pit latrines, the technology that circumscribed dangerous, but natural, human potential. Devil worshippers were held to throw babies into pit latrines as a sacrifice, or tithe, to the Satanic Church. Majini owners kept their occult properties buried inside their pit latrines; they acquired money by literally throwing household wealth and public futures into the toilet, where they were "eaten" by the majini. Similarly, witches prayed over the holes in their pit latrines, summoning up dark forces from the fetid ooze below to shower them with deceptively clean commodities, like brand-new passenger minivans. Wataita tended to be very proud of their public and private "VIP" pit latrines, just as senior men were proud of being able to keep their family's shit under their tails. The fact that politicians were appropriating the land on which pit latrines were located (a practice people called "toilet grabbing") through convoluted and invisible dealings with government officials in the Ministry of Lands was proof that boundaries were being breached in a way that allowed signs to become detached from referents (pit latrines and government from development). In the interstices separating these breached boundaries and disentangled signs, witchcraft erupted as explanation.

Witchcraft, then, referenced dangerous forces that resisted social control, as well as the absence of spatial and temporal order itself, but witchcraft was also the product of people's efforts to master spatial and temporal processes. Thus, one man explained that commercial competition unleashed witchcraft from social control. The desire to market the capacity to kill and, in turn, to protect oneself from new sources of death had the consequence of giving time a life of its own—moving constantly forward, while simultaneously driving people back, such that people now struggle, impossibly, to keep up with time *and* witchcraft: "Witchcraft has become this problem because of *modernization* [in English]! If I am making a beer, and you want to make one to compete with mine, you will find a way to make it stronger, cheaper, faster. So it is with witchcraft. Now this has gone completely out of our control!" Witchcraft also came to permeate space in pace with people's heightened capacity to move unmolested from one place to another. Thus, one man imagined a Taita past in which sovereign villages were internally at peace but externally in a state of potential war; movement from one space to the other was fraught with danger, and it required the construction of fictive kinship. Now movement through space has lost this symbolic meaning, and people are free, but they exercise no control over their relationships to others; this loss of sovereignty is productive of, and synonymous with, witchcraft: "Our fathers were terrified of going very far away, unless they had some relation, like blood pact (*mtero*) with someone there. Even if they were men of mtero, they could be killed when passing through a village on the way to their destination. In those days, the witches were always over there, and they used their witchcraft on us in warfare. But these days, it is all around us. They are our own neighbors! How does one control something like that?" Controlling witchcraft, then, meant controlling spatial and temporal process, which required strengthening social boundaries.

Imbuing order upon the sources and forms of danger began with the act of naming and representing them as a prelude to acting on them, and Taita understandings of social danger came to life in a tripartite typology of witchcraft: African witchcraft (traditional and modern), Arabic/coastal witchcraft, and transnational/American witchcraft.

Types of Witchcraft in Taita, and Their Underlying Universality

Wataita spoke of a wide range of witchcraft practices arranged on a hierarchical scale. As they ascended in potency, they allowed for a greater removal, and alienation, on the part of the witch, just as increased power in the real world allowed certain people to leave Taita behind. Thus, advanced urban witches could bewitch someone with a mirror, while less advanced witches actually had to put some poison in their victim's food or drink; unfortunately for the perpetrator, some of these poisons worked too fast, making the witch vulnerable to detection. More advanced forms of poison took years to develop and grow in the body of the victim, sometimes only finishing the job twenty years down the road—thus distancing the witch from the bewitched. These advanced poisons also assumed exotic forms, such as fine electric wires that resisted detection by both physicians and "traditional" healers. Less advanced witchcraft required more social mediation for its success: these witches had to use people as intermediaries in order to disguise their close connection to the victim. In addition to advanced and less advanced witchcraft, there was witchcraft for making oneself go forward (also called "witchcraft of money") and witchcraft for holding others behind (called "witchcraft of jealousy" or "eye"; *iriso*). The somewhat more worldly, and advanced, experts in the witchcraft of money also ended up "blocking" (*kurugha*) others out of the process of wealth acquisition, as their occult knowledge allowed them to monopolize business opportunities, kill off competitors, and easily exploit neighbors.

Overlaying these distinctions (advanced vs. less advanced, procapitalist vs. anticapitalist) was another distinction related to space and time. African, Arabic, and American witchcraft were of different types, originating in different places and having entered Taita at different historical moments. Each had different implications, which were related to people's anxieties about the respective place and time. African witchcraft had the most variation because some forms were more advanced and modern than others—many poisons were relatively available, while the skills needed to plant electric wires in someone or to "persuade" people to work as zombies while they slept (or thought they were sleeping) had to be purchased, usually outside of Taita. All African witchcraft involved learning some skill that enabled the person, or witch, to kill or to prosper without working. Purchased African witchcraft tended to be more advanced than traditional, inherited witchcraft, though no less African and no less dependent on skill. In contrast, Arabic witchcraft, discussed in more detail below, involved the use of spirit familiars (majini) that Wataita purchased from Swahili merchants in coastal towns. These majini also came in two types: majini of protection/murder and majini for making money, both of which required the sacrifice of social resources (children and livestock). Unlike African witchcraft, using majini involved no skill at all: the purchaser of majini became a witch by proxy, buying an animate life form that the new "owner" could not easily control. This form of witchcraft was particularly dangerous, because it was so easy to come by and use, the benefits were clear and tempting, and the majini were relatively independent actors. Finally, devil worship, sometimes called *ushetani*, arrived in Africa very recently; it was also global, though centered in the United States. Some described devil worship as a kind of pyramid scheme, while others spoke of a transnational, hierarchical crime syndicate with gruesome rites of initiation. Devil worshippers set up churches that mirrored, but symbolically inverted, Christian churches, and they offered converts vast sums of money, often under the guise of Pentecostalism. But they compelled their new recruits to engage in heinously violent acts of commerce (such as stealing and selling babies, blood, and human organs), which placed them in contact with fantastic new places, people, and temptations (underground skyscrapers and satanic megacities on the astral plane with sophisticated divisions of labor and manifold bureaucracy).

These spatiotemporal distinctions referenced the different sources of danger and conflict in Taita society in the late 1990s, as well as different degrees of power: African witchcraft signified the fear of violence from jealous kin and neighbors, as well as from people who were so desperate that they wanted to get ahead by any means necessary. Majini spoke to Taita's dependence on relatively close places and people beyond Taita—places that often drew Wataita away from what really mattered. And Satanism referenced and epitomized the lure of foreign things and values, which were transforming economies and polities in unprecedented ways. Satanism also indexed relationships with a defunct state, and with international agencies that were operating along with the state in inscrutable ways. Despite the general interest in devil worship as a commentary on world affairs, global commerce, and high-level national politics, Satanism in its strict form (the Satanic Church) seemed fairly remote to most Wataita. This antichurch, it was felt, had become a problem in major cities that were gateways to the world, like Nairobi. In daily life, Wataita were far more concerned about the scourge of majini from the coast. In the following section, I argue that this concern had to do with the dissolution of their historically important and vital relationship to the urban Kenyan coast and wage labor in general.

Of Spirit Possession and Structural Adjustment Programs

A Case of Spirit Possession

For two months in 1998, female students in a primary school in the town of Wundanyi found themselves the victims of majini possession. The affair was said to have begun with the affliction of a single girl in 1996, the daughter of a local Taita farmer and a mother who purchased clothes from Tanzania for resale on the local market; her family was comparatively poor, and her mother was clearly the primary income earner in her family. The girl had lived with her sister for some time in Mombasa, and had plans of returning there, hopefully to find work making clothes in one of the new, Chinese-managed export processing zones (EPZs) outside the city. But her father hoped that she would find an educated and affluent husband, perhaps one closer to home. The girl, torn between working in the city and being married and thus bringing bridewealth to her family, had fainted in class one morning, and then entered a trance state, moaning and writhing on the floor. The *jini* that possessed her then spoke through the girl in a thick, masculine voice, using Kiswahili (the language of commerce) to inform her (or rather, his) listeners that his name was Mohammed; the name denoted the jini's Islamic orientation and coastal provenance. Mohammed said that he had been brought to the area by a specific Taita man who, everyone knew, had been working in Mombasa as a civil servant and, like so many others, had suddenly lost his position. Upon being asked by teachers and the school headmaster what she, or rather the jini, wanted, the girl replied, "I want to destroy education [*elimu*] in Taita." She was apparently calmed by Christian prayer and later left the school to live with her sister, now a nurse in the coastal town of Kilifi. Mohammed's interest in destroying education implied that he and his spiritual brethren wanted to turn Taita backward by destroying a historically central site of articulation with urban centers.

The possession incident occurred again in late 1997, and the cases increased through 1998, as other school girls were seized by spirits; they now claimed they were being sexually violated by the majini. During the months of May and June, the majini penetrated eighteen girls between the ages of twelve and fifteen, all said to be among the brightest students in the school. For weeks, the girls ran around the school yard en masse, at times even into town, where they howled at passing adults and the town's many civil servants. The incident came to the attention of the district commissioner, who ordered that the school be closed down if the possessions did not abate within a fortnight. The headmaster responded by holding school prayers in the hopes that, as recounted to me, "the Holy Spirit would take away these demons." Christian, mostly Pentecostal, preachers were invited to visit the school, and they came from towns progressively larger and further away. One claimed he felt an intimation of complex evil associated with commerce and modernity: at the site of a tree stump he saw an invisible "skyscraper reaching to the sky, filled with demons." The preacher ejected the spirits in a mass ceremony that had all the girls writhing on the ground, screaming and, some said, foaming at the mouth.

A single girl could be afflicted by more than one jini at a time, each entity competing for access to the voice that would enable its needs to be met, while in the process slowly consuming the young body's blood. The girls screamed and moaned, and were heard to growl such commands as, "Bring me a chicken!" a comparatively expensive form of flesh that Wataita typically eat on special occasions. The majini's taste for chicken suggested that they came from an urban milieu and were suffering from their recent deprivation. The girls, for their part, appeared inordinately strong in their possessed state, and often held off the advances of two or three young men endeavoring to wrestle them to the ground. When they recovered from their afflictions, they tended not to remember anything about the possession. Sometimes they claimed to feel fine, but often returned to a trance state, repeating such outbursts as many as fifteen times over the course of a month. When the police and teachers asked them why they ran about the town in a frenetic state, the girls sometimes responded that they were instructed to commit suicide, or that they were approached by a knife-wielding bearded man donning a white *kanzu* (a Swahili robe worn mainly by Muslims) and an Islamic hat (*kofia*). When examined by the headmaster and the invited ministers, the girls, or rather their majini, openly identified their owners (those who purchased them) and described the terms of the contract under which they were purchased. They were, in effect, creditors demanding the payment of debt in kind, with interest.

Majini as Substitutes for Human Labor

Wataita held that their experience with majini was a by-product of their familiarity with Mombasa and other Swahili cities, and dated back to their entry into wage labor in Swahili-dominated towns on Kenya's coast during the colonial period. Majini are entities purchased with money, and they are rumored to live either in containers in secret places in the house or in the hole of a house's pit latrine. Though not biological beings, their desires are of a visceral nature: majini crave blood (*pwaga*) and interact with human beings solely for the purpose of having their hunger satisfied by their human helpers. Blood is of course iconic of many things for Wataita, in particular the relationships, values, and goods that are produced and circulated through "bloodship" (*upaga*, the Taita word for kinship). And so, in consuming blood, majini consume the social world in its entirety. Majini are also commodities that are owned (*kushamwa*) by individuals, but control does not accompany this kind of ownership. Rather, majini own their owners, because over time the latter are compelled to sacrifice their real, enduring interests in order to satisfy the needs of their occult property. In exchange for the blood they receive from their guardians, majini create wealth through the occult manipulation of the phenomenal world. They thereby produce value, that most capricious of human labor's products, out of nothing, making a mockery of the commonly espoused Taita moral ideal that would have work, prosperity, and virtue be indissoluble.

The goods that majini confer range from ordinary comestibles like tea and sugar to such sublime symbols of affluence as automobiles and passenger minivans. These objects are not, however, what they would appear to be, as today's shiny new Nissan minivan (*matatu*) may actually be a rogue elephant, or even a rock whose appearance has been altered by the jini's magic; often, the majini are said to live inside the thing (the elephant that appears to humans as a minivan) and to be the engine that makes it work. Majini thus produce simulacral goods of illusory value, and it is unclear whether the objects are actually transformed or if the majini distort the perception of those who touch or gaze upon them. People say the jini typically begins with an established quantity of cash (perhaps 1,000 shillings, or approximately $18.00 a week), and later supplements this allowance with luxury goods bestowed randomly, even whimsically, as if without design. Majini hold to a contract that assumes consistency on the part of the owner, but if conditions change, the jini becomes a violent repossessor, going after things (people, property) that do not actually belong to the owner.

Wataita say that, in exchange for the goods and currency they provide, majini have very strict and regular requirements the satisfaction of which forces their owners to discipline and routinize their daily lives. These jini owners become ironic caricatures of what many Wataita understand as "developed" people: they are punctual and follow a strict regimen, but all of their activity, and all of their household wealth, goes into the toilet as it were, where the majini often live. All majini are unique, having individual (usually Arabic) names, tastes, and needs, while their owners are progressively turned into automatons. Thus, a particular jini may demand a bag of rice and a red rooster every Friday, or a black and white cow once a month. It may even require its owner to wear certain kinds of clothing on particular days, and to provide blood food at a prescribed hour. The specific content of the requirement (e.g., black goat and rice) is unimportant in and for itself, for the jini is being arbitrary and capricious on purpose, as if to make a point. For example, in the town where I lived, there was one woman who could be seen wearing red every Thursday, a behavior sufficiently regular, disciplined, and yet apparently arbitrary to generate public suspicion that she was keeping majini. I believe it was equally crucial, though infrequently commented upon by Wataita themselves, that she illegally sold beer out of her house, in that many Wataita related this activity to the corruption of the family and the "problem" of uncontrolled commercially oriented women (we will see that ideas about majini relate to this fear as well). In any event, Wataita said that the jini owner's enforced conformity was extremely demanding and labor intensive, often requiring a family to go without food because of the energy and resources it spent satiating these spirit helpers. As one mother put it, highlighting the negative consequences of converting life into things, "Majini make families starve!" (*majini ghadabonya mizini bwagho ni njalo*). Thus, the jini resembles a Taita version of the commodity fetish, a purchased thing that appears to produce wealth out of nothing; assumes the character of a living being with individualized desires and personality; and produces, as a by-product, an alienated and dehumanized human subject, a slave to the products of her labor (Marx 1977, 127–28).

When individuals cannot satisfy their majini, they are set loose at public sites, which they then set about terrorizing. These sites are in a sense possessed, and it is important to think about the meaning of these places, because they are as much a part of this symbolic tapestry as the majini. In particular, schools and roads figure prominently in these discussions, and majini are often held responsible for many of Kenya's numerous road accidents, as well as the failure of schools to provide work to students. For example, majini appear on the side of the road to travelers and workers en route to the coastal city of Mombasa. On one level, this popular belief that the majini are responsible for accidents implies that an occult agency is responsible for the decay of roads. On a deeper level, schools and roads play a powerful role in the public imagination, as they have historically been the means through which people became respectable citizens by liberating themselves from the limitations of the rural, and accessing the city. At the same time, these very sites are said to be responsible for alienating youth, both physically and culturally, from their rural homes. Majini thus invade those places that symbolize connectivity for Wataita and that have facilitated their movement from "home" to an urban source of promise and danger.

Majini, Money, and Commodities

Majini are arguably iconic of money itself, not only in that they appear to create wealth *ex nihilo* but also because, like money, they effect the conversion of capital goods (labor, cattle, and crops) into consumption goods (sugar, tea, minivans, and more money). In the Taita case, the majini-mediated conversion of objects of one kind into objects of a different kind also collapses an idealized symbolic opposition, transmuting two opposed standards of value that encode an array of related distinctions. Thus, objects created by majini, such as alcohol, tea, meat, or household amenities, are more or less immediately and individually consumed, rather than being recirculated within and beyond the household. In contrast, Wataita (especially but not only men) describe livestock (which majini consume) as meaningful (*ya maana*) or enduring (*kilambo cha matuko mengi*), because they (1) maintain their value while continuing to generate surplus in the form of milk and offspring, which can be exchanged for needed money; (2) can be loaned, exchanged, or shared between two or more men in wealth and prestige-generating transactions called *vuturi*;[1] and (3) can be converted into children and, consequently, future generations, by virtue of their idealized role in bridewealth transactions.[2] In sum, then, the qualities, or qualisigns, that humans and majini exchange are ontologically antagonistic to one another (Munn 1986, 16–18). The jini actually gives nothing in the process of converting blood into commodities, because it has merely effected a physical distortion of things already existing in the world. In contrast, its owner sacrifices the very real future of his or her family, household, and even community—embodied in blood, pastoral animals, and children–for the immediate enjoyment of consumable commodities. By turning productive resources into consumer goods and destroying the means for the production of these resources (e.g., maize, children, and livestock), majini help to make a world where Wataita are no longer producers of value, but consumers. In the process of destroying the future, they obliterate the past, as relationships with the dead fail to be reproduced in offspring and communities. The result, according to many Wataita, is tragic, amounting to nothing less than the destruction of the means of reproduction of the family and the world.

Taita ideas about the qualities of money and witches are also symbolically linked to one another. As mentioned above, Wataita felt that commerce had increased the volume and diversity of witchcraft knowledge, had turned productive occultism into witchcraft, and had made people more inclined to resort to witchcraft out of perceived and real need. Wataita often said that "money is a witch" (*pesa ni msaβi*). By this, they seemed to mean two things: on the one hand, money breeds conflict between people over how it should be used. On the other hand, it allows people to turn one kind of thing into another kind of thing without regard for social consequences (e.g., land into beer). "Money is a witch because it can do anything, even if it's terrible," people often said. Also, in a way reminiscent of "bitter money" among the Kenyan Luo (Shipton 1989), Wataita commonly said that, if people followed money alone, they would become poor. Moreover, worrying about money, like "foods of money" (canned goods, sugar, and many cash crops), caused the heart to race and develop *presha*, or high blood pressure, which ultimately led to death. One woman linked Taita's increasing dependence on money to the jealousy of non-Taita in positions of political influence, suggesting that their witchlike characters had turned Wataita into "people of money": "We used to grow coffee and food together [in a single plot] back in the 1970s, but those Kikuyu agriculture officers told us we couldn't [they were encouraging mono-cropping]. Why? Because they were jealous of us, and knew that if we had both food and money, we would be truly rich, richer than them! So now they have left us poor, with money and no food, while our ancestors were rich and fat!" The symbolic equation between majini and money is epitomized in the jini's form, or rather in its lack of form, because majini are shape-shifters who render themselves beautiful (and feminine) so as to divert attention from their deadly nature. As one young woman put it, "Imagine now you have gone to a disco. There you meet a beautiful woman, and she invites you to her home. Of course, you go. When it comes time for her to serve you tea, she does not get up from where she is sitting. No! What does she do? She simply extends her arm over your head, to where the sugar is some meters away. Now, I ask you, is this a human being? It is a devil (*shetani*)!" Majini stories thus also imply that monetary wealth is seductive and erotic, that it opens a person to the dangers and promises of desire. Additionally, stories about majini transcending the limitations of space and time evoke the image of expansion, speed, and escape in Taita notions of progress and the good life, while also implying that this promise is itself dangerous because majini keepers are gradually lured away from the real, rooted, sometimes ugly communities that nonetheless generate enduring social futures.

Engendering Spirit Possession

Taita ideas about majini also reference the perceived intersections of sex, gender, and commodification. In some ways, majini resemble women: as mentioned, they often take the form of women and are said to be kept by women while their men are away, in Mombasa or elsewhere. Moreover, men at least associate many of the commodities that majini convert with women, and majini are attracted to goods that women like and use, such as perfume. On a more general level, men associate women with consumption, and themselves with production, despite the fact (or perhaps because of the plain reality of the fact) that, in most households, women have long been primary producers of food, though not always of money. More directly, majini are, these days, analogous to women in that they are the invisible producers of a household's wealth. As a Taita government extension officer informed me early on in my fieldwork, "If you dig deep, you'll discover something major has changed: women now own everything!" Indeed, women emerged as dominant owners of wealth in the 1990s, partly because of their increasing out-migration to work in the EPZs in Mombasa and partly because nongovernmental organizations preferred to support women's groups (importantly, women originally formed these groups because they were unable to secure loans from banks on the basis of title deeds, which were held in men's names). Moreover, the declining value of men's paid labor was matched by the fact that women increasingly traveled, often for extended periods, to distant border towns and cities, where they sold used clothes, food, and other goods. Many men disliked women's involvement in commerce (especially long-distance commerce and the making and selling of illegal beer in one's house), despite the fact that they depended on it. Stories about majini thus partly reference men's resentment about women's entry into commerce, because majini dramatize the inversion of women's idealized roles. Thus, ideally, women actualize the conversion of livestock, agricultural goods, and money into offspring via bridewealth, and, in so doing, they turn relationships between men over space into relationships between generations over time. However, in majini stories women do exactly the opposite: they convert children into commodities, and life into things, by feeding them to majini.

Thus, both men and women claimed that families had increasingly come to rely on majini as the value of men's work in cities had declined, and so linked the prevalence of majini with the declining power of male labor and masculine virtue. Demonic spirits stood in for absent male labor, and Wataita said that they had been doing this since the beginning of wage labor—making up for the inconsistencies of remittances and the uncertainties of employment, dangerously filling in the gaps in the not-so-seamless articulation of country and city. But many women contested the idea that majini and women were somehow synonymous. The jini's seductive and apparently innocuous exterior self may have appeared female, but on a deeper level, majini were male: they were fictive husbands standing in for absent male labor. Many women portrayed them as aggressive rapists, violating girls' bodies, in addition to families' control over female production. While their female appearance spoke to the beguiling character of majini and the commodities they produced, the fact that they were "really" male suggests that majini are fluid nightmares; they can index the danger of declining male labor and value, and the related violation of women's autonomy by men who draw on them as thinglike resources.

It bears keeping in mind that possession by, or because of, commodities and spirits that resemble and produce commodities has a history in Taita, and this form of possession seems to have emerged at the same time as male wage labor migration. Specifically, the possession of school girls in Taita in the 1990s recalled a phenomenon witnessed by the anthropologist Grace Harris in the 1950s, wherein Taita women afflicted by a form of possession known as saka entered into a trance similar to that experienced by the school girls. The possession was typically triggered by a young woman's exposure to objects associated with men, male labor, and men's movement to the city: "Sometimes a particular sight, smell, or sound is responsible: the sight of a motor car, the sound of a train whistle [denoting travel to cities], the sight or smell of a cigarette, the sound of a match being struck, the sight of a bright piece of cloth, the smell, sight or taste of bananas [at that time, a male cash crop]" (Harris 1957, 1048). As Harris noted, all of these triggers indexed "an activity, as well as a physical area, of which Taita women have little experience in comparison with men: the world of wage-labor outside the hills" (Harris 1957, 1051). According to Harris, the treatment for such affliction consisted in a kind of socializing homeopathy, as women were made to play out their longing to be male, as well as their longing for absentee men, by ritually indulging their desire for "masculine" things. Thus, "A lighted cigarette may be forced between her clenched teeth and this normally revives her" (Harris 1957, 1050) and "One standard prescription calls for drinking water in which a man's lower garment . . . has been washed" (Harris 1957, 1049).

Saka seemed to reflect women's frustration at being closed out of the city, as well as their desires for things from the city, and for experiencing the city itself. On the other hand, saka, and the healing rituals surrounding saka, also reflected men's anxieties and issues: mainly, that the value of male migrant labor invested in particular commodities was appropriated and consumed by women in a process that was detrimental to the wealth and authority of senior males, formerly embodied in land and livestock. Moreover, women's apparent hunger for commodities was akin to a blood lust, as it propelled men to work in difficult, life-draining labor to support their seemingly insatiable spouses.

Revisiting the Spirit Possession Cases of the Late 1990s

The school possession events of the 1990s built on the historically entrenched issues surrounding majini, but projected them to a new level. On the one hand, Taita rumors about the meanings and causes of this and similar events reflected widespread concerns about rapid change; on the other hand, the experience that young women had of being possessed is more difficult to interpret because it was more than a social commentary or "weapon of the weak," though it certainly reflected their experience of large-scale events and processes. Again, when asked why majini had chosen to possess primary school girls at this particular time, many men and women argued that unemployment in the civil service in the wake of structural adjustment programs had caused former jini owners to lose their jobs. As a result, they explained, majini owners could not continue to feed their occult properties, and the majini had therefore chosen to make their demands for blood public by possessing human subjects at community sites (e.g., schools). This belief linked the possession of Taita's future, embodied in adolescent girls, to Taita's now threatened connection to formal employment in Mombasa (the focus on schools drew this home all the more).

The majini's new behavior indexed a larger change in the social relations that have long fed majini–for if they were once symbolic of the dangers implicit in what could be called modernity's articulations, in the late 1990s majini were taking on the features of modernity's disintegration. Wataita's ability to access development had been breached because the currencies of articulation were unhinged, in part by the firing of one-third of Kenya's civil service corps in the 1990s, and in part by the rising costs of schools. Consequently, majini could no longer be contained within the outmoded system of relations that once fed them; they were forced to venture out of the private domestic sphere and into the public arena. In the process, their very nature had been altered. Once they were fictive husbands making up for the inconsistencies and insufficiencies of male labor. Now they were abortive would-be mothers, making explicit the impossibility of reproducing the recent past (not the experience of a generation of some time long ago but that of a recent previous generation of labor migrants) in the way that it was remembered.

But these interpretations do not fully enable us to understand the social conditions of possibility of the experience of possession. Clearly, we need to ask what it is about the subject position of these girls, and the urban, commercial Swahili culture with which majini are associated, that made the threat of possession by majini feel so real. Majini possession is a prism through which multiple social concerns are commented and acted upon, and gendered conflicts cohered around these representations and interventions. Thus, for men, the possession of schoolgirls confirmed women's openness to malevolent, commercializing forces and their complicity in the transformations that were ruining the countryside and disempowering masculine moral-political authority. Yet the experience of the possessed drew attention to the violent violation of their own boundaries and the physical appropriation of their sexuality by forces they did not control.

As mentioned, Taita women have increasingly migrated to nearby cities and to far-flung market centers in Kenya and Tanzania in search of employment and commercial opportunities. Most young women with whom I spoke about Mombasa had at least some practical experience with the place, and viewed it in positive and liberating terms; those who lived there rarely expressed a desire to return to Taita except for short visits, and they demonstrated a kind of behavior that could be characterized as at ease in comparison with their more restricted behavior at home. I did not know all of the possessed girls well enough to make a general statement about their motivations, or even enough about their social positions to be able to make a sensible sociological comparison with those who were not possessed, and would not wish to reduce their experiences to a single idea. However, drawing on my conversations with the first possessed girl—who seemed torn between being an object of value for others and a producer of value for others—I do believe that at least part of what they were experiencing emerged from a particularly structured feeling: increasingly, their families depended on them to survive, and this threatened their future ambitions from the very moment they began to realize themselves as women capable of difficult work and of giving birth.

Wataita commonly contrasted the bridewealth exchange patterns of the present with those of the past, asserting that, formerly, bridewealth consisted largely of "being there" (*kukaiyana*), of assisting one's in-laws in agricultural labor. Not surprisingly, young men were the strongest defenders of tradition and accused their fathers of disavowing the spirit of the past when they had converted to Christianity. As one young man put it, "Bridewealth is not supposed to end. It is the promise to always assist your in-laws in times of need. Say, in case your wife's father's hospital bills must be paid, or if his fields need clearing. You must help. It is not a purchase, but a relationship that lasts forever. Now these people, they see a young man who seems to be developing, and they'll ask him for 5 million shillings [nearly $10,000.00] straight out. That is trying to make your fortune out of your daughters, which is wrong!" Although most Taita bridewealth was paid with money, Wataita preferred to extend payment over time, usually continuing to pay the wife's eldest brother following the death of her father. They argued that, even if the agreed-upon funds were available, completing payment on the debt too early would be "like buying a wife," thereby commoditizing affinal relations. However, desperate times had led many to depend on received bridewealth to pay off debts and make ends meet. Schooling also contributed to the rising cost of bridewealth, as fathers raised the "price" of their high-market daughters, partly to make up for the drastically increased price of school fees under structural adjustment.[3] Furthermore, bridewealth had come to appear more like commodity exchange because the field of actual bridewealth recipients in a wife's minimal lineage had narrowed, and these in-laws increasingly pressured men for prompt and regular payments.

Thus, many people, both male and female, argued that women had increasingly become commodities themselves, in part because of men's personal indebtedness. These girls could soon expect to be the objects of negotiation over bridewealth, which appeared to be changing fundamentally as the result of economic transformations of a global scope. Thus, the girls may have been expressing their concern about the possibility that they would be transformed into exchanged objects, with a concomitant loss of social power. As one girl confided in me, "I am an educated girl, and so I will bring my father a high bride price. But this I do not like, because it means that I will have no power in my new household. My husband will say, look at all the money I spent on you. You must do everything I say." Another, very insightful young woman in her twenties put it this way: "Many girls they are tired of being treated little cattle. They know that their families are depending on them for money, and this makes them crazy. Sometimes, they revolt, and decide to go away [to Mombasa], just to show everyone that they can make it on their own, and they can bring back money to the family through their own work. But either way they end up turning themselves into slaves for their parents."

Thus, the girls' desire to acquire education in order to work and provide for their families was in conflict with their families' desire to use their education, and the possibility of future employment, to levy higher bride prices, and so control their daughters' futures. Perhaps the feeling of being possessed was instigated by these conflicting forces taking place in and around their bodies, plunging the girls into a state where they felt themselves truly transformed into a demonic caricature of money.

For both the girls and those who speculated about their possession, the incident drew attention to two interlinked processes: on the one hand, Taita was engulfed by processes that they did not control, and on the other hand, Taita was cut off from generative points of connection with the world outside of Taita (e.g., formal employment in Mombasa). This feeling of being cut off from modernity while also being absorbed by foreign things and values that society could not control defined Wataita's contemporary experience, as outlined in chapter 2. This experience was embodied in the belief in new, foreign forms of witchcraft that were held to have become a problem because national borders were vulnerable, people were moving to distant market towns in search of work, and formerly taken-for-granted means of making a living had disintegrated. Thus the concern about new forms of witchcraft was part of a larger patchwork of concerns that were related to Taita's experience of neoliberalism and the disintegration of an earlier model of development, in which nation-state sovereignty and the separation and codependence of urban and rural spheres were assumed. All of the processes discussed in chapter 2—imported food and liquors, spiraling prices, cross-border theft of local resources, violent crime, and increased AIDS and death—joined forces with the disintegration of the currencies of articulation of an earlier model of development now glossed as traditional (schools and wage labor, which were now understood as specifically Taita inheritances) to create a situation that local authorities could not control.

Conclusion

In this chapter I have argued that, in Taita, witchcraft was development through the looking glass, and vice versa. Witches were able do all of the things that developed people were able to do—such as distancing themselves from their surroundings and manipulating space and time—but they did so by curtailing others and by turning others, and often themselves, backward (*kuruduisha nyuma*). In turn, the fact of being turned behind, which all Wataita claimed was central to Taita's current historical condition, was synonymous with witchcraft, and witchcraft was most prevalent in those institutions that appeared most threatened by decline. Thus, roads, offices, markets, and schools were seen as places of intense witchcraft attacks, and also places that were sabotaged by witchcraft. The jini Mohammed's threat to "destroy education" in Taita drew attention to something that Wataita feared had already taken place—mainly, the unraveling of the totality in which schooling, formal employment, and households had ideally been bound. Thus Taita understandings of witchcraft drew attention to these two seemingly contradictory dimensions of neoliberalism and globalization (related to simultaneous engulfment and disconnection). Most Taita discussions of witchcraft and development were concerned with the problem of forging a sustainable development based on the selective appropriation of foreign things that were in harmony with Taita's perceived uniqueness.

Ideas about witchcraft encourage the selective construction of boundaries by presenting an oppositional foil that provokes strong emotions, for witchcraft is abhorrent, and the witch commits actions that should not be possible, but are. Yet the emotions that are the foundation of witchcraft are entirely normal, in the sense of being regularly experienced by almost everyone, which is partly why people who confess to bewitching tend to be forgiven. These emotions are also boundless, so much so that to represent them means to dabble in fantastic images and to flirt with the absurd: the witch turns dead things into living things, can alter the physical properties of things, and can obliterate normal spatiotemporal constraints. But the implication of these rumors is that the magical and fantastic do not belong only to the witch, but also to the virtuous person or community that truly desires the social good. These fantastic things are believable because the passions and desires that undergird them are real, and do make improbable things possible.

Witchcraft, Evans-Pritchard (1993) wrote, explains unfortunate events. No necessary relationship exists between the representation of reality embodied in the witch, or jini, and actual reality, but in these beliefs and accusations real issues and affairs press in at all angles, and from many different directions. Sometimes these beliefs seem to capture reality to such an extent that they approach classical political philosophy, and this is satisfying in part because some hint is evident that such representations could form the basis for a political community when one is sorely needed. For example, the devil worship rumors of the 1990s certainly approached political philosophy in arguing that Satan was at work in the IMF, that Kenyan political elites were selling out national futures as part of a global satanic plot, and that all the currencies of the nation's articulations (money, roads, schools) were contaminated by satanic forces that drove society back in time. But witchcraft also draws attention away from structural issues by blaming putatively evil individuals whose actions we, as outsiders and anthropologists, believe to be the effects of structures. As James Siegel has put it in relation to antiwitchcraft killings in East Java, "The witch, it is true, threatens political power. But 'witch' could be the basis against which a polity is formed only if the witch could be identified and thus built into an ideology. The fear of witches, as we have seen it, is directed against something unnameable" (Siegel 2006, 216).

There is truth in this statement: in Taita, girls blamed demons, and the people who unleashed them, not because they understood the failures of structural adjustment, but because they were giving a name to their own feelings of despair, inadequacy, and lost control. These people spoke metaphorically about structures, but did so in a way that was so awry, and so obfuscating to reality, that it made life seem more out of control, more alienated, than it actually was. But even if the evil is unnameable, witchcraft beliefs still attempt to fill this evil in with content—to contextualize it with a place, a time, an accent, a style, a set of specific habits and desires, an age, a sex. The images of witchcraft that people created were symbolically constituted, and they did instigate social change by causing people to reflect on abuse and unfairness through the invocation of an idea of essential evil that often convinced others of the need for change.

In the following chapters, we move beyond abstract representations of witchcraft and development to sites where people struggled over the meanings of development, invoking the concept of witchcraft as development's antithesis in their efforts to shape society and give meaning to their lives. I examine some Taita efforts to control the present by producing social boundaries that were selectively open to outside influence. I show where witchcraft and development came into opposition through particular social conflicts around different issues: family relationships and debts (chapter 4), the value of the past (chapter 5), interactions with the state and international patrons (chapter 6), and the irreducibility of sociostructural differentiation, which made any idea of pure evil shrink in the face of complex social reality (chapter 7).

CHAPTER FOUR

"Each Household Is a Kingdom": Development and Witchcraft at Home

Wataita often commented, sometimes in lament and sometimes with pride, that "In Taita, each household is a kingdom." Some said this to mean that people were selfish (the growing culture of *ubinafsi*, or individualism in Swahili), while others used the phrase positively to argue that each household exercised sovereign power over its own affairs (as the old men said, "an old bull hides his shit under his tail," *Njau mbaa yadavisa mavi ghake na kizeri chake*). Most also argued that social efforts to forge and protect boundaries on the basis of kinship used to center on larger social formations, such as minimal lineages—hence the use of the words *mnyango* (door) or *mbenge* (gate or fence enclosing several households) to refer to these social groups. The word "mbenge" is also used to refer to medicine planted in the ground at the entry point to a house's compound; it kills people who wish to do harm to those who live in the home and is considered by some to be a form of witchcraft (though this is a debatable point for Wataita). The use of the term "mbenge" to refer to powerful magic, a gate, an extended family, and a lineage of historic depth suggests that this level of social belonging is understood as powerful, and this power must be protected from competing powers that would subvert it. But in the 1990s, Wataita understood that the locus of family sovereignty was, increasingly, a more or less nuclear family, reflecting a progressive contraction of recognized blood relations at the very moment when people felt they needed to depend on larger kin networks because of declining income and price inflation. All Wataita with whom I spoke claimed that the home was supposed to be a private sanctuary protecting its members from a social world that was increasingly venal. If the household had come to appear in some ways sovereign and independent, the inhabitants of each individual household had also linked themselves to new, often transnational, networks of people, organizations, and ideas (such as the nongovernmental organization [NGO] Plan International or a new church or pastor). Often these networks seemed to undermine the autonomy of the household, even though the household's autonomy was the precondition for its participation in these new networks.

In this chapter, I first discuss Taita debates about how the meanings of development are embodied in everyday, taken-for-granted things and processes that cohere around the household. The household is the place where morally ambivalent forms of value are siphoned into the project of social production, a process that Taita men say is epitomized in "chewing tongue meat" (*kuzha nyama ya lumi*), a phrase that refers to serious and productive talk among men. Men often use this phrase to mean that the meat earned by men and cooked by women is transformed into productive words shared among men, which in turn generate value, embodied in real and figurative meat. And so household work is also the dangerous and promising work of making the future, and households become models for the production of alternative kinds of futures. The house is also one of the major sites around which gendered conflicts, often expressed as debates about what development consists in, or what kind of person is most capable of generating it, take place. In the second half of this chapter, I focus on a family whose members' efforts to progress forced them against the thin line separating development from witchcraft, while also throwing widespread gendered and generational conflicts into broad relief.

The layout and structure of each Taita home can be read as, in part, a statement about the family in question, and its connection to local and global forms of power. Of course, these statements are always constrained by a family's means. Because the construction of a household follows upon marriage, it is, in most Taita understandings, the outward expression of a man's physical and economic independence from his own natal homestead. It is also a symbol and a product of his successful payment of bridewealth—because the construction of a household follows upon marriage, its very existence implies that the husband's family has already contributed significantly to bridewealth payments. Thus, the household is supposed to be the outcome of a man's efforts to create and maintain social relationships through the circulation of gifts among kin over time. Moreover, the household is the place where values are converted through gendered labor, such that men and women come to take on the qualities associated with different kinds of work. Specifically, this is the space where, ideally, money earned by men in urban labor markets is transformed into blood-enriching food and local social relations (also understood in terms of bloodship, or *βupagha*) through women's work.

The household is thus a model of patriarchal authority that also entails an argument about the proper appropriation and distribution of wealth, the value of the past, and the nature of men and women. However, houses are also cut through with repressed meanings that subvert these masculinist ones. Of particular importance is the already mentioned fact that women have of late become the primary producers (arguably, they have always been) and are increasingly understood to be the *owners* of household wealth because of the "gifts" that national and international NGOs have provided to women's groups, women's increasing participation in long-distance trade networks, their entry into wage labor in export processing zones, and the predominance of matricentric households. Indeed, a survey of households that I completed in 1998 revealed that more than 80 percent were either entirely headed by women or headed by women with men in absentia. Few households received anywhere near enough money from men's wage remittances to satisfy a family's various obligations; most received a sum that was largely symbolic, communicating the desire to give something substantial without transmitting the substance.

Wataita consider their houses to say quite a bit about themselves and their society, and their reflections on the relative value of the past and present often turn to the social lives that different kinds of houses potentiate. For example, many men tend to associate the "traditional" house with historical and moral continuity; they said that the traditional house had the advantage of being "moist," referring to the way it caused people to feel as much as to temperature. But many of the relatively prosperous and educated Wataita identify these houses as generative of incest, and so also of social contraction, temporal reversal, and heat. Similarly, for men, "modern" households (*nyumba za kisasa*) are associated with privacy and detachment (ubinafsi), but also with social contention and the loosening of men's control over women's sexual lives and natures. Larger transformations influence the meanings of house architectures: For example, a former clerk in the Mombasa high court who had allegedly earned his millions (of shillings) by acting as a liaison between judges and high-paying defendants had the most ostentatious mansion in the hills—complete with a circular driveway and satellite television hookup. After the popular election of Mwai Kibaki to the presidency in 2002, the clerk was prosecuted for fraud. As the sums he had expropriated were gradually revealed to the public in painstaking detail, his neighbors were forced to reflect on the disconnect between the signs of development, ideally embodied in the home, and the realities of private greed, which many linked conceptually to witchcraft.

Houses of Thatch and Houses of Cards: Traditional and Modern Homes

While Wataita arrange their domestic spaces in many different ways, in discussions they tend to focus on the difference between *kienyeji*, literally native, houses, and modern houses (*nyumba za kisasa*).[1] While kienyeji houses are abundant in the lowlands and in places where land has yet to be "consolidated" by the government, few are found in the highlands. Kienyeji houses are round, mud and stick houses with thatch roofs, no windows, and a single entrance of hanging grass. At the interior center of the home is a pole (*mngio*) which supports the roof and acts as the central, supporting pillar of the house. In colloquial expression, the mngio is equated with the male household head and with the principles of patrilineal descent in general. Thus, Wataita say, "a man is the mngio of the house" or, "let us be like an mngio against divisiveness." In a previous generation, it was on the mngio that ascendant male seniors placed their personal lineage shrines, through which their own personal careers, and the identity of their independent households, were symbolically wedded to the development of patrilineal minimal lineages (cf. Harris 1978). The mngio rises up from the three-stoned hearth (*mafigha*), the uppermost stone propped up against the stove (*iriko*), as protection from the fires. The mafigha constitutes the experiential center of the household, the space around which people congregate to eat and talk, and is also the place where women work to transform raw substances into social things (such as food) that are also meaningful values. It is also likened to the womb or the vagina (both of which are called *kifu*), just as the mngio, with which it is physically connected, is colloquially likened to the phallus. The union of the phallic mngio and the uteral mafigha constitutes the central organizing structure of the kienyeji household, around which everything else revolves. In relation to the signifying elements of the household, the

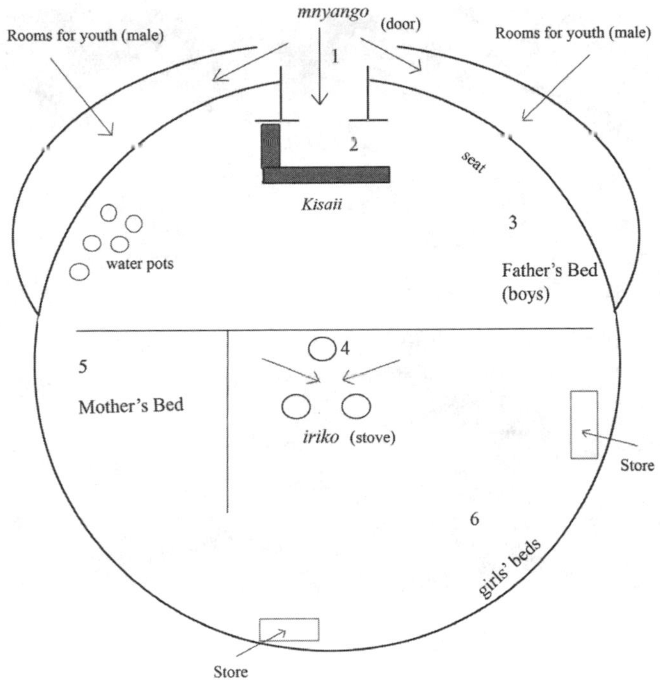

FIGURE 2. A senior man's depiction of a traditional Taita house, showing the important sites (numbers are his).

mngio is also the dividing line, separating the house into relatively interior and exterior spaces, which are cast as male and female, and moist and hot, in relation to one another. This use of space tends to reinscribe masculine ideology, as the passage of food from the female side of the house to the male side incorporates female labor into the male-dominated world (see figure 2).

While the markedly female hearth (mafigha) is the focal site of domestic discussion and eating, men say it is also that place where disruptive emotions are produced and circulated, especially when mothers and daughters-in-law share in the act of cooking. In their own poetic application of language, Wataita men often say that bad words climb up the (male) mngio and out into the world, where they would be heard were they not closed off by the leaves that tie the thatch roof (*nyasi*) to the mngio. These leaves are called *mwambari*, or "closing," because they seal the male household from the outside, protecting it from the destructive emotive

FIGURE 3. The decorated wall of a young man's bedroom.

forces that emanate from inside the house, where women sit. (As one senior man explained the function of mwambari, "man and wife should be one thing, and they must not be separated by words that tell the world that they have slept in hunger.") This male model of social control and boundary creation is founded on the presumption that, in order to create social peace and prosperity, men must first contain women's contentious and usurping natures (specifically, their diversion of household wealth to their brothers and other natal kin). "Woman," one man put it to me, "is a woodpecker gnawing continually at the branches of an expanding *mvumu* tree," an indigenous species whose long, thick roots are associated with historically enduring kinship systems.

Also implied is a homology between the heat of the iriko and the heat of women, and of women's gossip. In the traditional house, the mother and her daughters sleep in that part of the house called the "other side of the mngio," that farthest from the door. They thus inhabit the hot and smoky area of the house, and that most removed from the public. The male household head typically sleeps on what is called the "cool side of the mngio," near the door, where he is visited by his wife, who retains her permanent sleeping location by her daughters. Dependent sons occupy semiautonomous rooms attached to the central house, but separated by the exterior wall and accessible by a separate outdoor entranceway. Their comparative autonomy and independence in relation to girls, and the notion that the survival and expansion of a patrilineal lineage depends on a father's ability to control his daughter's sexual habits, is thus inscribed onto the household, which has become the visual model for a certain kind of social order.

Most Taita senior men praise the old kienyeji-style Taita house as an example of something they feel has been lost: mainly, men's paternal control over women, animals (now mostly absent), and the "hot words" that threaten civility (*sere*). Moreover, when Wataita remember these houses, they also remember the villages they comprised: at one time, these villages allegedly contained up to twenty agnatically related houses arranged in concentric circles around a central common space called *βaza*, where villagers gathered and ate around the old, who told them stories at the center of this social universe. Older Wataita often contrast the βaza to the modern school, with its less upright form of pedagogy, more individuated in its consequences. Senior Wataita often blame such social evils as AIDS, incest, and the atrophy of Kidabida language on the physical absence of the βaza in contemporary homesteads. What they are bemoaning is the loss of a social and historical center, a centrifugal point around which allegedly orbited concentric circles of decreasing moral community, represented by the relative genealogical and spatial distance of a village's inhabitants from its physical center, dominated by a small group of senior men.

Again, the modern household is distinguished from the kienyeji household by the wealth required to construct and maintain it, its spatial separation from the outside world and the neighboring community, and its internal compartmentalization. In modern houses, bedrooms are separated from the other rooms by doors or by cloth hung from a rope at the top of the doorway. In some cases they are even marked off with chalk messages that announce, in English, that the visitor is entering the "sitting room" or the "master bedroom." In contrast to the kienyeji house, the modern house is typically constructed of bricks, either mud or cement; these are sometimes painted red to match the color of red-bricked European homes. The roofs of "modern" houses are made of corrugated iron, and such houses are often divided into two main parts separated by an interior compound set off from the outside by a wall. In very modern homes, the entire household may be surrounded by another cement or stone wall as much as 10 feet high and topped with glass or barbed wire, accessible through an iron gate.

Wataita often refer to the modern home as prestigious, and argue for their comparative development with respect to other coastal peoples by citing the fact that they have many such homes. But many Wataita, including young men, also claim that the modern home is responsible for adultery and unwanted pregnancies, as their separate rooms allow daughters to sneak out to meet their lovers at night (hence gender and age subordination figure in these stories). The perceived "heat" of square houses is also rooted in the sometimes violent struggles that the construction of these houses have precipitated; indeed, many witchcraft attacks are said to be instigated by the construction of a new house. This contention is partly related to the fact that the late colonial and postcolonial governments have typically given exclusive ownership rights to those elites who have been able to invest in their land by building cement houses.

Despite the fact that Wataita often speak of their history in terms of rupture, and in turn project this rupture onto their houses (traditional vs. modern), in fact a great deal of continuity exists, as differentially positioned Wataita work to materialize particular interpretations of Taita values in architectural forms that appear European to an outsider but that are now Africanized. Consider the homestead of Zablon Mwanda, the head of the family whose affairs are the subject of the following section. Zablon was at one time an employee of East African Breweries, who rose through the ranks to become a quality control inspector. To gain access to his large, rectangular home, his visitors (who, Zablon says, are rain) enter through an iron door and emerge in the compound. There, the women of the house clean laundry and sort, dry, and grind maize. Within the compound one finds a machine for grinding maize, a chicken coop, and a water tank "donated" by the transnational NGO Plan International. The visitor faces one wall and has his back to another, which is topped with shards of broken glass bottles glued into the top surface. To the right (in Kidabida language, this is called the "male" side, *mkonu ghwa kiβomi*, or the hand of the male) is the main house, in which Zablon; his wife, Sarah; and his daughters, Lydia and Erminah, sleep. Thus the control of the male household head over the women of the house is inscribed in the layout of space in a manner similar to that of the kienyeji house, though less markedly so.

Both the modern/*kizungu* (European) house and the traditional/kienyeji (local) house have a mediating space called the *shighadi*, or enclosure. In the kienyeji household, the shighadi is located immediately outside the home, constituting a common space between two or more agnatically related households. In a more individuated modern house like Zablon's, however, the shighadi is located within the nucleated homestead itself: an open-air space between the walls that separate the house from the outside, it lies centrally between the left and right spheres of the home. In the left side (in Kidabida, literally the female side, *mkonu ghwa kiβaka*, or the hand of the female) of Zablon's home, one finds the kitchen, where Sarah and her daughters spend most of their time cooking, chatting, and greeting mostly female visitors. The kitchen is hot, filled with smoke and soot from the often-lit fire. Within the kitchen, a small granary is placed above the far wall of the room, where Sarah stores dried maize and vegetables, cooking utensils, and her own private items. The granary is the most secret domain of the house, and the most likely place to find witchcraft paraphernalia (cf. Auslander 1993). The female kitchen is spatially and symbolically opposed to the "moist/cool room" (*chumba cha mbeo*) on the right, male side of the house, where Zablon and his brothers, kin, and male friends meet to chew tongue meat. Indeed, from the dominant male perspective, this room is cool because it is the space where men chew tongue meat, while women, over in the kitchen, share those hot words that sometimes poor out of the house to the detriment of everyone, as the kitchen is more open to the outside than the sitting room. For men, the kitchen derives its heat in part from the commingling of many women and, thus, many hot words and hearts in one place. Thus, whether the house is traditional or modern, witchcraft is said to originate in the kitchen, usually entering prepared food in the physical form of poison, and moving from there out to the cool/moist sitting room where unsuspecting male visitors meet and converse in seemingly peaceful dialogue.

Modern rural houses like Zablon's contain many references to urban lifestyles and experiences, and these signifiers (photographs, diplomas, letters, books, and depictions of wildlife reminiscent of what might be found in tourist hotels) are situated in the masculine areas of the house (in particular, the sitting room) and typically reference the male household head's success in the world beyond the Taita Hills. As in the homes of other relatively well-off families, the rooms of Zablon's house are meticulously decorated with posed photographs of the family, calendars, framed Biblical verses, diplomas, and certificates from schools or training sessions organized by state and nongovernmental organizations. The family displays greeting cards sent from relatives and neighbors living or working in Mombasa and Nairobi, hung from strings that criss-cross the sitting room where the walls meets the rafters. These cards wish the addressees great success in all their endeavors and bear photographs of modern young people in suits having picnics by brooks or dining in Nairobi's fancier hotel restaurants. In the main sitting room, a picture of Job and a Biblical verse warn of the adverse effects of jealousy on the human condition.

The eldest son, Rasta, has made his most personal surroundings, his bedroom, a testimony to his desires and ambitions, though his room also suggests to a visitor the ineffable gap that separates these dreams from reality. In the style favored by many rural young men, Rasta has covered his room in a collage of advertisement images culled from eviscerated magazines, most of which he secured from itinerant Peace Corps volunteers. They depict pulsating nocturnal cityscapes, women bathing suggestively, sports cars speeding furiously, and men seducing themselves, presumptuously, in the mirror while applying cologne. These are images of people preparing for something to happen, or hurtling toward that thing, while those around them remain stuck in one place, unable to "develop" or "go." For Rasta, all of these photographs are evidence of the existence of something higher and more grand than rural life, including what he considers to be the petty interests and squabbles that surround him—the epitome of which is the desire among some to bewitch others and anxiety about this desire among the remainder.

Masculine Households and Female Wealth

Again, the placement of icons of what could be called modernity in spaces explicitly identified with male ways of being (such as sitting rooms) coimplicates masculinity, development, and chewing tongue meat, linking all of these values to places that transcend the local. These places are often counterposed to women, who are enmired in a world of smoky kitchens, back-breaking physical labor, food preparation, and sexual reproduction—and who are thus antithetical to masculine conceptions of development, predicated as they are on escape. So too does the structure of the house (the opposition of cool room and kitchen, and the location of women in the left side of the house during the day and under the father's scrutiny in the right side of the house at night) iterate a model of masculine moral authority that is historically entrenched and layered. But I have already highlighted the central irony of the contemporary domestic sphere and, arguably, of Taita society: although the home is the emblem and, ideally, the outcome of men's labor and progress through life, and although it is inscribed with the material emblems of masculine virtue and male-driven development (such as wage labor in the city), women are now the primary producers and owners of household wealth. All Wataita were very aware of the discrepancy between the ideal of the household as masculine sign and the reality that women's *sometimes* illicit work (most notably, beer brewing and prostitution, but also such formerly male activities as cattle herding and small business ownership) was the real substance behind it. As discussed in chapter 3, and again in chapter 6, this disruption between the is and the ought fed into Taita ideas about the simulacrality of formerly dominant models of development (those centered on the state and men), ideas that were fleshed out further in new conceptions of witchcraft (now figured as *majini*, or out-of-control commercial property owned by women).

These gendered and generational conflicts were acted out in real life against the backdrop of the house, which often became important to the dramas that engulfed individual families. The story of the Mwanda household makes this particularly clear.

Witchcraft and Development Up Close: The Mwanda Household

Mzee Zablon ("mzee" is a designation for a senior man), a fifty-five-year old retired mid-level manager for East Africa Breweries, fell seriously ill one day in 1998 at his home in Werugha. Two nights before, his "saved" (Pentecostal) wife, Sarah, had been up all night speaking in tongues, and in the morning had awoken with a fever. With difficulty, her son, Rasta, and her daughters, Lydia and Erminah, had walked Sarah to the clinic by the market. It was a steep uphill walk, and the diabetic, heavy-set Sarah was not entirely up to it, but she had proved too large for the village's stretcher. At one point, she sat by the side of the road and, in tears, screamed, "They are killing off the family of Mwanda!" Some thought she was referring to witches, while others spoke of a curse (*njoβe*) of uncertain cause spoken by someone long since dead (perhaps Zablon's mother's co-wife, of whom see below). Now Sarah's health had improved, but Zablon was incapacitated. Zablon had been sick with a fever and malaise for weeks, but so had many people in the neighborhood, what with the cold weather and the stagnant water following upon six months of torrential El Niño rains. But Zablon could not rise at all on that day in May, so Rasta and his sister Lydia hoisted their father onto the village stretcher and began the downhill descent to the hospital in Wesu, assisted by relatives, neighbors, and passersby they met along the way. At one point, Rasta returned home to gather his father's clothes for what could well be an extended stay in the hospital. Eventually, Rasta came upon his father's shoes and, when he picked them up, noticed a bank statement tucked deep inside one of them. Succumbing to this opportunity to know how much money his father and his family actually possessed, Rasta examined the statement, only to discover to his great surprise and dismay that his family had no savings at all. Rasta was shocked because he thought that his father had received a pension for thirty years of service at the brewery, and had expected the savings to come to nearly a half-million Kenyan shillings (around $10,000).

Rasta placed the folded piece of paper back in his father's shoe and hurried down the hill to join his family at the hospital. He did not share his discovery with them. When I returned from Nairobi a few days later, Zablon had returned from the hospital and was drinking milk tea and reading the *Kenya Daily Nation* in the sitting room, while Sarah sat beside him, knitting. Zablon was feeling stronger, but had not recovered completely. I greeted them, offered my sympathy, and chatted for awhile. Then I pulled two pounds of beef wrapped in newspaper from the small knapsack I carried so that Zablon's neighbors would not see that I was bringing meat to his family: the eye causes the heart to feel jealousy. At length, I took my leave and went to the other side of the compound, where Rasta sat reading a paperback entitled, *The Truth about the UFO Crash at Roswell* in his own, smaller sitting room, adjacent to his bedroom. We exchanged greetings and prepared for a game of chess.

Rasta's Story

Rasta shut the door to block out the cold wind and the cat, and we sat, pushing pieces across the chess board, exchanging horror stories about Nairobi, and sipping our very sweetened tea. Gradually, he shared with me his frustration over his father's lost funds, and speculated as to where they might have gone. He told me with some disdain that his father, like "all old men," had many secrets, and that the money might have gone to a lover, or even toward a second, secret family in Mombasa. He knew his father's habits, he said, because they had once lived together for a while in a rented house in Mombasa, when Rasta was in secondary school. Or perhaps, he speculated, his father had been part of a commercial transaction that had gone awry, leaving the family with nothing. Old men, he explained, have the secretive habit of keeping their affairs to themselves, and he blamed this tragedy in part on his father's unwillingness to share information in the spirit of "transparency," a word that the political "opposition" had popularized and deployed against the aging President Moi and the rest of the old guard. Rasta had had plans for that money. A portion of it would have been set aside for bridewealth payments for his eventual marriage, though Rasta had not initiated a relationship for some time. He also had various business ideas that would have required his father's assistance, including opening a small kiosk in town, acquiring an education in computers at a private "college" ("college" is the word used for any privately owned school teaching a professional skill) in Mombasa, or even beginning payments for a passenger minivan to ply the streets of that city. Now he was compelled to return to one of his various get-rich-quick fantasies: illegally purchasing gemstones from garnet miners in the lowland mining town of Mwatate to sell to an Indian jeweler in Nairobi. This required very little start-up money, but was an extremely high-risk venture because he knew nothing about gemstones, and the business was secretive and illegal, largely monopolized by affluent Kikuyu women from Nairobi. "I am certain," he declared between sips of tea, "that my father's sickness and his [financial] loss are part of the same thing. He is being punished by someone—maybe one of his own [family]. Perhaps by God Himself."

The then thirty-year-old Rasta personified many of the tensions afflicting relatively educated Taita and Kenyan youth, though in a somewhat exaggerated form. For example, his English exceeded that of most American undergraduates, though he was only educated through high school. Rasta had picked up his fluid, notably Americanized English, as well as his familiarity with a variety of popular and political topics, from global media and film. He considered himself to be a citizen of the world, and felt very alienated from the life of what he considered to be his remote town. Indeed, his Kidabida was very poor, and he felt much more comfortable with English and Swahili, despite the fact that he had spent most of his life in the Taita Hills. When it came to English, Rasta was adept at moving from "high" to "low" and back again, highlighting the eccentricity of words like "xenoglossia" and "corpus delecti," picked up from the

Webster's dictionary he had memorized, by casually throwing in a "motherfucker" here and there, then blending in Kiswahili and Kidabida.

The form of Rasta's speech embodied the globalized world he inhabited, while consciously drawing attention to the absurdity of the fact that he was stuck on his parents' *shamba*, or small farm, in Werugha. Most importantly, it was partly through historically enduring local kinship relationships that he was able to gain access to the world beyond the hills. His mother's brother, Mwachofi, worked at a hotel in Mombasa, and he often brought Rasta the pulp novels tourists had left behind. Rasta liked science fiction (Ben Bova and Philip K. Dick) and—not surprisingly, given his generation's concern over witchcraft attacks from apparently friendly kin and neighbors—appreciated those genres that draw attention to the lurid, repressed secrets that at times erupt from beneath the surface of the mundane and familiar (horror, particularly the work of Stephen King). In the evenings, Rasta visited his mother's brother's house, where he watched bootlegged action videos, which Mwachofi had picked up in Mombasa, on a television that ran on a car battery; other times, he went to one of the rural video houses in town. Later, when I returned home, he kept in touch with me by writing letters by hand, then passing them on to a friend of his who worked as a *matatu* (passenger minivan) tout. The tout would dutifully pass the letters to one of Rasta's sisters, who for a time worked at an Internet café in Mombasa, and typed well (this was a few years before the Internet had reached the hills and created the generation known as "dot com").

Rasta had spent the past several years moving back and forth from the city of Mombasa to his rural home in search of some sort of work, and was painfully aware of the fact that he was going nowhere fast. For a while he had sold used clothes that came in to Mombasa in bulk. Then there were the "Stretchers," a portable abdominal exercise device that had been unloaded at the port in the thousands from Nobody Knew Exactly Where. Rasta's efforts to sell those things in Werugha had met with very little success—while the thin physique was becoming more popular among the educated urban crowd, in Rasta's community fatness was still synonymous with power and beauty for most. Rasta had also tried getting some used computers together in the hopes of taking advantage of the new fascination with the Internet by opening a "cyber-kaf" in Mombasa, but he was very short on funds.

Rasta's interest in things from beyond the hills, and his vision of development, was not limited to the material or the mundane. He was really more interested in alien visitors, Mars probes, and miracles than in making a buck, so to speak, off used clothing, although he did have practical ambitions. Rasta was also an eternal social critic, and, for him, future development required a radical transformation, a breaking with the past, which partly accounts for why the new religion of Pentecostalism was so appealing to him (Meyer 1999). In particular, he often spoke against the customary Taita practice of naming one's children after one's parents or in-laws (like most Wataita, he held that this naming practice caused something of the person who possessed it before to inhabit the new namesake and, in Rasta's own words, he did not want his children to inherit the characteristics of those who had lived before him). Neither did he want to inherit land from his father or his mother's brothers, and he proposed to his parents that, when he married, his wife be provided with a separate kitchen so as to avoid disagreements between her and his mother. When his parents retorted that such innovations would incur curses from those who had died, Rasta invoked the idea of romantic love, and he once informed them, pointedly, that he had no intention of marrying just so they could have someone to help out in the kitchen.

Rasta's search for a higher truth, and his desire to escape what he regarded as the parochial and petty relationships and historical entrapments that characterized Taita life, was epitomized in his religious practice. He had followed his mother's cue some years before and become a saved Pentecostal at the same church that she frequented. For Rasta, being saved (*kuokoka*) was part of an ongoing process whereby one ritually surrendered oneself, as an individual, to God, and thus established a personal, communicative relationship with Him, which was otherwise obscured by one's various, unholy social interactions. The religion was growing rapidly: preachers were in every market center and nearly every abandoned store house and town hall, some claiming to be able to heal the sick and insane by exorcising demons, others denouncing all forms of medicine as a rejection of God's will. All of them spoke in tongues and publicly revealed the secret sins of fellow villagers—from masturbation to theft to witchcraft. They thus also provided villagers with a great deal of information and detail about the nature of these practices and established a kind of compendium of possible human activities—all with a view to beginning afresh. In these churches, converts confessed their sins openly, often admitting to having murdered and bewitched people, to say nothing of more minor sins, such as having sex with water. These religious communities thus hoped to create a clean slate (as usual, Rasta stunned me by using the Lockean expression tabula rasa, thus incorporating an element of Europe's past into his potential future) as the precondition for a new social order. At the same time, they sought to establish the extent and nature of public malfeasance, much in the manner of reconciliation committees, laws forcing public officials to declare their income, and investigations into torture and corruption—all of which were either happening or imminent in the Kenyan public sphere at this time.

Rasta had developed a close relationship with one of these preachers, a man named Hector, who was about ten years Rasta's senior. Hector had befriended Rasta's mother, Sarah, in church, and had later left to found his own church in a neighboring village. Rasta soon became Hector's principle disciple, and together they prayed often at Hector's house. When he prayed, Hector entered into a trance, during which God spoke through him, referring to the vessel Hector as the prophet Elijah, and promising Rasta great success in the future. Sometimes Rasta was asked to provide an offering, to undergo a certain ritual, or to journey with Hector to another town or city to pray, with Hector, for a member of the latter's congregation. Later, Hector relocated his church to Mombasa, and Rasta followed him, combining his search for work with the spiritual search for truth through Hector, in whom he believed fully. Rasta once told me that Hector was impervious to disease; was immortal; and could read the thoughts, as well as the state of the soul, of those who came to him in search of guidance.

Rasta believed that building a relationship with Hector was the surest way available to him of "developing," and this belief suggests an interesting shift that was taking place in his society. In particular, it represented a simultaneous rejection and devolution of the patron-client relationships that formerly bound big-men politicians to their citizen-clients and, in an even earlier period, senior men with large herds of cattle to their dependents (cf. Bravman 1998). Rasta established a similar patron-client relationship with Hector, performing certain tasks for him and assisting him in his entrepreneurial religion in exchange for a promised material and spiritual return at a guaranteed, but unspecified, future time. It is not hard to see the obvious parallel between the religious lives of Hector and Rasta and the structural transformations shaping Kenya at this time: the relationship was supposed to be generative of wealth and respect, but it was detached from any institutional structures, consisting in an unwritten contract between two enterprising individuals with links to God, who was for some reason interested in their success. Neither Hector nor Rasta had any sustainable employment outside of praying for others and changing their personal habits in accordance to an imagined moral and aesthetic ideal. Their work was in many ways suggestive of what Foucault (1980, 39) refers to as capillary power, wherein practices and dispositions that have long been encouraged by state and religious officials from on high (such as sobriety and thriftiness) were personalized, and in the process came to appear original and transgressive. Moreover, their religious practice was committed to the idea that God recognized them as individuals and had plans for them on earth, which would manifest as miraculous rebounds (an in-flow of much anticipated aid) after a prolonged suffering and a pronounced personal structural readjustment consisting in the containment of what Hector and Rasta each recognized as polluting desires (pertaining particularly to sex and dissipation through alcohol and irrelevant conversation).

As Rasta and I sat playing chess in his sitting room in 1998, he told me about how he had once, years before, tried to protect his father from the advanced witchcraft of his competitors and superiors in Mombasa. Around the time that Rasta became saved, his father was still working for East African Breweries and was having a difficult time advancing in his job. Zablon had returned home from Mombasa one weekend to hold a meeting with Rasta and Sarah. He declared that life had become more difficult in Mombasa, and that the only Wataita who succeeded there were those willing to purchase the advanced witchcraft of Muslims and Indians, or to become owners of Arabic spirit familiars (majini). He told them how, the last time he went to Mombasa, a *jini* appeared on the side of the road in the form of a beautiful woman, forcing the bus driver off the road. Zablon felt that someone had sent the jini to warn him. Rasta and his mother counseled Zablon to speak with Hector, who would be sure to offer prayers for him. Agreeing that no harm could come from this, Zablon agreed to allow Hector to pray for him, and some days later the minister paid the Mwanda family a visit. Hector prayed for Zablon and his family, and went into a deep trance, during which time God told Zablon that Kikuyu and Swahili witches in the company wanted his position. Hector said that with God's assistance he could make these unfair barriers to success go away, and that Zablon was certain to receive his pension from the company upon retirement. What God asked in return, according to Hector, was that Mzee Zablon give a tithe of his pension to Hector's church, so that he could continue his work of saving Wataita from sin, disease, and death. Zablon had agreed, but never followed through on his word and so, according to Rasta, had been denied his pension.

Zablon's Story

Zablon was in his late fifties, and like so many others of his generation in the 1990s, had fallen dramatically from the position of relative prosperity and prestige he had attained in Werugha in the 1970s, when his job with the brewery was paying him a moderate salary. He possessed an elementary school education, which placed him in the ranks of the educated of his generation, and he had married Sarah Mwachofi, the only daughter of the first Catholic convert in the neighborhood. The marriage was a good one, and elevated Zablon from his own social position, for his parents had converted later in life, and were recognized as βatasi, or non-Christians who performed the central rite of *kutasa* (see chapter 5). Even in Zablon's more prosperous days (the 1970s) his gradual progress was marked by difficulties. He had purchased the land on which he lived from Sarah's father, and this placed him far away from his brothers, who immediately complained that Zablon was being controlled by his wife. In keeping with the by then entrenched aesthetic of modern houses, in the mid-1970s Zablon began building a new house with an interior compound and several rooms. One of his brothers contributed to the expenses and the labor, with the expectation of moving into the household as well, but for reasons that are unclear, and which angered his brother greatly, Zablon's plans changed, and he lived there alone with his wife and children. From the beginning, Zablon and his family were nervous about the "witchcraft of jealousy": they found a dead mole (an animal that represents nocturnal secrets) at the foundation of the house during its construction, and after it was built they were plagued by "night runners," people who knocked on the door, then disappeared—one was alleged to have smeared feces on the compound walls. They had paid local diviners to come in and ritually "cleanse" the household, but the attacks continued, and the family's fear increased.

Then, Zablon's only son, Rasta, an adolescent at the time, was expelled from a school that was considered to be excellent for his rebellious behavior. Zablon and Sarah interpreted Rasta's failure to progress in school as the product of someone else's jealousy, for witches were known to subvert the most intelligent before the latter had a chance to parley their education into employment and wealth. Rasta was known to be extremely gifted, and though he often told me that he had simply become disinterested in school, his parents insisted in identifying who, in fact, had caused him to detest books. This time, rather than resort to local witch doctors, the family decided to take matters to a more advanced level and hire a renowned Kamba diviner in Taveta, a large town and transit center on the Kenya-Tanzania border. Wakamba are widely rumored to be among the most powerful witches in Kenya, while the transregional traffic and intense market competition that characterize border towns make these areas laboratories for the most advanced and contemporary forms of witchcraft knowledge and technology (cf. Auslander 1993; Geschiere 1997). Rasta had stayed there for two weeks, having alien objects removed from his body by this female surgeon-diviner. At that time, the diviner had revealed that these objects were the material manifestation of a sinister prayer enunciated by Zablon's mother's co-wife, a very old lady who was apparently angered by the relative prosperity of Zablon's mother's line and wished to derail its development. After the divination, Zablon and his brothers confronted their stepmother, and this episode was followed by a series of counterdivinations in which the stepmother tried to demonstrate her innocence. Eventually, the families made an uneasy peace, and blessings and gifts were exchanged to cement social ties, although both Sarah and Zablon felt that the name of my friend Rasta remained cursed.

Since the 1970s, Zablon's brothers had tried to convince him to join them in a business venture; they spoke of purchasing a matatu to ply the passage from Mombasa to Taita. But nothing came of this venture, and Zablon continued to struggle for recognition, advancement, and salary in the brewery. As the 1990s proceeded and the economy declined further, Zablon sometimes had to forgo his salary for several months, and the upper-level management at East African Breweries refused his attempts to secure his son, Rasta, with meaningful employment. Moreover, Zablon continued to be indebted to Sarah's brother Mwachofi, to whom he tried to make regular bridewealth payments. When at home, Zablon sat on his couch drinking *chofi ya asali*, a fermented honey drink made locally, rather than drink expensive bottled beer in the pub. He complained that too many envious witches stayed around the market, waiting patiently until finding the right opportunity to slip a touch of black poison into one's beer. He had developed a new favorite topic of conversation: bridewealth, and how it had been transformed of late, from being the material expression of a social relationship to being a form of payment akin to a commercial transaction. Now, wives had become a commodity (or rather *mali*, property), especially among the educated, who used their high-market daughters to acquire income in a period when no other options were available.

As Rasta told me the story of his father's sickness it became clear to us that Zablon was at the end of the line: out of a job, out of his pension, and besieged with requests for assistance from his brothers and bridewealth payments from Sarah's brother. And now there was this sickness. While in the hospital, Zablon began listening to his son and his wife, who told him that he needed to abandon his habits, that he had enslaved the family to Satan when he had decided to visit diviners and witch doctors to solve the family's problems. If he became saved, like the rest of the household, then a barrier would protect them from others, and they could continue to develop as before. Not surprisingly, Sarah was the primary instigator.

Sarah's Story

As mentioned above, Sarah's father had been one of the very first Christians in this community and had built his house on land given to him by the church. His was the first square, modern-style home in the village, now inhabited by his eldest son, Mwachofi, who worked in Mombasa. Sarah's father had sold most of his family's livestock to the butcheries that sprouted up during the 1940s and 1950s, and used this money to put all of his children, even Sarah, through primary school. Mwachofi was perhaps the most financially successful person in the village, and the only person I knew in Werugha who possessed both a television set and a video cassette recorder. In the 1980s, Sarah had been active in Maendeleo ya Wanawake (Women's Development), a national women's organization established by the wives of colonial administrators to teach women domestic skills and the habits of civility. Maendeleo ya Wanawake received funds from the government and the international community to fund community projects headed by women. Prior to the liberalization of politics in 1992, the organization was legally a branch of the Kenya African National Union (KANU), and much of the money donated to this organization actually went into the hands of local KANU politicians, who in turn influenced the election of women to the organization. In some cases, KANU politicians dressed up as women and participated directly in the elections, from which men were legally excluded (see also Aubrey 1997, 45–89). Sarah had been a vocal critic of politicians who used their authority to, in her words, "steal what belonged to women and their families."

Sometime in the early 1990s, the period of structural adjustment, state downsizing, and political liberalization, Sarah turned from politics to religion and became a saved Pentecostal Christian, abandoning the church that her father had in a sense pioneered.

When I knew Sarah in the late 1990s, Maendeleo ya Wanawake had imploded into numerous village-centered groups composed of neighbors, and had no direct connection to KANU. Sarah often expressed disdain for politics, which, like so many other Wataita, she equated with witchcraft and contrasted negatively to development. She continued to head a couple of women's groups, all of which had empty savings accounts at the Kenya Commercial Bank and had ceased to receive patronage from politicians. However, they did receive some funding from the locally prominent NGO Plan International, which allowed the groups to purchase a few dairy cows by putting up only 10 percent of the cost. Moreover, because of her family's relative development, attested to in part by their house, it was at the top of Plan International's list of worthy recipient households in the town. The family soon came to be identified as a "Plan family" by the organization's employees, and Rasta's sisters were "adopted" by a donor family from Texas. Off and on, they took pictures to send to the United States, and the Plan representatives would suddenly return some weeks later with gifts from the Texan family. The Mwanda family could not understand why the Texans sent their daughters crayons and paper, gifts they considered insultingly unhelpful. They suspected that the Kikuyu Plan employees were pocketing the actual gifts, especially as Plan International would not allow the Mwanda family to communicate the mistake to the family in Texas via writing (the Plan employees read and censored all communication between the donor and recipient families). Nevertheless, neighbors saw this transnational relationship and the wealth that it promised, and Sarah was often visited by kin and neighbors seeking money for school fees or contributions to rotating credit unions.

As mentioned, Sarah had shifted her attention these days from politics to religion. Until the early 1990s, she had been a major participant in the Catholic prayer groups devoted to specific saints, and she had served as treasurer of the church council. Soon after becoming saved, Sarah became a medium like Hector, directly communicating with God, speaking in tongues, and praying for others. Sarah acquired a great deal of power in her homestead and in her natal family, for God communicated His wishes to her, including how best to distribute household resources such as livestock. And she was personally responsible for engineering a number of feasts over which she presided in prayer, and these ritualized ceremonies brought together her affines and natal kin, supposedly at God's behest. They always culminated in prayers, during which Hector was often present; both communicated directly with God, who then relayed to them His plans (typically positive) for those present. Though she thus acquired a certain amount of prestige and power, this positive potential was tainted: rumors circulated that she had joined the new church because she had embezzled money from the Catholics when she was treasurer of the council and had used the funds to make ends meet during one of those times when Zablon had not received his salary. Some even suggested that she had used the money to purchase blood-sucking, livestock-eating majini for enriching her homestead.

Part of the issue was Sarah's relative household authority and, up to the time of her sudden sickness, her apparently abundant health. Many people, men and women alike, spoke disparagingly of the fact that Zablon was in such a deplorably thin condition while his oversized wife continued to be so obviously healthy. Neighbors laughingly observed that Zablon was overpowered by his wife, and some suggested, more seriously, that this inversion of idealized gender relations implied that Sarah had sacrificed Zablon to demons, which accounted for the family's apparent prosperity. Thus, the Mwanda household became iconic of the overall reversal in gender relations that many believed was occurring in Taita, and in turn bore the weight of all the moral valuations that have attended this reversal. In particular, Zablon's brothers claimed that Sarah was the source of Zablon's reticence to join in with them in the matatu business, that she had magically bound him to her, preventing him from progressing in ways befitting a mature man with children. Sarah's brothers also blamed their failure to develop on her: her brother Eloji had failed, by the age of fifty, to marry or bear children, and Eloji believed that Sarah wanted to inherit his land and pass it on to her son, Rasta. Eloji's anger at his sister's witchcraft, foretold to him by a Taita diviner, encouraged him to assume proprietorship over a piece of land that his brother-in-law Zablon had loaned to him, and he had paid off a Kikuyu in the Ministry of Lands to have the land registered in his name. Zablon contested the registration, and the case made it to the chief's office, where Eloji lost. Eloji's inability to become a socially adult male and reproduce his line was a serious problem, and the idea that Sarah may have been responsible is probably what encouraged her to level an analogous counteraccusation against

Mwachofi's (Eloji's elder brother) wife, Agrippina, whom she accused of trying to kill Eloji with slow poison. These accusations and counteraccusations culminated in a fistfight between the two wives, with each party publicly threatening to murder the other. When Agrippina died of diabetes in the late 1990s, rumors circulated that Sarah was responsible, and also that her witchcraft was too advanced for local divinatory methods to combat.

It was, however, Sarah who steered the two families toward a temporary peace in the late 1990s, by engineering a feast (again at the Holy Spirit's behest) between the two, with a view to healing strife and hastening Zablon's recovery.

A Temporary Peace

Thus, the Mwanda family had a number of problems, many of which an outsider could relate to national and global economic and social circumstances. These problems included the loss of Zablon's pension, Rasta's failure to find a job despite his relative education, and the whole family's poverty and increasing reliance on bridewealth to make ends meet. However, the Mwanda family, despite their understanding of the larger issues that affected their lives (Rasta in particular was well aware of his nation's problems and had a very cosmopolitan view of the world, even accommodating an unusual belief in space aliens), tended to dwell on local relationships and to see these as being the most important issues to deal with if any meaningful development, or future progress, was to take place. In particular, the family had long been convinced that their problems were due to the jealousy of Zablon's mother's co-wife. The reason for this preoccupation with the local was not simply cultural or cosmological, in the sense that they were somehow deluded into thinking that local matters were more important than global processes. Rather, they were grappling with an ineffable reality: regardless of how informed they were about the state of the world, they were forced to deal with kin and neighbors in their immediate environs. This was now more true than ever, because, in their poverty and joblessness, they depended increasingly on each other, and on traditional institutions like bridewealth. But this tendency toward reproducing the familiar generated change, because old institutions came to appear sullied by what were understood as modern dispositions (greed and selfishness, which turned relations among people embodied in marriage payments into relations among things). Specifically,

Zablon's brother-in-law Mwachofi began to see Zablon as his most likely source of income and of development, and so sought to remind Zablon of his obligations. Yet his requests came at the most awkward time for Zablon, who had recently lost everything and was intent on smoothing over conflicts among his own brothers. Zablon thus sought contraction and retention vis-à-vis his affinal kin (though not among his agnatic kin), while Mwachofi invoked the contradictory ideology of cooperation and flow (cf. Taylor 1992).

The family's response to their problems was to recreate social cohesion within the family, and the form in which they did so embodied the new transformations taking place in their society. Thus it was Sarah, the empowered woman, who managed the show, a response that went against the time-honored practice of senior men gathering to restore order. Sarah called all of the people who could be potentially responsible for the family's setbacks, including her own brothers and Zablon's brothers, to a goat roast. There she prayed to a universal God, and no attempt was made to communicate with ancestors, although the possibility of an ancestral curse was recognized. After the roast, God informed her that it was her brother Mwachofi whose anger had spoiled the family; God said that Mwachofi was not bewitching them, but that his hot heart was bringing misfortune. Here Sarah invoked a historically entrenched Kidabida understanding of hearts and their impact on events (see chapter 5), but grounded this notion in an evangelical idiom. The family members involved apologized for any bad feelings they may have harbored, and blessed one another. Then the old men shared organ meat (the meat of senior males), much in the way that age mates and blood brothers did years ago, and even performed kutasa, though with water instead of beer. A few days after the ritual, Rasta informed me, happily, that his father had become a saved Christian. Their dairy cow had disappeared, and Rasta said that his father had sold it to the butcher, and that some of the money would be used to make good on the family's debts to Mwachofi. Rasta began visiting Mwachofi's household to watch videos again, after a long hiatus. Moreover, the eldest daughter, Maria, a secondary school–educated secretary who lived in Mombasa, was marrying a Kikuyu, and the Mwanda family was expecting a marriage payment from that family shortly.

The Mwanda household seemed to have resolved its crises for the time being, although they remained incapable of satisfying their household's needs. Moreover, the family bore the additional burden of possessing all of the signs of development without any material substance to support the image (Rasta once called their house an "empty shell"). All of their accouterments—their large square house filled with Plan improvements, their education and their various international contacts, and their daughter who would soon be married to a non-Taita male with a job in Mombasa—encouraged others to seek them out as potential benefactors for their various household-centered projects. Yet the family was unable to meet these demands and was widely and inaccurately seen as a well-off family that kept to itself, refused to cooperate with others, and had many "secrets" (*malagho*). Perhaps, some said, the household's cow had suddenly disappeared because the family had fed the animal to its jini in order to obtain money. Perhaps, it was implied, they had sacrificed something real, enduring, and virtuous for something socially destructive—for an unsustainable development that had now become difficult to maintain.

The Mwanda Household Five Years Later

When I returned to Taita after a five-year absence, I found that the Mwanda family had taken a turn for the worse, again. The household had very little in the way of income, Zablon never having recovered his pension, and Rasta remaining unemployed, working as a *kibarua,* or casual laborer, from time to time on other people's farms. Sarah was bringing in more income than the others, for she still acquired some donations from the locally based transnational NGO Plan International, and occasionally received money in exchange for offering prayers, but the substance and value of what she produced through prayer was ambiguous and subject to contestation. Most of the household's currency came from the eldest daughter, whose husband sometimes sent bridewealth from Mombasa, much of which Zablon gave to his brother-in-law Mwachofi. Zablon had been unable to pay for his young daughter Erminah's schooling, and so sent her to live with her elder sister Lydia, now a secretary in an Internet café in Mombasa. There, the young Erminah was impregnated by a Luo businessman who had pledged to marry Lydia. At first, the Luo sent marriage payments to Zablon in Taita in compensation for impregnating his young daughter, but he eventually stopped, and no one could trace him. This situation drove a rift between Rasta and his parents, and fueled the latter's suspicion that his parents were witches (see below) because they had fallen for the lure of lucre when, according to the governmentally minded Rasta, they should have contacted the police in the beginning so as to have this man punished for impregnating a legal minor.

As for Rasta, he had been engaged in a five-year journey of self-discovery, visiting preachers and diviners throughout Kenya in an attempt to figure out who was obstructing his development—his personal attempts to move away from home, marry, find gainful employment, and initiate a sustainable business venture. Rasta's attempt to come to terms with the source of his misfortune, and his eventual confrontation with his family, is a story that he is currently writing himself, and I hope that in the future it will be told with all of the immediacy that presence affords. I will, however, draw together a few major points. Soon after I finished my main research stint in 1999, Zablon and Sarah had a falling out with the preacher Hector, claiming that he had gradually siphoned money in the form of church donations from the family and suggesting that it was he who had made Zablon sick with a curse when the latter had refused to pay that tithe to Hector's church. Rasta had refused to stop seeing his guru, and, according to Rasta, his father responded by cursing him, allegedly claiming that Rasta would not inherit from him and would "die when he died." Hector countered by informing Rasta that God had communicated to him that his parents were witches, and that his mother had been using majini to keep Rasta "bound" at home as a personal sacrifice to enrich herself. God had revealed to Hector that Sarah possessed a stool (*kiti*), which she used to communicate with demons. An earlier generation of initiated senior men had used these stools to communicate with ancestors; the stools referenced men's ability to generate prosperity and peace by sitting and chewing tongue meat with each other and with those who had died (Harris 1978). Sarah's alleged appropriation and misuse of this icon of gerontocracy suggested that the perceived ascendance of women, and their usurpation of men's economic and political power, was polluting and dangerous. This suggestion was underscored by Hector's not so subtle transformation of "ancestors" (*βarumu*) into "demons" (*mashetani*). Hector had also told Rasta that his mother was "tying" her two younger daughters at home, preventing them from marrying and giving birth. According to Hector, Sarah hoped to force her daughters into prostitution and bring the revenue earned from this infernal nocturnal commerce into the house. This idea represented the epitome of a now standardized Taita nightmare: that women were becoming commodified and were in turn responsible for the increasing commercialization of the home, and of blood relations in general.

Rasta continued praying and traveling with Hector, and they even entered into some commercial ventures together. But Rasta eventually grew disillusioned because no substantive results seemed to be gained despite the promise of future rewards, and he began questioning Hector's teachings and refused to travel with him to pray. When he made this decision, God began delivering angry messages through Hector and curtailing his promises of material success, which made Rasta furious with God Himself (perhaps more so than with Hector) and disillusioned with the prospect of salvation. Then, suddenly, the apparently invincible Hector died, which sent Rasta into an emotional tailspin, causing him to wonder aloud, was it his mother who had killed Hector, for revealing to him that she was a witch? Immediately after Hector's funeral, Rasta returned home and began asking his mother's and father's brothers about the possibility that his mother Sarah was in fact a witch, only to discover, much to his surprise, that they had apparently known this all along and were simply waiting for Rasta to discover this plainly evident fact on his own. When Mwachofi claimed that some years ago Sarah had admitted to him that she kept majini in the house, Rasta became convinced that his mother had been unable to satisfy the demands of her spirit helpers and that he was being used as a sacrifice.

Rasta astutely mobilized senior male ideology against the more current phenomenon of female mediums, whose ambivalent potency Rasta and his male kin now sought to control. He succeeded in assembling his uncles and his father's brothers at his house, and they proceeded to voice their own concerns about Sarah's witchcraft. Mwachofi accused Sarah of spoiling the family with majini, but Sarah countered that hers were majini of protection (*ya kulinda*) and not the majini of money (*ya pesa*), which provide gifts of cash in exchange for blood. Anyway, she and Hector had disposed of all the majini years ago, when she became saved. At one point, Rasta, apparently disgusted, asked the assembled crowd whether these people who cursed him and harbored majini were indeed his parents, and he again reiterated his refusal to name his children after them and so reproduce their legacy. But ultimately they agreed to make amends: everyone present performed kutasa, Zablon retracted the curse, and Rasta agreed to accept them as his parents. However, later Rasta refused to eat with them, out of fear that it was through the food that his mother cooked that he had been bound to the house and thus turned into a failure. Instead, he set up a kitchen in his part of the house and at night boiled spaghetti, an exotic food, for himself.

Rasta's refusal to eat with his family and to accept their cooking as nourishing rather than destructive struck at the core of everything Wataita hold dear, for he had in a sense refused the total process through which food and male property is converted into moral and social values, as well as futures, through the feminine act of cooking (see also Weiss 1996). Rasta's actions also implied that he had not really abandoned his belief that his mother had bewitched him. His rebellion became news throughout the region and was widely interpreted as polluting the entire area. Soon, church congregations were camped outside their house, praying and exorcising it of demons, but Rasta went on cooking macaroni with the kerosene stove that I had left for him, until he eventually saved up enough money from working on other people's fields to return to Mombasa again in search of paid employment. However, things did not look good for Rasta: the young woman he had expressed an interest in for some time, and who had at one point agreed to marry him, suddenly withdrew her affections at the request of her family when they forbade her from seeing the insolent Rasta, whose actions were perceived as tantamount to witchcraft. Now it was Rasta's turn to be accused of being a witch, despite the fact that many people had made similar claims about his mother.

Conclusion

This chapter has focused on the family in two ways. The first approach was to examine how materialized embodiments of local social relations (houses and households) become models of development and antidevelopment, while standing for the morality and orienting the desires of people seeking to progress and accumulate. These constructions are the most familiar and shared icons of how individual families, and Wataita as a whole, are doing, what they believe in, and what they want for themselves and their families. They are also iconic of limitations and restrictions, not to mention conflict between those who are capable of accumulating and those who are not. While they often appear to resemble homes in the West, they are cut through with local meanings and valuations, which are sometimes contradictory. These contradictions (such as the conflict between the ideal of masculine control and male-driven development against the reality of men's diminished potential and women's increased power and productivity) incite the local imagination, influencing collective action on the ground. Houses also tend to express a tension between the desire to articulate with urban centers and foreign ways of life (the greeting cards hung from the rafters) and the dependence of people on neighbors and kin. Always, these houses acquire their symbolic meanings in relation to an imagined "true" Taita house that existed in the past, and sometimes exists in the present; the modern house is in some ways a reiteration of this traditional house, and in other ways a transformation of it, and Wataita reflect on changing social relations by indexing these shared icons that dot the landscape, presenting a ready-made palimpsest for social commentary.

The second section of this chapter moved away from the household as a model of the past and the future to examine the actual kinship relations that take place within the home. There too, people's actions were understood in relation to the way things were imagined to have been in the past, and an uneasy attempt was made by everyone in the family to accommodate the desire for innovation with the need for historical continuity in the face of change. If houses—their structure, the decorations found in them, and so forth—communicate people's desire to escape the confines of the hills and their simultaneous dependence on local social relations, so too did the actions of the various members of the Mwanda household. For example, Rasta wanted to free himself from the influences of his family and forebears, from their habits and tastes in cooking as much as their direct control, and envisioned a future life manufactured of his own devices—one where wives cooked alone, shared ideas with their husbands, and were not afraid to try new foods (a big issue for Rasta, who found Taita food to be uninspired, to say the least). His iconoclasm was fueled by a combination of Pentecostalism and the liberalization of Kenya's politics, including the vanquishing of old men long in power and the implementation of anticorruption measures. Yet Rasta found that his desired freedom was impossible when public opinion was leveled against him, for suddenly he was unable to marry. Moreover, despite his self-made cosmopolitanism, Rasta's worldly success turned out to be hampered by the emotions of a dead paternal co-wife who had never left the hills.

The story of the Mwanda household demonstrates how global processes and transformations become personalized, and how generations are thrown into structural and ideological conflict with one another in this neoliberal moment, a time of simultaneous disintegration and promise (Ashforth 1999). Certainly Rasta's conceptual resources, combined with his simultaneous alienation from and dependence on his local community, suggested that Wataita were as subject to "deterritorialization" as

space divided by gender + age

the most cosmopolitan citizens of the globe. Moreover, his family's reliance on independent prophet-entrepreneurs who made no bones about the fact that spiritual, financial, and intellectual progress were self-same processes, confirmed their belonging to a global ecumene in which the market had altered preexisting social and institutional sources of power and respect. Of course, Rasta saw most of his actions as culminations of his own individual thought and choice, believed that the parochialism of others was rearing its head to stop his development, and called this destructive desire on the part of others witchcraft. It was not simply that global events and processes imposed themselves on people and altered preexisting social hierarchies, though this certainly did happen. Rather, people like Hector, Sarah, and Rasta appropriated the concepts and ideologies of the new era, with its emphasis on personal empowerment, public confession, and the revelation of nocturnal secrets, circulated not least by "political" NGOs and churches. Thus it was that the Mwanda family tried to save itself by ritually mimicking larger social transformations: specifically, elevating women to positions of spiritual authority and developing a connection to God through charismatic intermediaries instead of institutionalized church authorities (although they later resorted to the moist hearts of senior men to counteract the damage Sarah and Hector had allegedly done).

In this chapter I have called attention to competing temporalities in Taita notions of development and witchcraft, and have shown how the members of a particular family sought to domesticate these different potentials in their efforts to develop. In the following chapters, I explore two opposed spatiotemporal dimensions of this dynamic: chapter 5 examines Taita attempts to produce development by creating harmonious relationships with the local past, while chapter 6 focuses on people's efforts to control highly contemporary processes and institutions that were marked as foreign. Chapter 7, on the witch hunter Maji Marefu, examines Taita efforts to deal with historically enduring resentments with a view to creating the conditions necessary for people to use the past and the present, the foreign and the domestic, in a way likely to be generative of development.

CHAPTER FIVE

"Dot Com Will Die Seriously!" Spatiotemporal Miscommunication and Competing Sovereignties in Taita Thought and Ritual

This chapter offers a different point of entry into Taita understandings of development and witchcraft by focusing on how certain Wataita made sense of the present by reifying the past, deploying it as a conceptual and material resource at once positive and negative. I argue that Taita ritual practice and Taita reflections on ritual suggested that many people were concerned about probable misrecognition by forces emanating from a past that was also coeval—that ritual specialists did not know how to perform rituals, that ancestors did not recognize the living as their own descendants, and so forth—and that this concern reflected the fact that their home increasingly confronted them as an entity that they did not control. I show how senior male ritual specialists sought to ensure the safety and prosperity of their communities, as well as their own moral authority over these communities, by closing the gap between sign and referent, but found themselves challenged in fulfilling their mandate. I then argue that many Wataita of divergent social backgrounds tended to view gift giving as generative of viable moral and political orders, and focus on *fighi* shrines as emblematic of a particular form of sovereignty forged through the exchange of objects and affections. I examine fighi as a symbol of, and mechanism for the production of, a counterfactual sovereignty based on perceived cultural values and identity that stand in stark contrast to lived experience. The implication is that the contrast between development and witchcraft in Taita has to be understood in terms of spatial and temporal unfolding, where development work refers to the attempt to control spatiotemporal processes. In stark contrast, witchcraft indexes breach and loss of control, as well as the gap that separates the sign from the thing to which it refers.

Recuperating the Past

People may correctly remember the events of twenty years ago (a remarkable feat), but who remembers his fears, his disgusts, his tone of voice? It is like trying to bring back the weather of that time. —Martha Gellhorn, *The Face of War*

From May until September of 1998, Wataita endured a drought (*kilangazi*) that everyone I spoke with claimed exceeded all others in living memory in duration and intensity, ruining crops and forcing households to purchase most of their food. While those who had managed to save money earned in Mombasa or elsewhere fared better than those who had none, the drought placed a heavy financial strain on all families, and people complained bitterly of hunger and poverty. Family members and neighbors turned against each other in complicated disputes over land and money, and Wataita were more vocal than usual in their castigation of the rich, who somehow managed to prosper without working. One chief informed me that he was forced to listen to three times as many disputes than in the year before. According to many, when the area experienced drought, it was not only because rain had ceased to fall but also because people had stopped loving one another, both across space (in the case of neighbors) and across time (in the case of ancestors). The idea, as I came to understand it, was that the land, facilitated by spiritual agents (God and/or ancestors), mimetically reproduced the substance of people's collective actions by becoming either moist or dry. This was not a purely mystical belief, as it was supported by the fact of deforestation, which, for good reason, Wataita associated with the loss of cultural values, political autonomy, and rains. While one might expect seniors to be quicker to assert the importance of ancestors, because senior men have historically mediated between the living and the dead through sacrifice, I found that this was not the case. Youth often asserted that the generation of men that was senior to them had turned their backs on their own seniors by converting to Christianity and buying into the culture of *ubinafsi*, or possessive individualism.

During the drought, a young man died in his home in the lowlands *nyika* (wasteland or scrub), and his body was awaiting burial. His family had been among those that had left the highlands for want of land, and had constructed their home in an area once used for grazing cattle. The deceased's bereaved family invited Mtula, the local *mkireti*, or man of the wilderness, to visit their household and "cleanse the land" (*kuhora mbuβa*) with a goat so that the man might be buried beside his *shamba* (agricultural plot) without being disturbed by the fighi defender shrines. Every person I spoke to about the matter, regardless of age or sex, asserted that people were not supposed to live near fighi, and that eliminating fighi so that people might live was no easy task: as mentioned in earlier chapters, fighi shrines are supposed to protect communities from outsiders, but, because the areas they survey are sacred, many otherwise ordinary acts are forbidden within them, which makes fighi very dangerous to living populations. This family was certainly not unusual: because of land scarcity in the highlands, many people had been moving into these lowland areas, in the process infringing upon the sovereignty of the fighi protector shrines. People offered different reasons for why the fighi killed off innocent people: Perhaps the fighi were unaware that the area had become residential, and suspected the innocent Wataita of being intruders or foreigners—all the more so since they spoke Swahili, the language of commerce and the city. Or perhaps the fighi were angry with living Wataita, who failed to pay them proper respect. In any event, the family of the deceased decided to seek out the mkireti, Mtula, reasoning that he was the only person who might be able to domesticate fighi. Mtula visited the homestead and, after performing a rite called *kutasa*, or libations, and divining from entrails (*kushoma βula*), prayed to "create understanding" (*kureda masikirano*) between the family and the land.

Kutasa and βula are the mainstays of what most Wataita would call non-Christian or "traditional" ritual, although the old men who perform these rites tend not to view them as inimical to Christianity. In particular, they refer to kutasa as "prayer" and make a direct comparison between the act of giving libations and the pouring of holy water by Catholic priests. Kutasa and βula are important acts to discuss briefly, because they are suggestive of the symbolic politics at work in senior men's rituals. Both rites are centrally concerned with the creation of moral and territorial borders within which positive sentiments and values are both protected and positively mandated. In kutasa, senior men take home-brewed sugarcane beer into their mouths, but, instead of swallowing it, they spray the beer out through their partly closed lips. In my experience, they sprayed in the direction of the thing they wanted to heal or bless: a group of friends (the space in the middle of their circle), a household (the door jamb), or the face of a sick person. These were all sites of vulnerability and exposure of self or family to the world outside, and the act protected those who were the objects of prayer at the same time as it expunged violent emotions from the hearts of those spraying out beer. These men said that the hate, or violence, in the heart was expunged through kutasa, which also suggests that this violent potential in all people was transformed into something socially productive through an act of personal sacrifice, or deferral.

Whereas kutasa can be performed anytime old men assemble, βula, or intestines, are read by senior male specialists (*mlaghui* or diviner), either when something has gone wrong or when something with great potential, and attendant risk, is about to happen: the opening of a new house or plot; the acquisition of a new job; or the discovery that someone is lethally sick, infertile, or impotent. In βula, the large intestine of a sacrificed lamb or goat is flattened out and becomes a text that is metonymic of the relevant Taita social landscape, relative to the situation at hand. The practitioners read the text, like a book, from left to right, scrutinizing the central vessel at the center of the palimpsest and the blood-carrying arteries that radiate out, perpendicularly, from the center. The central vessel refers to the general health of the event, place, or situation, while the arteries refer to social groups whose actions or sentiments can have an impact on the event.

In the central vessel, the men look for abundant fecal matter, which portends prosperity and good fortune, while the arteries, each of which is given a number, are investigated for blood clots, which reference social breach. The mutual imbrication of society and landscape is thus embodied in a mediating figure, the pastoral animal (goat or lamb), which consumes the land and contains it within its belly. These animals are, not accidentally, also mediums of exchange between social groups and the means through which the social body has historically been reproduced in bridewealth exchanges. For male ritual specialists, then, the sheep or goat epitomizes and produces the social world and bears the trace of that world in its belly. Senior men were very explicit about this relationship, stating that they preferred to use sheep intestines because "Sheep do not choose what to take in. So everything, good and bad, is in them." The good and bad referred to here were the emotional products of human social interaction and activity (the social shit), whose effects were impressed on the landscape, which could in turn be interpreted through the socially significant animal. In cases where clotting was found, the diviner announced that the vein was closed and tried to determine the kinds of social breaches that had caused this abnormality. In all cases, the arterial blockage indexed that social relations had been breached—that boundaries had been eclipsed or that gifts were not circulating properly within those boundaries. Taken together, kutasa and βula enable senior men to carve out a protected space within which they exercise control and to then monitor that space to ensure relative reciprocity and peace (*sere*) is maintained within this bounded domain. Thus, there is good reason why staunch Christians of all ages recognize these rituals as acts of rebellion or sabotage, which is partly what they mean when they refer to them as demonic. For this ritual knowledge forges alternative sovereign orders, which interlopers cannot easily understand, penetrate, or undermine.

During this particular case of divination, the entrails revealed, through the clogging of their arteries, that the people of Mgange had to perform a rainmaking ritual to "heal the wounds" (*kuhoresha vonda*) inflicted by innocent lowlands Wataita engaged, of necessity, in the transgressive practice of downward migration to the hot (and because of this, also polluting and "un-Taita") plains. Mtula, the mkireti, said that the ancestors would require the sacrifice of one goat, and informed the chief, Alex, an official state figure. Word made it around the neighborhood and, as always, Father Muteyi, the Taita Catholic priest, protested against this backward "devil worship" to the same chief, who had already begun to raise funds from the community. He said that the ritual would "turn people backward," by which he also meant away from the church, and so the perceived disintegration of a social-symbolic articulation (church-development) became morally significant when he gave it temporal implications. Assuming that the area chief was accumulating some of the money that the community had contributed to the project, he insinuated that the state's officials had aligned themselves with the village's seniors to selfishly drain the community's meager resources: an act of *karaptchan* tantamount to witchcraft. This view was strengthened by the fact that the chief went house to house, aggressively persuading people to contribute to the ritual—thus lowering the state (*kuenda chini*) while simultaneously driving people back in time, processes the priest depicted as synonymous. But Chief Alex did not consider his actions to be destructive, because, from his perspective of how such rituals operated, the community's contribution was a necessary gift to the ancestors, without which their blessings would not flow, and the state was therefore merely acting in the public's interest.

Whereas most other rituals, such as fighi renewal, are held in dry, open plains or the open space that surrounded a compound, *kuora mbuβa*, or cleansing the land, usually happens in a moist, secluded glen. Men produce rain by penetrating the guarded space of the forest, where they extract water from the forest's medicines by ritually invoking ancestor spirits. Ndolwa, the high-altitude forest spring chosen for this particular ritual, is a place of ambivalent magic, where many say that strange, capricious spirits live. Now a tiny watering hole not more than three feet in diameter, it was, according to those more than fifty years old, at one time a sizeable pond (it had diminished due to deforestation and intensive cultivation). Some people said that the spirits who lived there were ancestors, while others were not so sure, referring to them as trickster spirits, called *visugha* (see below), and it was not clear to me that these different perspectives corresponded to any sociostructural pattern. Some senior men and women said visugha and ancestors were the same, but that the former had not produced recognized offspring and so could not have their skulls placed in hidden family caves, called *ngomenyi*. Older people who were less familiar with the Swahili coast said that they had seen ghosts wearing Islamic *kofia* (caps) there, insinuating that the powerful Islamic spirits called *majini* lived in the forest, and that the forest was therefore as "other" as the labyrinthine towns on Kenya's coast. However, Ndolwa was also a place of heritage, and one that served the community in very direct ways; it was, after all, from this spring that the entire town of Mgange drew its water. Ndolwa's existence was also threatened because people had slowly been moving up the hill and cultivating land in rocky places that previous generations avoided; they helped to dry up Ndolwa when they used its waters to irrigate their fields. The town's relatively prosperous shop owners compounded this problem when they built pipelines directly to the source against the wishes of the public.

The Accidental Traditionalist

For good reasons, all Wataita I spoke with perceived Ndolwa, like Taita tradition in general and Taita as a whole, to be in a state of decline, and people wondered whether it would be an effective site for the ritual, or if the spirits still had the powers they once did. Moreover, a school and shops sat just down the hill from the spring and, as one woman put it, "the din of the school is a sound that the dead won't understand" (*Ndoghoi ra skuli βandu βifuye ndewirelelwa*). More importantly, even those who were supportive of this ritual in principle were unsure if the senior male *wakireti* would be able to create conditions recognizable to the dead. In particular, younger men and women questioned the wakireti's capacity to mediate the relationship between the living and the dead by presiding over a gift exchange. As one educated Catholic woman in her forties put it, accusing the wakireti of secrecy and witchcraft: "If rainmaking has value, why do they hide it? If they opened it up for us, there are those among us who would be interested, who would like to be able to use this thing for the benefit of all. But they sit on it, trying to control the rains we need, eating our money. They act like witches!" A young man, accusing the wakireti of deception, put it this way: "These days a rainmaker may dream that he should slaughter a white calf, but instead he'll slaughter a black goat and put a white tail on it to fool the ancestors. Or he may be told to sacrifice one of his own, but fears losing the money he might make at the butcher's. He convinces the chief to make the whole community contribute. Now, instead of raining, it got drier!" In the views of these unlikely defenders of ancestors, rainmakers had turned into drought makers by distorting reality, in the false assumption that the ancestors would not recognize the ruse. Also, in the young man's view, the man who should have "owned" the ritual and served as patron for the entire community had participated in his own emasculation by directly depending on women's money. Since he felt compelled to raise funds from female-headed households, it was highly unlikely that his actions would be recognized by the dead, whose masculine virtue and productivity had been beyond reproach.

But, for many in this community, the wakireti were the only available recourse and the only viable defense against the drought. The word "mkireti" (man of the wilderness) references familiarity with things of the forest, including indigenous trees, medicines, and poisons, as well as spirits of the dead (visugha or *mashetani*). While a mlaghui, or diviner, explains what has gone wrong in a community and who is at fault, a mkireti is a kind of traditional police officer. One young man argued that the mkireti was "in charge of security, and fighi." Another offered, in English, that "he sets up ordinances and statutes on how people should live on the land." His is also an officially recognized position, and so the mkireti has a kind of titular authority over certain spaces, as well as times, whose control many Wataita of all sexes and ages feel is crucial to the community's well-being. At the same time, his position references an earlier, largely imaginary sociopolitical order; each mkireti represents a bounded geographical zone that has no legal existence, conforming to the remembered boundaries of earlier neighborhoods (*izanga*) that existed before land consolidation.

The position of mkireti is often coveted by former civil servants and police officers, as it confers some influence and a small income in one's senior years. But, like the treasurer of a Florida condominium's board of directors, any mkireti is likely to be subject to a great deal of inspection and reprobation from members of the community. This is partly because this kind of work is intrinsically contradictory: although his life and biography are as contemporary as anyone else's, the mkireti is understood to be an expert in tradition and, like the Catholic priests whom Wataita know intimately, is expected to be somewhat detached from the world. And he takes on the burden of communing with ancestral forces that the vast majority of people, male and female, young and old, feel incapable of interacting with successfully. Indeed, the mkireti is called upon to mediate two epochs that Wataita as a whole imagine to exist as shadows of each other—the present and long ago—and is compelled to carry the antagonism between these types within himself. This obligation makes him tragically incapable of succeeding in any of the tasks that Taita society has entrusted to him.

Mtula had inherited the position from his father, but his life was certainly far from pristine: he had been a clerk (some asserted that he had corrupted his position) in the Kenya Ports Authority in Mombasa for nearly thirty years, sold beer (*chofi*) out of his house illegally, and made little secret of the fact that he expected monetary compensation for his work. And he did not seem too concerned that most people felt that his work had to include some personal sacrifice if the ancestors were to pay any attention (not everyone agreed with this, not least the mkireti, who asserted that the community as a whole had to bear the brunt of any sacrifice). One man I interviewed surprised me by insisting that Mtula would die within one year, so greatly had he offended the ancestors by charging money for "opening" new land: "The fighi are enraged at Mtula. He will not live past January!" (he turned out to be right). Another person offered, "Of course our fighi don't work! If Mtula even tried to go near one, he would die instantly!" because he was more interested in accumulating than reciprocating, in selfishly earning money than in protecting Taita as a whole. It did not help that Mtula was also accused of consistently swallowing the beer that he was supposed to spit out during the act of kutasa—more evidence that his heart was selfish and witchlike, for he consumed selfishly rather than redistributing.

Furthermore, during the previous rainmaking ritual, Mtula had demonstrated his lack of control over junior subordinates when his son-in-law, acting as his assistant, made a tremendous reenactment error: he prepared Swahili *pilau* for the ancestors. Pilau is a "foreign" dish, made of meat, rice, and spices not grown in Taita, for which Wataita have acquired a taste in Mombasa and other coastal Swahili cities; they typically eat pilau during celebrations. In his defense, Mtula's son-in-law's decision made a certain amount of sense, because pilau is served to respected visitors and guests and is a sign of distinction and generosity. Yet Mtula's pilau offering was said to have spoiled the rains for an entire year, because the ancestors only respond to foods they remember, like *kimanga*, a dish composed of a variety of mashed tubers and legumes, which Wataita these days seldom eat. After all, one family rarely has all of these different foods at one time, due to the scarcity of land and the fact that a single individual rarely owns land in many different climate and soil zones. Maize is cheaper and faster to grow, and it has more harvest seasons, but most Wataita believe that it is not as nutritious as the foods that previous generations ate. By offering kimanga as gift, senior men and women contrive to communicate the continuity of an earlier moral and political order and to downplay contemporary transformations in ways of making a living. Likewise, by preparing sugarcane beer, and not the more typical, and commodified, beer of refined sugar fermented with the pods of the sausage tree (*mwasina*), the specialists recalled a past when men cultivated large fields of sugarcane and used the product to brew beer, which helped create friendship, hierarchy, and indebtedness among socially adult men. Because the ingredients used to make pilau must be purchased, the introduction of this delicacy caused the city and commerce to intrude in the protected temporal enclave the old men were working to create through ritual. It also suggested their waning power, partly because pilau is especially, though certainly not only, favored by women and is considered a somewhat feminine food (as opposed to, say, roast goat, the quintessential masculine food).

In this particular year, Mtula had postponed the ritual beyond the date prescribed by the diviner (mlaghui, or enunciator) Mwachofi, and so had threatened the harvest. When the day of the postponed ritual finally came, Mtula, the principal mkireti, was late to arrive, and the first people at the scene were his supporting mkireti from the lowlands nyika and the old βula diviner, Mwachofi. When Mtula finally did arrive with his son-in-law, the other men were angry: they still remembered the pilau debacle from the year before. Mtula was agitated, claiming he was late because he had left the medicines he had collected from the forest in a shop in the market, which he visited after coming to town on a matatu. When the others heard this, they rebuked him harshly for allowing the "moist" medicines to be spoilt (*kunonwa*) by the "heat" of the shop. And why had he visited a place of commerce, something unknown to the dead, and ridden who-knows-where in a matatu, one day before the event? Clearly, these actions were not of long ago (*ko kala*), and any one of them could undermine the effectiveness of the ritual: "If you have come to spoil like a witch, then move away!" warned the diviner. When I later tried to ascertain if there was a deeper source of conflict between Mtula and the mlaghui Mwachofi, I was told that the mlaghui and the mkireti argued with one another because, while they were supposed to work together and carry out distinct functions, they tended to usurp each other's duties and to act alone in specific instances. Some said they acted this way because of greed, and others said it was because of lack of communication, or the desires of the people seeking out their services. In any case, this kind of fragmentation and divisiveness did not augur well for the success of the ritual, and it confirmed the suspicions of many younger people that Taita's seniors were incapable of representing true Taita autochthony.

An Ambiguous Effort

Eventually we all settled down for the cleansing, and a few others, mostly young men, stopped by to watch. Clearly, the practitioners were on the defensive: Mtula's son wrote down every detail of the ritual in a logbook, in case the wakireti were later called to task and asked to prove that they had actually cleansed the land in accordance with the wishes of the ancestors, and not bewitched the entire community. Mwachofi counted the medicines to publicly verify that Mtula had fulfilled his charge as required, and Mtula's son-in-law wrote the names of the plants in his logbook. The three specialists then sat around the medicines and performed kutasa with the sugarcane beer Mtula had brought: each promised to "leave discord behind" and to continue the ritual with clean hearts. They then commenced pounding the medicines with rocks, causing them to emit a sweet smell, which was itself meaningful: "This is what Taita used to smell like long ago," Mwachofi told me. As the day progressed, it became clear to me that these ritual specialists were trying to encompass the entire landscape over which they had authority by deploying aspects of it, while also securing this space from exogenous polluting forces. Thus, the mkireti had collected forty different types of plants taken from densely forested nearby hilltops, and later sent emissaries to three mountains that constituted the perimeters of their charge. No one was to carry money to the ritual, or speak Swahili, both because these symbols would confuse communication with the ancestors and because they implied division and fragmentation. As they pounded the medicines, they merged in a unified voice, alternating in reciting the following lines:

> We're saying this, witch who would destroy this neighborhood: Let him be struck with hiccups and die! (*Daamba βelee, msaβi unonaa izhi izanga... ukabo ni ngengefu ufo!*)

> We don't want people from beyond the hills to benefit from us, when we don't benefit from them! (*Ndedikunde dendefughwa izha chiya na isi disefughaa!*)
> Rain is what we want! Of *pitch* black! (*Vua nizo dekunde... Ya chilu fii!*)
> Banish sickness! We're saying death should disappear. Get lost! Cease to be. (*βikongo isiye! Damba vifwa vilaghaye—Toe! Visekaiye.*)
> So much food that some will be carried and the rest left to dry on the stalks. (*Vindo viduko na vimu vedeomiyaa matasenyi.*)
> This, what we've said, is true. Let it be fulfilled. We're following footsteps. (*Agha daghora nighegheni. Ghikeniye. Damigha nyayo.*)

Here Taita was posited as a united, sovereign community, exploited by outsiders who wanted to take vital resources from them, from water to timber to gemstones, and no longer nourished by "those on the other side," who may have been Taita people living in the city or non-Taita interlopers. Similarly, the final phrase, "We're following footsteps," had several implications, one of which was continuity with the past. But "Nyayo" was also then President Moi's, and the Kenyan African National Union's (KANU), official slogan, screamed from the football fields by KANU youth wing supporters at election times and during national holidays. I think, then, that these senior were also expressing the fact that what they were doing supplemented, rather than preempted or foreclosed, the sovereign authority of the state; that is, their work went beyond the state's spatial control by accessing the power of another time.

The perceived disjuncture between the values embodied in authentic Taita tradition, and the real interests and attitudes of actual Taita seniors, was incorporated into the ritual in the form of an overriding concern with assessment and codification. After the blessing came a gift aimed at cementing the continuing relationship of Taita generations across apparently bounded times: Mtula prepared the kimanga, while the other men distributed chofi in small gourds. Everyone present joined together to ensure that the ritual was carried out according to the proper recipe, and the younger men participated in the act of authentication by recording their seniors' acts in English: "Mzee Mtula cuts the seven pieces of organ meat, and places them on a skewer, then sets them aside"; "The kimanga is cooked, and he places it on a broken piece of gourd. There are seven pieces"; "Seven men carry seven pieces of food. There were also seven pieces of tobacco." By holding the elders to a rigid and legalistic idea of how rituals were performed in the past, youth implied that Taita culture needed to be legally codified so that its purity could be guaranteed. For example, Rasta, who was not yet thirty years of age, was convinced that the rainmakers were charlatans bent on consuming as much roasted goat as possible. His youth did not prevent him from citing numerous violations of traditional orthodoxy, including the high number of specialists (too many); the fact that the old men ended up carrying most of the meat home with them after the ritual; and the privacy of the affair, which implied a lack of transparency and, hence, accountability.[1]

The ritual was not finished without a hitch. After the goat had been slaughtered in the correct, bloodless manner (through "peaceful" strangulation with a rope, rather than violent cutting with a knife), Mwachofi the diviner cleansed and unfolded the intestines to read the veins. He found a clot in one of them. Instead of calling out the anticipated "We are full!" (*Daguda*), he intoned, "There is hunger!" (*Njala yeko*). Mtula leapt in to verify, and immediately challenged the artery's number: Mwachofi said the clot was in the first artery as one reads from the left, referring to the owner of the ritual, who was none other than Mtula the mkireti. Mwachofi publicly explained that the ritual had not succeeded because Mtula had delayed holding it in an effort to extort as much money from the community's women as possible. Then, instead of buying the goat with these funds, Mtula had, according to Mwachofi's reading of the βula, pocketed the money and borrowed a goat from his in-law. Mwachofi pointed at Mtula and intoned menacingly, "Our children will suffer and die for this man's love of money!" Mtula's protests grew weak in the face of Mwachofi's confident anger.

Moreover, during the final stages of the ritual, while Mtula was roasting the goat, he had prepared an herbal mixture for his sons to drink. He had then sent them, with the medicines, to three different hills, which together comprised the limits of the area they wanted to cleanse. The formula was designed to render the young men invisible while making their feet light. But when they returned some two hours later, they reeked of alcohol. Now Mtula's junior dependents were accused of insubordinate, disrespectful acts (drinking illegal beer in someone's house-turned-bar) that would anger and confuse the ancestors. The men tried to salvage what they could of the situation by taking the remaining food to the *mvumu* tree at Ndolwa as quickly as possible, taking great care to leave their gift of food at the base of the tree without looking backward afterward (they did not want to suggest to the ancestors that they were giving regretfully). But the old man Mtula surprised me when he suggested that the ritual, in its current operation, was actually performed in accordance with received understandings of biblical events: "If we look back, we might be turned to salt," Mtula mused, much like Lot's wife in the Bible. Thus, in his perspective, their selective enclaving of Taita tradition did not preclude all foreign introductions, such as Christianity, which he instead conceptualized as an aspect of Taita tradition.

Mtula grew silent before his accusers on that day, seemingly admitting that he had expropriated some of the town's scarce funds. But later he retorted that the ritual had failed because the community was not supportive: in the old days, everyone would have shown up, and not just a few old men and their sons. The next week, the three men went to Chief Alex's office with the logbook, where, despite the apparent transparency of writing, various versions of what happened, and where the money for the goat had come from, were presented and dissected for hours. In the end, Alex humbled all three rainmakers by disallowing the entire ritual and demanding that the three go together to visit the venerable old healer, Mwarasho. At the same time, he confirmed that the government was unable to provide for people, that authentic Taita tradition was therefore essential to development, and that these womanly seniors were mocking it, and thereby driving Taita back in time: "Let me tell you a secret. I am a chief, but I will say that the government cannot support us. No one is looking out for our development but us. So if you do not have the heart for this work, if you want to fight like women, then go ask for help from someone who does."

Only a Living Anachronism Can Recreate the Past

I had some experience with the healer, Mwarasho: After about a year in the Taita Hills, I had experienced sharp stomach pains that lasted for hours at a time. I had visited doctors in Nairobi, and when I returned to the United States for a short period I was examined and treated, unsuccessfully. No one could find anything wrong with me so, when I returned from the United States I went, with my friend Rasta, to visit Mwarasho. The old man was odd and abrupt: he did not greet us or engage in any of the normal colloquial exchanges that confer fluidity to everyday social interactions. He even seemed to ignore us while we explained my symptoms, and at one point he disappeared for nearly a half-hour without saying a word. But when Mwarasho returned, he came with quiet confidence, as well as some powder and bark, and gave complete instructions on preparing a tea. And his charge was small indeed. But within two days of taking the tea and ingesting the powder I received the greatest surprise of all: I felt entirely healed.

Impressed, I returned to Mzee Mwarasho, this time to request that he teach me about Taita's medicinal plants and of his form of healing in exchange for payment. Mwarasho's response surprised me: "I wish that I could help you, teacher," he said, in Kidabida, "But I do not know anything about plants or medicine." "But what do you mean?" I countered, "People come from across oceans to see you. You have raised the dead so that they "chew tongue meat" with the living. I myself am better." Mwarasho, ever patient, was unfazed: "Teacher, let me explain to you how this thing works. When someone comes to me, those who have died talk to me. Those spirits know everything about the forest [where these medicines come from], and they tell me what to give you. I do not know if this thing is going to kill you or cure you. It is beyond me. But I am pleased that you feel better." Mwarasho went on to explain that his ability to heal was the product of his particular relationship with those who had died, who in turn held a kind of sovereignty over the "natural" environment, which included medicinal plants. Their power flowed through Mwarasho because of his disposition, so the fact that he charged little money for his services was not incidental at all. Rather, Mwarasho's moistness (*kinyoshi*) and lack of greed put him on good terms with those who had died and caused them to recognize him as a person who shared their nature—which everyone agreed was fast fading in this age of intense market competition, jealousy, and heat. Thus, Mwarasho's power emerged in part from the exclusion of markedly "modern" social phenomena—such as the logics of competitive capitalism, which motivated most healers.

Mwarasho was not a rainmaker because he had not inherited his position from one of the rainmaking families, and technically he should not have been performing this work. But he embodied the spirit of tradition as most people in the community understood it: what was so striking about Mwarasho, in stark contrast to the apparently self-serving Mtula, was that he held to a standard of value that seemed hopelessly out of touch with the present day, and thus confirmed his ascetic disavowal of its excesses. If the stories told in the neighborhood were true, Mwarasho came up with something useful in his gourds of plants and powders and put "those witches" to shame, initiating the torrential El Niño downpour that lasted for the remainder of my fieldwork.

The fact that someone like Mwarasho even existed suggested the possibility of a separate Taita moral order that could also be the basis of a political order; for this reason, Mwarasho aroused the suspicion of authorities whose political legitimacy rested on other spatial, cultural, and temporal assumptions. One day after the rains had commenced, two young male police officers visited Mwarasho and informed him that they were taking him to the University of Nairobi, where he was to translate all of his medical knowledge to the professors at the Kenya African Medical Research Institute. Mwarasho refused, repeating to the police officers that he knew nothing about medicine. The police, taking this as a direct affront to their authority, beat Mwarasho with their rifles, stopping just short of killing the old man. While the police beat Mwarasho, they repeatedly called him a witch. In their stated view, they were justified because he was concealing a form of knowledge that was potentially destructive, and could only be made legitimate if it was rendered transparent, so that all might learn from and improve it. In this, the policemen's perspective superficially resembled that of liberal Western humanists, who encourage the institutionalization of "local knowledge," as if all knowledge could simply be rendered transparent to empirical observation (cf. Scott 1998). Or, rather, they drew on this known, global ideology when justifying their act of violence and their generation's distrust of the power of senior men. In contrast, Mwarasho held that the policemen's plan was impossible, because his knowledge did not exist as a natural object, but was the outcome of a social relationship from which the police, the Kenya African Medical Research Institute, and the state were necessarily excluded. Through an act of violence on a man's vulnerable, isolated body, the young men reinscribed the spatiotemporal reality and power of the state themselves, and also reinscribed a particular version of the present; in so doing they tried to destroy historicity as it flowed through, and came to rest in, old man Mwarasho (cf. Feldman 1991). Far from succeeding, their actions proved and vitalized the past's sacrality, and its incarnation in real people and places, which would surely provoke future ripostes from central authorities.

The Power of Gifts

Though they claimed to be recreating an authentic tradition, in truth, like Walter Benjamin's "messianic historian," these senior men mobilized a reified vision of the past to change the present in a moment of danger (Benjamin 1968, 247). The crisis they worked to transform was written on an increasingly endangered landscape that, most people felt, registered the moral failings of Taita people as a whole. What they were wrestling with among themselves, and trying to protect from the corrupting force of the present, was the past's moral and political integrity, and thus also its sovereign exceptionalism. Ultimately, the specialist Mtula, redefined as witch, was blamed for exposing the hopelessness of their efforts without any pretense of shame. For when communication with the dead and with God failed because of a misrecognition or falsification of signs, blame was assigned to individuals such as the mkireti, whose position drew attention to his society's inadequacies, and so provoked contempt. In presenting the ancestors with staple foods and beverages, pure language, and the distinguishing smells of a bygone time, these men also tried to present an image of unquestioned patriarchal and gerontocratic authority. Their aborted gift to the ancestors was a sense of temporal continuity and coherence, but they left themselves, and their vigilant observers, with a certainty of the fact of change and the impossibility of return. For despite all their efforts, the present was bound to intrude, rupturing the relationship between sign and referent and leaving the ancestors confused. Or perhaps the ancestors were left in peace, leaving the living hungry and adrift.

Clearly, Taita society was increasingly incapable of solving Taita problems, as even those things that should have been synonymous with Taita people resisted their control and had even been transformed into exacting enemies. The idea of a reckless, murderous past took many forms. For example, some people—especially returned civil servants who had spent many years in the city—argued that it was not in fact urban majini who were afflicting Taita (see chapter 3). These former urban workers tried to draw attention away from the dangers that they represented for others by blaming Taita social ills and possession incidents on local spirits called visugha. These formerly benevolent spirits lived in the Taita forests and had grown hateful because they no longer received sacrifice. As one retired Mombasa police officer put it, "Listen. God brings many things, but some things humans bring on themselves. Long ago, visugha lived apart from us, but they would interact with us peacefully. They helped us. Sometimes they would clear our fields! Sometimes they gave us bananas as gifts. In return, we offered them animal sacrifice. Now, these days, visugha have become bad. They have become demons, and they are thirsty for our blood. But why? It t is because of what we have done to them!"

The police officer went on to explain that Wataita had, against their natures, allowed themselves to inhabit a "culture of *shauri yako*," (your responsibility) based on selfish individualism (ubinafsi). According to him, over time visugha had been forced to give up their territory as forests were cultivated, and so these embittered spirits had been evicted to progressively smaller and overcrowded reserves at the same time as people stopped sacrificing to them. Inequality and land pressures in the social world had turned these visugha into a refugee population, belonging, much like their human Taita others, nowhere, with no place left to go. Their conversion to Satan, forced upon them by hunger, transformed them, as they began to crave that which they formerly represented as objects of sacrifice (blood and, by extension, kinship). These formerly free agents ("sometimes they would give us bananas") having morphed into useful things owned by greedy people, now annihilate the social relations that they formerly helped produce when they give unearned money in exchange for human life: they have become objects yearning, impossibly, for life and producing death as a product of this desire. People and spirits of the dead thus suffer from a reciprocal degeneration that binds them together, as they join to destroy their livestock and children, the productive foundations of the world. But by virtue of recognizing this, those who told such stories posited an alternative model of social behavior, and even a potential plan of action.

Dot Com Will Die Seriously! Thoughts on Competing Sovereignties

Wataita in general perceived their region as possessing competing forms of power, and different groups of Taita people worked to control these powers in the name of development. These powers were indexed by, and embodied in, real places, practices, and institutions (the office of the chief, a school, a spring, a fighi shrine), and sometimes these iconic things, existing in a mutually constitutive tension that was sometimes productive and sometimes destructive, leached power from each other. In moments of perceived crisis, these apparently conflicting powers that were embodied in things (say, schools and fighi) appeared to share in the same essence, whose power seemed to recede on the horizon of history. Fighi were particularly important in this regard, because they were represented as competing forms of governance and sovereignty, spatiotemporality, and moral order.

Recall that fighi are said to have been borders that protected people and things within from people and things without, and that also guaranteed moral order, by pain of death, within those borders. The sites that Wataita refer to most commonly as places where fighi either exist or once existed include borders separating highlands neighborhoods that existed in the past, borders that separated the places where people lived from the places where they planted food, and borders separating the hills as a whole from the flat plains. Livestock (the lowlands), crops (the midlands), people (the highlands), and water (hilltops) were the social resources that fighi protected. As Wataita of all ages explain it, fighi's ability to exercise sovereignty depended on people exchanging gifts with the dead: tangible gifts of food when they were climbing from the lowlands to the highlands, and the more diffuse gift of recognition, or belief, which Wataita today sometimes speak of as a gift withheld. Now fighi have stopped working in the "right" way because Wataita have stopped giving them gifts, out of selfishness. The problem is compounded by the fact that fighi are no longer protecting the right social spaces, because the social landscape has changed irrevocably, and the fighi are still where they always were. Thus, the areas where one finds fighi are no longer borderlands, but central residential areas, a fact that provokes some Wataita to satisfy their fuel needs by cutting these misplaced guardians down.

Most Wataita agree that fighi embody an essential Taita power, which used to be managed by senior males, is not easily separated from the power of Taita ecology, and resists other forms of governance associated with the state. One middle-age man explained that, when the *Wazungu* (whites, Europeans) first came to Taita, they soon realized that they could not govern, because large swathes of the area had been rendered invisible by fighi's magic: "They would come to an area, and they would see only forest but, Ai! there is a whole town living there! (laughs) You cannot govern a place if there are thousands of people there and you think that it's a forest! (more laughter) So they taught people to destroy the fighi!" According to this man, and many others who held similar views, there was, for a window of time, a shadow zone where Wataita exercised sovereignty over their own affairs outside the purview of the colonial regime, which sought to control the region with a view to taxing its population and which already exercised legal control. According to this view, the transference of sovereignty, or the erasure of Taita autonomy, could be blamed on Taita people, because it occurred through a gift exchange between colonial authorities and Taita seniors, who became indebted to colonial missionaries and administrators when they accepted their gifts in exchange for leaving fighi behind. Thus this transference of control over space was finalized by the refusal to give gifts to the dead, and so also the past, which happened when Wataita began going to church. The net result was that they became an uprooted people, ever more vulnerable to manipulation by foreign others: "Our grandfathers listened to them [the Wazungu], because they said, 'Oh, these people have given us sugar! They have given us writing! They are very good people!' But then all of the sudden we had nothing."

Wataita held somewhat different views about the original source of fighi's power. Educated people tended to liken fighi to a church and referred to these spaces as "sacred," in English. For example, when I asked an engineer in the Ministry of Forests whether medicine was the source of fighi's power, he was a bit offended, probably because to him, "medicine" implied witchcraft or magic, as opposed to religion: "Would you ask if there's medicine in a church?" he demanded. "Fighi is like a church: it is sacred." The engineer continued by explaining that the power of fighi came from the positive force of people uniting in belief and ritual: "Fighi stopped working because people stopped believing," he offered, calling to mind Durkheimian notions of collective effervescence. His view was more benign than that articulated by those who live near fighi, who frequently maintain that the power of fighi originated with human sacrifice: specifically, the sacrifice of young virgins or, in some stories, infants, in forests. It is tempting to argue that this belief in human sacrifice is derived from the Christian missions, and it is certainly perpetuated by many contemporary preachers who incriminate traditional ritual as being satanic. But I believe that the continued resonance of this idea for many people suggests a more complex and ambivalent relationship to the past: specifically, the idea of a founding sacrifice that produces a generative sovereign order constituted by violence over those who have the power to give life on their own (women on the verge of reproductive promise, or virgins), or who symbolize life in its purest, presocial expression (children). This sovereign Taita community had, according to all Wataita with whom I spoke, the power to impose law and to exact violence over its members, but this form of sovereignty was renewed through repeated exchanges of gifts (food and bloodless animal sacrifice), rather than through repeated acts of violence. This idea that each fighi was constituted by violence, and understands itself as having the "right" to exercise violence over others, accounts for the common assertion that fighi is both curse, because it can kill, and medicine, because it protects and nourishes.

Not only did Wataita see fighi as somehow threatened by the exigencies of modern life, but they also thought of it as an institution that was in creative tension with commercializing institutions that opened Taita up to the world outside the hills: "Education destroyed fighi," my old friend Marki used to say. In part, this implied simply that the Christian, school-educated Wataita had ceased to be interested in maintaining fighi shrines. But Wataita also contrasted the "opening up" (*kufungua*) that schooling enabled with the closure and historical continuity that fighi ensured. As mentioned earlier, many people of all ages expressed the idea that schools drained authentic Taita power: in particular, they often argued that people lost their inherited traditional knowledge and power when they attended school or began visiting church, as churches and schools are linked in the Taita imaginaire.

On the surface, institutions like fighi and schools were antagonistic: the former militated against change, while the latter ideally connected people to urban labor markets, English language, and nonlocal knowledge. If the educated were sometimes "lost" (*kulegheriya*) and physically hard to find, fighi sought out those who were lost and punished them with death. But, ideally, Wataita envisioned these institutions as operating in tandem, for schools have allowed some Wataita to appropriate wealth and respectability, while fighi are supposed to ensure that these appropriated things benefit Taita society and are in accordance with Taita values. After all, Wataita were never able to live fully in the city or the country, and so needed institutions that allowed for the coexistence and productivity of both. It is in their perceived mutual decline, and in the eroded relationship between the signs and the things they stand for, that Taita glimpse the demise of earlier articulations (between the rural and the urban, for example) and begin to conceptualize ways of reconfiguring these relationships so that they actually work.

The interlinked themes of sovereignty and multiple, coexisting temporalities came out clearly in a discussion I had with Ignatius and Agrippinna, a married couple in their forties who made a small income by selling very fine sugarcane beer in plastic jerry cans out of their home. Their neighbor had just died because, according to them, he had annoyed the fighi that was nearby. The deceased had been in his mid-fifties and, according to the couple, was supposed to be taking care of fighi, because his father had done so more or less successfully when he served as the mkireti of that village some years ago. But he rejected his father's charge and faith, and tried to protect himself from danger by becoming saved, along with his wife, but within the Catholic church. Their salvation was part of an effort, on the part of the new Catholic priest, to mimic the increasingly popular Pentecostal religion by allowing people to express themselves as saved and to offer personal testimonials about their individual struggles to acquire salvation. According to Ignatius and Agrippina, he visited the nearby fighi with the Catholic priest and other parishioners, and together they tried to exorcise what they referred to as the "demons," or mashetani, from the forest by spraying holy water on the site.

He died two weeks later. "No one else there died," Ignatius explained, "because only he had sinned against his father. He thought that his power, from God, was greater, but he insulted his father by underestimating the power of his father's belief." Ignatius went on to explain that people were dying in the area because of fighi, and that ultimately there were two reasons for their death: purposefully insulting (he used the Swahili *kudhirao*) fighi and being ignorant (Swahili *kutojua*) of where they were and what they wanted. His explanation led to a discussion about knowledge: there are different fields of knowledge, Ignatius explained, and they have a tendency to conflict with one another; survival in Taita space requires that people inhabit a particular representation of culture, which is available to them as knowledge. "The only way we can live with fighi," Ignatius declared, "is by acting like people did in the past. But most people do not know, and they are in danger of dying."

My friend Rasta immediately picked up on the inversion that Ignatius was suggesting when he referred to fighi as specialized knowledge, implicitly in opposition to education and high technology. "So what about dot com?" Rasta, asked, referring to certain youth who expressed no interest in fighi but were fascinated by cell phones and the Internet. Drawing attention to the contrast between the foreign knowledge of computers and the local knowledge of fighi magic, Ignatius shook his head and laughed: "Ai! Dot com will die seriously! They think they know something, but they don't know the power that is here!" Ignatius's comment suggested that different forms of subjectivity were realized through symbolically opposed modes of spatiotemporal extension: specifically, communicating rapidly with people over vast distances via the Internet, and communicating with local spirits, which required accumulating knowledge and dispositions slowly, over time. Ignatius and Agrippina also seemed to be acknowledging the existence of an alternative legal-bureaucratic order that paralleled that of the state. For example, they listed a series of activities that one was not supposed to do near fighi, many of which made no sense to anyone present but which could easily culminate in death: menstruating women are not allowed to walk near fighi; a person cannot use a walking stick when passing fighi; one cannot have sex, argue, fight, curse, or bury the dead near fighi. Some of these things have to do with conflict and violence (arguing, cursing, fighting, and even the walking stick), while others are concerned with death and, perhaps more pointedly, the intervention of humans in matters of life and death. Specifically, the actions referred to included ritualized efforts to overcome death (funerals) and the power of people to create life (sex and childbirth, which can also be generative of conflict). Thus, the idea seemed to be that these acts offended fighi by challenging, or drawing attention to the limits of, fighi's power to grant life and take it away. But no one could easily explain the walking stick, although Rasta offered that "seeing" an old man with a walking stick challenged the fighi's "feeling" of omnipotence. I feel that part of the idea Ignatius was conveying was that Wataita were required to know certain rules even if the reason was unclear, and this opacity was constitutive of fighi's sovereign power.

At this point, I asked what I considered a vital, if obvious, question: how was it possible to live surrounded by fighi without having sex? Ignatius, laughing, acknowledged that people in the area did indeed have sex, and offered that either the fighi's power was waning or the fighi was forgiving about certain practices, because it recognized that people had to live there, after all. "The fighi has grown weaker, but it is still strong at the core," Ignatius offered. "There is a fuse at the center, and you have to be careful near that." At other points in the conversation, he referred to this core as a magnet and a battery, indicating that it possessed a kind of electricity that was equivalent to other, foreign, forms of technology. Perhaps, he offered, fighi was weakened because of the schools, churches, and shops that were nearby: "Mgange is very modern," Ignatius reasoned. "So much that people here can't do anything about them [fighi]. We have to go to other people for help. There was a time when the elders from here wanted to strengthen the fighi, because they were afraid that Pentecostalism was destroying its power. They went to the owners of fighi, in βumingu."

βumingu is on the far side of the Taita Hills. It is not connected to other areas by a main road, and it is not reachable by public transportation. According to Ignatius, "Our people went to βumingu, and the people there said, 'Mgange should forget fighi, because of the way people there are living, with electricity and many shops.'" In other words, fighi would either kill people or be inhibited from functioning in Mgange. βumingu and Mgange inhabited different temporalities that were incommensurate; one was moving forward, for better or worse, while the other resembled what all of Taita was like in the past. Too, Mgange's moving forward could also be conceptualized as a moving backward: Mgange people felt they had to go to βumingu for fighi, while βumingu people felt that fighi could kill innocent people in Mgange and, by walking to βumingu, the elders of Mgange enacted Mgange's modernity *and* its backwardness.

One point that emerged clearly from the discussion was that Agrippina and Ignatius felt that, while fighi was something important, it did not fulfill the functions it was supposed to: mainly, protecting Taita communities from outsiders. Rather, fighi tormented Wataita in the present, who were incapable of doing anything about it because of their alienation from the past. As Ignatius put it, "The area we are living in now was once a forest, with wild animals. There were lions, and people were very afraid to venture here. Fighi were hidden in this dangerous place to protect those who lived high up from the Maasai. But now there is really no need for a fighi here at all." That our new companions felt themselves imprisoned by the ancient actions and interests of people who were now dead, and who should surely want to protect their offspring, clearly dismayed my friend Rasta. He shook his head and complained, "There are some things I still don't understand about this place," meaning Taita. Invoking notions of self-government and planning, he demanded, "Why don't you pull out the fighi medicines if they're causing people to die, or relocate the fighi to a place where they will actually protect this area?" "We can't, because we don't know how," came the reply. Again, they depended on the fighi donors from βumingu. Perhaps, Agrippina offered, somewhat apologetically, they should organize a delegation to go to βumingu to enlist the help of its elders in relocating Mgange's fighi. The irony was clear: modern, but in many ways equally poor, Mgange was compelled to listen to backward βumingu's experts and to use their now foreign technology if they wanted to survive.

"OK. Good!" said Rasta, his temper clearly increasing. "In the meantime, what about placing a sign, or plaque, near the fighi, alerting people that it's there, so that they don't die?" Ignatius explained that this would upset the senior men in the village, who knew that fighi's power, like the power of the state government, depended on its being secret. Exasperated, Rasta proposed that they ask the government to create a sign along the perimeters of the area around which fighi held sovereignty, so as to avoid alerting strangers or governing officials to the exact location of the fighi itself. This would then become, in Rasta's words, a "protected area," and a "cultural heritage site." Ignatius and Agrippina claimed to agree that this was a sound idea, to which we could all drink.

Rasta's intervention in this discussion is interesting, because it draws attention to one of the ways in which some younger, educated Wataita who felt themselves stuck at home were conceptualizing the past as a natural resource that could be managed by local populations, in collusion with cooperative state authorities and, perhaps, nongovernmental organizations (NGOs). He had begun by taking seriously the idea that fighi existed to protect Taita; indeed, I had once heard him refer to fighi, in excited and optimistic terms, as "nuclear silos." He offered what he perceived to be a rational-utilitarian and developmental solution: move the nukes to a safer, more strategic location. When this was declared impossible, because of the multiple temporalities involved, Rasta offered that the state was partly responsible for protecting people from "out of control" fighi, and should be asked to intervene in this cultural realm in a way that would not interfere with fighi's sovereignty. In a sense, the state would perform the function of traditional culture by educating people, in the way that they had presumably been educated in earlier times but without direct interpersonal mediation. And so two forms of sovereignty, which were also two temporal orders, would be allowed to coexist, a compromise that would not necessarily make fighi any more functional but that would at least minimize the danger to innocents. Rasta focused on creating a sustainable solution that would allow Wataita to manage Taita space and history, rather than being tormented by it. By calling it a cultural heritage site, Rasta also suggested that this culture had prestige value and was worth something to both Wataita and the world community. Clearly, he viewed this conversation as an opportunity to develop in people a healthy respect for tradition, based on reason rather than fear. No doubt he also saw the proposed warning sign to be a gift of recognition, which would also potentially appease fighi and transform it from a mechanism of death into one of peace.

Thus, Wataita saw the past and the local as powerful entities that needed to be controlled, in much the same way as they saw the forces of "globalization" or "neoliberalism." In addition, as we have seen, their perceptions of the past were linked to their experience of the present, framed as it was by important structural transformations that were global in scope. Thus, in Taita understandings of the past, we begin to see an emerging argument about the appropriation and containment of powerful forces (foreign and local) as a viable development strategy.

Development as Sovereignty Forged through Exchange

A major point to be derived from this discussion is that, clearly, Wataita tended to view the ideal sociopolitical community as a complex of relationships constituted through magnanimous exchange, and development implied the creation of conceptual and territorial borders within which this could occur. As the editor of Taita's first indigenous language newspaper, *Mwanedu*, or Fraternity, wrote (Mwachofi 1998),

> When you look at why Taita has no development, you see the Mtaita, or Taita male, doesn't want to join in with his fellows. He does not like helping, even when others are sick. If you look at businesses here in Voi, most of them are in the hands of people from outside, and be advised that he who is in business is the one who has strength. Unity of Taita has a lot of things.... The biggest thing we want to bring in the middle of Taita right now is love and helping one another. Again, right now Taita language is nearly dying, and this is truly a big danger for the coming generation. Many are using Kiswahili, and leaving their mother tongue. For this reason, there are no secrets [a term which also implies ritual knowledge]. Another thing, we want to call the old men to sit down together and chew tongue meat so that they can give us their ideas.

This passage begins by invoking a taken-for-granted maxim: Taita has no development, some places do, and therefore Taita is behind. The writer then goes on to assert that this has to do with a lack of unity ("love and helping one another") produced and epitomized by reciprocal exchanges: Taita is sick because Taita's people do not like to help each other when they are sick. This new habit emerges from forsaking that which has been essential to them—including language and cultural secrets, which are being abandoned at the same time as Taita is overrun by foreign businesses. The posited turn toward Swahili ways and language is particularly galling, and telling, because it implies a new propensity for deceit and manipulation.

The author then goes on to explain that Wataita need to listen to the old men, a position distinct from arguing that they need to be governed by the old men. Rather, they will use these people as consultants with potent, morally ambivalent, resources: chewing tongue meat with them, a phrase that nods to the cultural practices and linguistic usages of the senior men the writer is courting. In this formulation, talking, like men eating meat together, epitomizes generative social production, as opposed to the selfish eating of witches or rapacious elites. Words are food, and they can generate positive futures. They are also materialized in things, hence the visceral image of chewing tongue meat: the word *malagho* refers to spoken words, as well as secrets, tangled intrigue, nonproductive politics, conflict, and controversy. Malagho, like shit, are ambivalent things that have to be contained to be productive and valuable. Thus we see an emerging theory of development as managed appropriation and circulation of powerful forces, whatever their provenance, for the public good. But what and who is the public?

Most Wataita implied that the reciprocal circulation of positive values was inherently positive, and they represented this circulation in terms of flowing water and blood, which reciprocity also produced. This widespread Taita idiom of flow and retention emerged, in part, from people's experience of sharing water resources, which was also shaped by the scarcity of land and water within Taita's overall context of incarceration. If flow was synonymous with personal and social health, thwarted circulation and unrequited gifts caused physical and social disease, whose symptoms mirrored the breached social relations that begat them (see Taylor 1992 for a similar analysis of Rwandan thought). A person's failure to make good on a social debt brought sickness, sometimes to the giver and sometimes to the recipient, such that the disrupted flow of things was reflected in the disrupted flow of bodily fluids and processes. For example, a senior female acquaintance of mine was told, upon divination, that she grew thin because her brother had not given her a promised gift of food, a symbol of his affection. She embodied, as disease, this failure to circulate wealth and love. A man who had not made a gift of beer to his grandfather's skull[2] acquired an aching headache and eventually went insane, where insanity (*isu*, also meaning twisted or compacted) consisted in a blockage of the mental processes and of the brain. A newly married young woman who had not received a gift from her brother-in-law could not recognize him as *anguo* (person of clothes) or *apesa* (person of money). She became completely constipated—unable to take food in or release it. Symptoms indicating retention and disconnection also emerged in people who had been bewitched through slow poisoning. These people eventually died because they could not eat, defecate, or urinate; their disease, characterized by disrupted and stunted flows, mirrored the social breach that preceded their bewitching.

But it was not simply that Wataita disliked retention, in the sense of selfish accumulation or refusal, and saw the free circulation of things and words as good. Rather, in practice, closing (*kufunga*) and opening (kulegheriya) implied one another, as the opening of one social relationship entailed the closing of another potential one, and without producing closure Wataita could not create viable communities. Thus, the door of the house (*mnyango*) figures prominently in Taita understandings of the creation of inviolable spaces that become staging grounds for accessing desired things while also protecting people from dangerous forces they cannot control. Wataita of all social backgrounds used the word door, or mnyango, to refer to a homestead as well as a small lineage, the implication being that when one visits a homestead, one enters into a semienclosed social world that has historical and spatial depth beyond this domestic unit itself; moreover, this semienclosed realm is always potentially threatened, and uplifted, by outsiders who pass through the door and who can also bring rain. Thus, when a man took up with a woman without paying bridewealth (called *kuchagira*, or abduction—allegedly, an increasingly common practice), he breached this increasingly fragmented and unprotected domestic sphere: people said that he had "left the door open" (*kusigha mnyango ghuari*) because he had taken something away and yet was still not a part of the family. In contrast, successful bridewealth transactions began with a gift of prepared food from the wife's family to "open the mouths" (*kufungua momu*) of the husband's family, facilitating the flow of words, emotions, and things. One of the most frightening aspects of the present was that it was permeated by ambivalent forces that entered through invisible doorways to the soul: preachers spoke often of these doorways to devil worship, and argued that demons were able to enter into the apparently bounded, but actually permeated, body without the victim realizing that he or she had brought this violation upon himself or herself by leaving the door open (by watching the wrong movie or listening to the wrong music, for example). Freeing oneself from these pernicious influences, foreign and domestic, was the ultimate development goal for many people: thus they said that the door was opened when a curse was lifted, or a person was no longer bewitched, and so could begin to "develop," or "go" (kuenda) by marrying and earning money. At the same time, becoming saved closed the door to destructive temptations, emotions, and experiences.

If a semienclosed social field was the emerging Taita ideal, a balance of exchange and enclaving was their inchoate strategy for dealing with neoliberal capitalism: this idea responded to the need to be flexible, so as to better capture the flow of things and opportunities across borders while also protecting Taita resources from others who were in a better position to capitalize on the market in those things. Thus, all Wataita claimed that they needed to unite against Kikuyu land grabbers, loggers, and gemstone dealers. They needed to preserve a place for themselves in their own markets against Kamba and Kikuyu traders and imported Tanzanian maize brought by local elites. They needed to assert their shared rights to animal resources in the Taru desert and to Mzima Springs, the Taita-based mountaintop water source that provided tap water for the non-Taita residents of the coast city of Mombasa, leaving Taita dry. They needed to abandon their docile soft-heartedness and mimic their neighbors and historical enemies, the Maasai (it bothered people tremendously that, because of their characteristic aggressiveness, or heat, these arrogant poseurs had managed to have a part of the Amboseli Game Reserve given to them for herding, while the polite and developed Wataita were forced to endanger and humiliate themselves by entering Tsavo National Park at night to illegally hunt abundant dik-dik, a small, tasty antelope). When people complained that members of Parliament and permanent secretaries gave Taita land to their Kikuyu or Kalenjin friends, when they talked about the weakening of the protective fighi shrines, and when they complained that their children did not speak Kidabida, they were speaking of analogous things. They were arguing that Taita was no longer protected from the world outside, because Wataita were not open among themselves—meaning they did not work together, trust one another, pool their money together in cooperative banking projects, or whatever the case appeared to be at that particular moment.

Thus, a political protest was evident in this discourse of bounded circulation, and which reflected current historical contingencies while projecting them backward onto the past (by saying that fighi once allowed for this kind of selective enclaving, or that schools and fighi once did this work together). But the issue of Taita unity was paradoxical, as discussed earlier, because Taita was a socially complicated place, with many people occupying multiple, overlapping, and conflicting subject positions. Wataita were well aware of the fact that the laudable idea of Taita unity and identity made less sense all the time, for they were struggling over increasingly limited resources in what appeared to be a zero-sum game. For example, a high-ranking minister and member of Parliament provoked a bloody battle for land that lasted for weeks when he extolled his constituency to extend their cultivation into an area already cultivated by the residents of another location. Within a single neighborhood, certain groups claimed to be the "true" natives, tracing their ownership to land back several generations; others were called "strangers" because they allegedly came under the auspices of the church or were relocated, later, by land consolidation. For instance, a young government employee in the Ministry of Social Services justified his efforts to have a vegetable cooperative placed in his town's market, rather than in a more road-accessible bordering town, by arguing that the residents of the other town were actually Kamba who had used witchcraft to displace the people of his town from their land in the mid-nineteenth century (the so-called "Kamba" in the village to which he referred claimed to have no idea what he was talking about). Other lines of social cleavage were irreducible to territory, but rather cohered around socially differentiated groups whose members each, in principle, extolled the idea of a true Taita essence that could be harnessed for development. However, as the failed rainmaking ceremony made clear, young men and women drew attention to the inadequacies of senior men and sometimes suggested outright that they should seize control of traditional ritual production themselves.

Conclusion

In this chapter, I have explored Taita understandings of development, with a specific focus on spatiotemporal orders and competing sovereignties, and have examined Taita thoughts about how to protect their local resources in response to exogenous threats associated with contemporary capitalism and the attendant decline of state regulating mechanisms. Clearly there was general disagreement about how Wataita should position themselves with respect to the past, and which elements of the past would constitute a genuine autochthony. In general, most Wataita articulated a flexible vision of Taita traditional values; as Rasta put it, when I asked him if he would perform kutasa over his father's grave, "My father drinks [bottled] Tusker beer. When he dies, when I want to remember him, I'll just poor some on his grave." But many wanted to enclave certain moments, such as rainmaking rituals and fighi renewal, as authentic spaces and times to be rigorously scrutinized by interested observers, and it was these fundamentalist efforts that were most vulnerable to critique and failure. The flexible vision was more pervasive, probably because it allowed for culture to be mobilized as a social resource, and even a marketable commodity, without incarcerating people in a past that completely rejected the existence of markets, capitalism, and state authorities. This was a malleable, moral political philosophy based on notions of retention and bounded reciprocity, which could be deployed to make sense of how Wataita should act in relation to new contingencies, such as structural adjustment and globalization.

But the attraction of locality and the past went beyond its promise of selective protection from capitalism and market logics. The past was positively romantic, even for those who held that people in the past inhabited a satanic realm where they intermingled, unwittingly, with demons: Wataita as a whole felt that, in the past, a close, unalienated relationship existed between people and their compatriots in the then present, people and their forebears living in a past that was very much present, and people and their physical environment. Beyond this, we could say that Wataita believed that the relationship between desire and fulfillment was seamless and uncomplicated in the past. Wataita suggested that in the past, people believed in what they did, and did it in an unquestioning and correct manner, and today they do not. In this way, Wataita drew attention to their awareness of their own alienation and cynicism.

This feeling of alienation from the past, nature, and the spirit world is, for the contemporary West, a hallmark of the modern, and it is easy to see evidence of "African modernity" in the Taita sense of dislocation. But what is most telling and interesting is that Wataita feel that their past refuses to go away despite the fact that people are dislocated from it and cannot communicate with it: indeed, the past goes on blithely killing people with a stupid, Kafkaesque persistency. This would seem to be a consequence of Taita people's particular experience of being dependent on the region and the historically deep social connections that tie them to it, at the same time as they wish to escape. Yet this alienated relationship to a powerful, murderous past is productive, because it provokes people to assume more creative ways of dealing with the past, whether by developing better defense mechanisms, as in the case of those who are saved; by integrating the past with modern institutions, like schools and government; or by trying to reproduce it wholesale in enclaves, as in the case of the rainmakers. While one could reduce this interest in the past to the fragmentation of the national project and its false promise of citizenship, it is important to remember that the past had a revolutionary potency, for it incited Wataita to imagine alternative futures by embodying a challenge to the present. And so Wataita's tendency to dwell on the past cannot be easily reduced to structural logics inherited from indirect rule (Mamdani 1996), for they are, more importantly, incitements against the present.

Finally, Taita interest in tradition took place in the context of perceived state transformation. It was clear to everyone, even state officials, that the state was retreating from development, and this was widely perceived as synonymous with decline: after all, state retreat opened up a space for traditionalists to enter and assert their authority over development (see also West 2005). Rather than retreating completely, however, state officials interjected themselves capriciously, at times paying lip service to traditional authorities while simultaneously punishing them when they adhered too strictly to their traditional understandings of how processes such as healing worked (as when the police, who wanted to use Mwarasho to cure AIDS, ended up nearly killing him because he claimed his knowledge could not be isolated scientifically and reproduced by just anyone). Such events made the state seem all the more chaotic and uncontrolled, even retrograde—thus, the antithesis of development, as Wataita had come to understand and use this concept. In this context, NGOs emerged as powerful moral and political entities that promised to revitalize the household and the family as sources of genuine, sustainable development.

CHAPTER SIX

NGOs, Gender, and the Sovereign Child

During the 1990s, the institutions and practices that had shaped Kenyan political life for at least a generation were becoming unhinged: new, Pentecostal-inspired churches arose to challenge the hegemony of the historically entrenched Catholic and Anglican churches, and the state appeared hopelessly segmented, each nominal part seemingly pitted against the other, as the promise of the developmental state became the object of national ridicule. Into the vacuum left by a retreating state apparatus entered a panoply of national and international nongovernmental organizations (NGOs), resulting in a rapid transformation, and simultaneous continuation under new conditions, of politics and patronage. This chapter examines how, in specific cases, the locus of politics shifted from the state to NGOs to the local population, thus conceptualizing localization (as opposed to globalization) as a political process involving the appropriation of the symbols and instruments of government by civilian members of the population. Through this process, localized social conflicts, such as those that pertained in the domestic sphere (gendered and generational conflicts with a long history), acquired public prominence, at the same time as the terms of public political debate (progress, development, transparency) penetrated domestic relationships. This chapter also demonstrates that political rumors about sinister occultism, or witchcraft, tend to wax and wane in relation to the perceived remoteness and attendant secrecy of governance, which is itself always in flux, depending on the actions of socially differentiated political actors.

The Eruption of Repressed Power in the Form of Witchcraft

During the mid-1990s, I visited a state agricultural fair in the dusty lowlands railway town of Voi. Fairs like these have a long and loaded history in Kenya, being rituals that work, and often fail, to fuse the image of government and, during the 1980s and 1990s, President Moi with the ideal of progress. They are also pedagogical forums, through which citizens are supposed to be instructed in the virtues of scientific rationality, record keeping and accountability, and export production. This instruction often occurs implicitly, through the organization of space in straight lines and the display of symbolically potent bureaucratic objects for public inspection. At such fairs, officials from the various government ministries (water, land, energy, etc.) try to communicate, and hopefully establish, their dominion over the constitutive elements of local geography, social life, and production (from water to women to commerce). They set up tables and sit, prepared to answer questions that almost never come their way, because most people are more interested in eating ice cream or riding on a camel's back, attractions that civilian entrepreneurs offer at the margins of fairs. This particular fair was interesting, in part, because of the multiple, seemingly contradictory projects that jutted against one another within its confines, calling attention to the "chaotic polyphony" of Kenyan life (Mbembe 1992). State officials competed with mermaids for the public's attention. A hospital ambulance (which, as far as I could tell, had never been used, save for display) sat next to a wooden sign describing the services offered by a traditional healer: everything from curing gonorrhea to locating missing persons. And the ideal of collective prosperity through state intervention was undermined by the fact that unofficial, even illegal, business thrived on the outskirts of the fair, and of the state's control: young men illegally sold gemstones to Kikuyu and Indian businessmen, sometimes in the guise of a haircut, for impromptu barbershops are often covers for all kinds of trade in this region.

At a table showcasing the work of the Ministry of Lands, I found a stack of books amid the labeled display of tape measures, sextants, and telescopes—icons of the ordered rationality and scopic knowledge-power of the state, presented here in museum style. The books contained the recorded minutes of the state-sanctioned Village Development Committees. Upon picking up one and randomly perusing its pages, I quickly came upon the following remark, dated 1993, the year following the first multiparty elections and the beginning of public revelations of massively destructive kleptocracy in the Moi regime: "The villagers of Mwatate requested that the government investigate the incidents of blood theft in the area. They claimed that the District Commissioner's truck [interestingly, not the district commissioner himself] has been silently waylaying people on the road, siphoning their blood, and selling it to an international organization. The villagers of Mwatate are afraid to go to their fields because the truck may capture them in the evening while they are returning to their homes." I had heard this rumor before: when I stayed with a family in Mgange, occasionally the women and children would run home at night, out of breath, claiming they saw bright white lights approaching, without sound. They assumed it was the blood-sucking truck, which they always said was a hospital vehicle (not a district commissioner's vehicle). Indeed, rumors of vampiristic state agents with access to blood-sucking machinery have a history dating back to the colonial period in East Africa, and have long expressed Africans' skepticism concerning the putatively beneficent intentions of government (White 2002). The passage above also resonated with contemporary pamphlet-spread rumors about the transnational Satanic Church, an anti-Christian corporation alleged to deal in bodies, children, and blood. By depicting state agents as illegal traffickers working for an international, probably outwardly philanthropic, organization, this rumor suggested that the state had been hollowed out and that its possessed shell was dangerously out of control. Rather than safeguarding life, it destroyed and sold life.

I immediately showed the passage to Mr. Muthai, the bored extension officer staffing the table. He read over it, laughed nervously, and quickly closed the book, placing it on the ground behind him, where it would be safe from prying visitors. Then he leaned in and, smiling sheepishly, intoned, "You know, these people are very backward. They think the government is trying to sell their blood to some NGO. (snickers) They think the people who are trying to help them are witches, but we know that it is they [the villagers] who are in fact the witches." Muthai went on to explain that all of the displayed instruments of his craft were in fact impotent against the insurrectionary, backward-looking witches of the Taita Hills, who refused to accept the inherent rationality of land adjudication, privatization, and consolidation. According to him, they had used witchcraft to compel the government to back off from these demarcation and privatization projects: "Our engineers, they are mostly Kikuyu, and they have refused to go out there [to the villages] and do their work. Why? Because their tape measures are being turned into snakes by those people! It is very frightening, *bwana*. We fly overhead in helicopters. We take photographs of the land [for demarcation]. But later, when we come to look at these very photographs, we find there is nothing! There is nothing there at all! So now what can we do, when that is what we are left with?"

In this exchange, I was exposed to two different accusations of witchcraft. In the first rumor, state agents were depicted as being in league with an international organization that wanted to harvest sovereign citizens in order to perpetuate the lives of foreign others. In the second rumor, a state official argued that the occult power of those who were defined, rhetorically, as being outside of the state sapped the state's power, rendering it flaccid and ridiculous. In each case reference is made to a power that threatens the sovereignty of the group in question, be it the state or the citizenry acting independently of the state, and that power is experienced as being occult. More specifically, this uncontrolled and competing power is depicted as being extraordinary, by which I mean that it tramples upon ordinary limits and expectations, such as the laughable laws of physics. Government trucks suddenly appear without a sound. Instruments of order and permanence (tape measures) are turned into animals that symbolize mutation and intransigence (snakes), while photographs designed to capture the world as it really is return blank, allowing that world to remain invisible, and thus inviolable to the governing efforts of others.

In each case, the specifics of the rumor are important, because they draw attention to the self-perceived frailties of the group that utters the rumor. The state official references the fact that the conceptual and practical foundations of his office—the ability to measure, standardize, and apportion terrain that is understood to be pure matter, unencumbered by spirits or history—are vulnerable and challenged, and this weakness affects his ability to perform his job as well as his attitude toward his job. He recognizes that the state's power is limited, and accounts for these limitations by imagining a contrary power, located outside of the state, that is resistant to change and that has the capacity to reverse history. The citizens at the state's *baraza*, or state-managed public assembly, suggest that the state, augmented by unseen international others, possesses the ability to extend itself abruptly and silently into their neighborhoods and homes, and that its interests are not always benign, especially when it pretends they are (when the state appears in the form of a hospital truck, for example). More than this, the state has the capacity to intervene in life at its most elemental form—blood and family—and to take this life away, while also turning people and their milieu (now characterized as a resource by both state and citizenry) into something that can be purchased on markets that ordinary people cannot access, or even know to exist for certain. Finally, the power of the state is congealed in particular objects that are contested—not in the sense of there being people who deny the power of the objects, but rather in the sense that there are other powers that are perceived as running counter to their power. These alternative powers lay hold of the state's fetishes and seek to transform them, and this competition between powers over objects is part of what makes the objects appear to come to life (as when a tape measure, which has been able to wield a considerable amount of power over people's lives, and so has a kind of life, is turned into an animal and is thus imbued with a different kind of life).

In another context I have discussed how, in colonial Kenya, particular bureaucratic objects came to symbolize the power of the state to order life, and to take the means of producing life away, and how this power reflected the actual power of bureaucracy and all of its forms, including but not limited to reading and writing, in daily life (Smith 1998). Thus, armed conflicts between competing factions in the late colonial period (most notably Mau Mau insurgents and the Kenyan government's military and police forces) were as much symbolic struggles to control these state icons (their ownership, placement, purpose, and meaning) as they were violent struggles over territory or bodies in territories. In the postcolonial period, state figures—most notably politicians and chiefs, but also government extension officers whose work was directly concerned with "development" in terms of scientific management and planning—often represented the state, or *serikali*, as a remote, mysterious, and powerful entity that only certain types of people were capable of accessing and controlling for the good of the public ("serikali" is often pronounced, in jest, as *siri kali*, or fierce secret, to draw attention to the secretive nature of politics and the state). "Bringing development" home to the countryside, as Kenyan politicians have long promised to do, meant being able to plunge into this powerful realm and master the secrets that were to be found there (specifically, secrets for bringing money, infrastructure, and projects back home). In the late 1990s, ordinary citizens continued to struggle over these symbols of (formerly) state power, to invest them with meaning, and to use them to frame local conflicts that had a long history. The presence of NGOs on the local scene facilitated this process, arguably extending the apparatus of government into people's lives while also making procedures associated with the state available to the public.

Challenging an Old, Emasculated State

In making this claim to bring back development (here configured as a material thing and a symbolic value located somewhere else), Kenyan politicians and chiefs have long invoked the image of masculine conquest, and this image has been supported by another: that of the self-composed and upright male household head who goes out into the world and comes back home with things of value for women, children, and seniors. Wataita often refer to these appropriated possessions as an inheritance, or legacy, and sometimes also as bridewealth. Conversely, when politicians failed to sponsor projects they had initiated, they left behind half-constructed buildings that remained in limbo for generations—ruins from a possible future. When such aborted relationships occurred, people said that the "marriage" between the politician and the public had dried up (*kuoma*) or that the politician's "seed" (*mbeu*, also meaning semen) did not take. In this way, the moral ideology of the household—or rather, a particularly exaggerated, patriarchal moral ideology of the household—was transplanted onto the Kenyan public sphere, with mixed effect. The image continued to be deployed long after the state ceased to be a provider of development projects, and was later transposed onto the international world of foreign NGOs, which politicians and chiefs endeavored to court. Importantly, the projection of family relations onto the public sphere contributed to the weakening of those relations in the domestic sphere. For men often complained that it was women's dependence on male politicians that had allowed these land-grabbing thieves to become powerful and to expropriate resources for themselves: during campaign drives, many women lined up by the roads and pledged their eternal loyalty to politicians in exchange for the feminine gifts that husbands are supposed to provide for their wives (cooking fat, sugar, and gardening implements). In this way, these politicians called attention to men's inadequacies, claimed their superiority to ordinary men, and signaled their respect for masculine cultural values glossed as traditional.

For example, Darius Mbela, the Kenyan African National Union (KANU) member of Parliament (MP) from Taita during the late 1990s, presented himself publicly as an aggressive ex–prize fighter (he had boxed for years while working on the docks in Mombasa). His nickname was *Mabonyo*, or Doer, a word with multiple meanings (he who gets things done, as well as he who kills, conquers, or screws people). His ubiquitous T-shirt campaign slogan was *Kiboko Yao*, meaning "Their whip," as well as "Their hippopotamus" ("kiboko" has two meanings), a phrase that many took to mean that he whipped people into supporting him. Mbela elaborated a mythology based on his sexual conquests, and became a paternal patron-provider for men when he bought them cases of bottled beer during election campaigns; he also hired young men who were referred to as his "sons" to beat up political competitors and their supporters. Men widely regarded this kind of patronage as a payoff or bribe in exchange for the right to transgress men's authority over women in the domestic sphere. Mbela presented himself as the true husband and provider for the area's women, and, by gathering to receive gifts from him and cook for him, many women gave objective substance to this image. Mbela also made a habit of unexpectedly entering into men's households to berate them in front of their wives (in an infamous incident, he was alleged to have beaten up a political opponent in the man's own sitting room, on the main table, in front of his family). Most egregiously, one widespread rumor told that, during the parliamentary campaigns of 1997, Mbela hired a company to manufacture women's undergarments emblazoned with his portrait and the catchphrase "Mabonyo," or Doer/Fucker, on the front. Though I never saw these provocative panties, people said that Mbela distributed them throughout the constituency and, at barazas and meetings of women's groups, instructed women to wear them on voting day and when they slept with their husbands.

In a 1997 campaign speech before the second multiparty election in recent history, the incumbent Mbela chastised the upstart Mwashengu Mwachofi, the candidate from a relatively new, competing party, for his marginal status. This condition was supposedly embodied in Mwachofi's "beards," a stylistic marker loosely associated with Mau Mau and resistance to state authority. During the early 1980s, following the aborted coup against President Moi, Mwachofi had been affiliated with a group of critical politicians (who were also KANU members during those single-party days) that the then state-monitored newspapers had derisively nicknamed the Seven Bearded Sisters. In his speech, Mbela claimed that he would make development flow, like water, from the state, but that the comparatively indigent Mwachofi would shore it up for himself, given the opportunity (political figures and chiefs often warned people not to vote for poor people, because they extract wealth for themselves, while rich people's wealth flows out to loyal clients). Part of Mbela's speech is worth quoting: "When we come to development, I am called Doer (Mabonyo) though some make this name into something bad [specifically, fucker]. I don't care. When my opponent left Parliament, he left no inheritance at all, no project to be remembered by! I initiated Mazhungu water project, which assures him of water in his compound, so he can wash his beards. The problem is the compound is so dirty there is grass up to his doorstep."

In this speech, Mbela justified his political position by referencing the masculine inheritance he had bequeathed the public, thereby proving his masculine virtue in contrast to Mwashengu's, whose contracted social status was embodied in the state of his household. Mwachofi's inability to govern his own household and to conceal its secrets from the public view made him ill-suited to capture development from the state. In turn, his inability to access the state's recesses implied that he was an inadequate provider at home and an incomplete man in general. This was certainly not the first time the populist-Marxist Mwachofi had been so insulted: at a 1992 *harambee* for a secondary school, President Moi had publicly humiliated Mwachofi when he offered a relatively small donation of 1,000 Kenyan shillings (about $17.00) for the construction of the school. The president refused the gift and insinuated that Mwachofi was a poor husband and father by extending his sympathies to Mwachofi's family. According to Mbela, Mwachofi's relationships with others were contracted, such that water did not flow into his compounded without the assistance of men like him, while Mwachofi's body grew thin because of this alienation. In contrast, the sovereignty of the physically powerful, aggressive, and fat Mbela was sociospatially encompassing and transgressive—his capacity to act and to do (*kubonya*) meant that he penetrated ordinary social and natural boundaries, entering into men's homes, screwing their wives, and taking away their masculinity to the accompaniment of resounding applause. Mbela's power allowed him to be many things at once: human/warrior, animal (hippo), and violent instrument (whip). But for this very reason, Mbela's efforts were never completely successful, for many saw him as a parodic caricature of masculine authority, an abuser, precisely because he usurped the authority of other adult men.

Many Wataita were outspoken in their fear of this man's brutality, and in his use of his position as Minister for Energy to withhold meaningful benefits like electricity (denied for decades to towns whose denizens had voted against him). Despite the fact that they openly feared voting against him, and although men and women tended to be divided over his candidacy, the public did manage to domesticate, even to humiliate, Darius Mbela in 1997. At his request, the election had been carried out under the queue voting system (voters lined up in front of pictures of their chosen candidates), an intimidation tactic that had the ironic consequence of making each candidate's relative success visible to all. Though Mbela had the shortest lines throughout most of the region, and was popularly declared the loser, he managed to have himself announced the winner over the radio (according to unverified rumor, through a kin connection at the station), and his broadcast victory was supported by then President Moi. Despite this public display of official support, people speculated that Moi had only supported Mbela's declaration to ensure peace and that, in truth, Mbela's deception had provoked the president to relieve Mbela of his powerful ministerial post, which Moi, it is true, later bestowed upon another parliamentarian. Reduced to a mere MP, Mbela suffered final humiliation when he lost even this position in the subsequent election of 2002.

Certainly people were beginning to realize their power over men like Mbela, and the consequences of this empowerment were far reaching. One major effect was that gender relationships, which had always been invested with the potential for discord, became sites of intense discussion, critical thought, and action. As mentioned earlier, Taita men have long struggled to present themselves as primary producers, both by controlling productive rituals like rainmaking and by asserting proprietary rights over cash crops; but, in reality, women have always been the main producers of wealth, and so men's rhetoric and ritual activity has been aimed largely at the production of a falsehood (see Donham 1999 for a similar analysis with respect to the Maale in Ethiopia). State figures like Mbela continued in this masculine rhetorical tradition, but during the 1990s, these political figures, like men in general, were less successful than before at presenting themselves as masculine providers. Furthermore, their increasingly farcical appearance fed into an ongoing conversation about men's capacity to govern and, more generally, to produce development. Underpinning this discourse was the fact that Wataita of diverse social backgrounds increasingly described development as something that had to be generated locally: somewhat ironically, international NGOs encouraged this idea and made it financially meaningful by funding women's groups. And women—the generators of the household par excellence—were identified as vital and honest mechanisms for "home-grown" development at precisely the same time as men were struggling to contribute to their homes and families.

Moreover, the state as unified father figure was visibly crumbling, and its various, predominantly male, officials were competing with one another, often violently, for meager resources. This competition was most evident in conflicts between politicians and government extension officers, such as water engineers: during my fieldwork, it was quite common for the latter to complain of death threats (often phrased in the idiom of witchcraft) from the former, presumably because they refused to locate projects that were popular in places that, from the experts' point of view, were unfeasible. Similarly, biologists in the Ministry of Forests complained that politicians encouraged their constituents to cut down forest reserves to make way for markets, despite the fact that this activity was plainly against the law and punishable by chiefs, who controlled the police. Chiefs and politicians also increasingly came into conflict with one another, as when the chief of Mgange exhorted his subjects to defend their lands against people from Werugha, which a politician from Werugha had encouraged them to seize. This speech precipitated violent clashes in which some people were killed. On a somewhat more symbolic level, in 1997, new legislation mandated by the international community forbade chiefs from campaigning for politicians in elections, or from publicly supporting what had formerly been the only political party, KANU. As chiefs withdrew from politicians, they invoked a common point of contrast when they asserted that now their work centered on development rather than politics; for many, it was not clear what their work entailed anymore.

This perceived fragmentation of the state, and the concomitant demise of the masculinist model of political rhetoric, was coupled with the rise of international NGOs on the local scene, whose employees tended to focus their activities around women and children. Many of these organizations controlled a great deal of money, and they visibly upstaged the state as provider of development. As a district water engineer (a government employee) put it to me, in reference to the global NGO Plan International,

> Plan International is changing the power base of this society by handing over the process of distributing aid to popularly elected citizens. If you are a chief, what power do you have if there is another person in the community controlling several million shillings at one time? And you represent a government that has absolutely nothing to offer and has stolen from the public countless time? This

> new system, it goes to the root of everything, and the chiefs and the people don't know what to do next. The chiefs hate it, but they also don't want to interfere, because these people [the NGOs] are helping the communities in which they [the chiefs] live.

Increasingly, NGOs came to be seen as the real, if sometimes inscrutable, economic and political forces behind the false presentations of state authority, much in the same way as women were the invisible, but real, producers of value behind the false presentation of men's productive power. Every time an NGO picked up a project that the state, personified in a politician, had initiated, it was an official embarrassment, and government extension officers frequently expressed the concern that they, and the government, had lost legitimacy in the public imagination. At state assemblies (barazas) and harambees, politicians publicly announced that they had single-handedly funded projects that were in fact funded by NGOs, and few people were fooled, though most cheered and ululated. Indeed, when the Danish International Aid Organization (DANIDA) moved its operations away from the Taita Hills in 1998, one former Taita employee of the NGO complained that its personnel had left because their hearts had "grown hot" from the area MP's claim of responsibility for the projects DANIDA had funded. Of course, not all NGOs were the same: many were fly-by-night organizations that came to towns promoting pyramid schemes. They raised start-up funds from people, promising great benefits in the future, then immediately disappeared, never to return (Rasta lost his entire bridewealth savings on one of these schemes). The fact that NGOs were typically invited by chiefs or politicians led everyone to speculate that state agents made up for their lost salaries with such ruses. Other NGOs, such as Plan International, stayed for long periods and involved themselves in every aspect of Taita life; their intrusiveness, and apparently great resources, was widely seen as simultaneously promising and dangerous (see below).

Again, the changing nature of governance was expressed in gendered and generational terms, and so mirrored transformations at work in the larger society. This relationship became visible to people at barazas, one of the principal locations where state agents and citizens have historically come together in staged performances that have helped to generate the vertical, paternal power of the state (Haugerud 1995). Orchestrated applause, repeated cries of *Nyayo*! (or Footsteps, the slogan for President Moi and thus a show of allegiance to Moi on the slow, laborious path toward development), the unequal distribution of food and drink, and the organization of public space to reinstate the authority of the state against society were symbolic elements of the baraza that conferred gravity to the Kenyan state in the late 1990s and framed interaction between the state and the *wananchi*, or citizens. At these assemblies, the branches and offices of government were displayed and named before the public in a way reminiscent of the state fair, described above. Moreover, the authority of the government over civilian leaders (priests, school headmasters, and village chairmen) was inscribed in seat placement and in the order in which individuals were invited to speak. Tables, chairs, bottles of soda, and plates of *pilau*, a meal of meat with rice (offered to some and withheld from others), were the simple but crucial symbolic differentiators of social status.

At any given baraza, local leaders sat behind a large table facing the people, who sat on the grass, while bottles of soda were distributed to those seated behind the tables (rarely to people in the crowd). When an important politician was invited to address the public, those seated behind the table were fed pilau, while onlookers consumed the leftover rice without meat. The meat eaters, seated in wooden chairs before a table decked with distinctive global commodities like bottled Coca Cola, were representatives not only of the government but of educated modernity. While these "modern elites" were differentiated one from the other by virtue of their names and their positions, laboriously enunciated by the chief at the onset of each meeting, the public, seated on the ground, was not individuated, but called upon to respond to visiting officials as social groups that were internally undifferentiated. Thus, the *vikundi vya kina mama* (group of mothers) represented women as a whole and typically sat in a huddled mass near the table, while the elders (*wazee wa vijiji*) typically sat in a line on the outskirts of the assembly and gave the impression of being simultaneously autonomous and connected to one another. Youth (*vijana*) sat in clusters around the assembly and were typically spoken for by an unmarried young man in his twenties.

Over the course of my fieldwork, the transformation of the state, and the outsourcing of its functions, could be read in the form and content of the baraza. For example, government administrators evidently felt it necessary to use barazas to explain to the populace that the state still existed, despite the conflict and heterogeneity that characterized the multiparty election campaigns. Administrators and politicians implored, "The government is still here!" and insisted that chiefs were crucial social and political figures, despite their contracted social and political roles (as of 1997, they were not in direct control of the police and were not supposed to adjudicate in land disputes, for example). Despite such assertions, the state officials were now joined—at times supplanted—by the young, cosmopolitan (often urban Kikuyu) employees of NGOs, whose stylishness (crisp blue jeans and leather jackets from abroad, purchased used in large markets) made the chief's official, colonial-style uniform look antiquated and tired. While chiefs and politicians were relatively remote male figures, NGO representatives were often young women, and villagers had come to know them through their work and their regular visits to households. These NGO employees spoke out of turn, sometimes criticized the officially orchestrated applause of the baraza, and were openly critical of people's dependence on the government and local political figures. Representatives of NGOs and state officials drew their authority from entirely different spheres, each deploying concepts and symbols that undermined the legitimacy of the other. For their part, chiefs, who were Kidabida-speaking locals born and raised in the community, did their best to use the barazas to create an impression of state control over NGOs by introducing speakers, treating them as "guests," and organizing the labor that was sometimes required for NGO projects. But guests could often steal the show and draw the public's attention away from the state and toward forms of development that bypassed the state, or particular state representatives.

For instance, at one baraza, a university-educated Kikuyu representative of the Young Women's Christian Association (YWCA) publicly vilified politicians and the administrative government represented by the chief, who officiated the baraza. The woman introduced herself as Ms. Wangui, an educator from Nairobi, and claimed that she had come to speak to the women of the town of Mgange, though it was unclear from the meeting whether the YWCA planned any projects or programs of material consequence for Mgange. The chief, Clement Hesabu, was the official host of the ceremony, and throughout the meeting he cringed silently behind his official guest, begrudgingly confirming the legality of the assembly, perhaps despite his personal feelings. In opening the assembly, Clement reminded the crowd, in Kidabida language, of the importance of treating a guest with respect and kindness, as "a guest is rain" (*mghenyi ni vua*). In doing so, he associated himself, and the government he represented, with local space and society, while marking Ms. Wangui as an unknown quantity from Nairobi. In thus localizing the state, the chief concocted a cultural and linguistic community that was inclusive of the state and society:

CHIEF: This woman has come all the way from Kikuyuland because she says she wants to help Taita. [This is a very ironic statement.]

Show her that Taita hearts are warm and that, although we may disagree with each other, we do not violently attack each other. [Probably a reference to violent Kikuyu-Kalenjin land disputes in the Rift Valley, which were taking place at that time.] Now. . . . One, two, three:

Open [the hands in preparation to give applause]!
Close!
Open!
Close! . . .

Here Ms. Wangui entered, abruptly shifting the tone of the meeting, turning it against the chief and the culture of arguably obsequious display that had preceded her. She began by appropriating the terms of state discourse, such as progress and backwardness, and deployed them against the state and the citizenry, whose conviviality and lazy corruption she condemned:

MS WANGUI, *after the orchestrated clapping and ululating had subsided*:

Thank you for inviting me here today. I look around me and see a land that is green and filled with opportunities for development. . . . But I must tell you the truth for we are all human beings, and I do not have time to waste on greetings. You Wataita are living in the past! Let me tell you now what I mean by this. You have remained backward [*mumebaki nyuma*] because you allow yourselves to be humiliated before your leaders.

At this point, Ms. Wangui asked her audience to reconceptualize elections and development: politicians, like good husbands, are supposed to bring development, but the politicians of today have become abusive husbands, and so women have to recognize that development can be generated through local work, which implies a form of government grounded in harmonious, feminine social networks outside the state. This requires a transformation of women's attitudes toward one another, and toward the state, if it is to be realized:

Let me ask you this: Why do you elect leaders? (long pause) Is it so you can get iron pots and lamp oil [as gifts during election campaigns]? (pause) Don't

> you realize you gave them their jobs so they can represent you in Parliament? So they can bring you water to drink. So they can bring you roads?!
>
> You shouldn't vote for people because they have given you *kitu kidogo* [small thing, or bribe]. They are giving you your own money back! Yes, they sell your what? They sell your land and then turn around later and sell it back to you. Look around you: there are no roads, no water, and here is your bwana *mkubwa* [big man, or powerful husband] strutting around like a baboon. "Me I'm *bwana mkubwa*"! And he has done nothing but steal! The money he says he has given you has come from outside! He has not seduced these NGOs with his sweet words—they have come because of you!
>
> The other day [the 1997 elections] your homes were split apart, brothers were turned against sisters, fathers against sons, for politics. Now your politician is sitting in his job. He is eating his money. [In English:] He's OK. You were so worried for him, but he's OK. And where are you?!

Ms. Wangui's decision to refer to politicians, and especially the area's MP, as baboons was striking and even courageous. It was also symbolically loaded, for baboons are despised throughout rural Kenya, although they are also objects of pornographic fascination: they steal food from shambas, are prone to brutal acts of violence, and are perceived as hypersexual (the females have pronounced sexual organs and the males are rumored to occasionally rape human women). In referring to them as violent, uncontrolled animals, Ms. Wangui cast politicians as beyond the pale of society, even presocial, and so these animal-humans became a foil against which to imagine a more humane political community. She also suggested that politicians dabbled in diabolical occult power, for witches allegedly keep baboons as familiars. Furthermore, Ms. Wangui implied that Mgange's women had been relegated to the status of prostitutes and/or abused wives because they did not grasp, conceptually, their power as citizens. At the same time, by saying that politicians had given the public *kitu kidogo*, or bribe, she inverted local understandings of power, for kitu kidogo is something received by people in higher sociostructural positions than the giver. By saying that the public had been given kitu kidogo, the speaker placed male politicians below the (female) public and argued that politicians should be servants of the people.

After this segment of the speech, an undoubtedly insulted woman in the crowd expressed the opinion that exploitation was eternal and would not change easily: "But this is the nature of human beings!" she cried. Ms. Wangui became antagonistic:

MS. WANGUI: Forget about human beings! The nature of humans is a different matter. These are Kenyan affairs. This is Kenya!

What will you do when you cannot even afford oil for your lamps? Go back to your big man and beg, please bwana give me 500 shillings? He has gone! He is in Nairobi eating your money with the other baboons! And who suffers the most in the end? Who has to care for children, carry firewood, cook? Who has to take care of the household, and make sure the children can go to school? Who is enduring *presha* [high blood pressure, but, more generally, wasting] because of worries?

THE CROWD OF WOMEN (understanding the cue): The mothers!

MS. WANGUI: Yes, the mothers. But let me tell you something. It is your own fault that you suffer the way you do. Instead of standing like beggars on the side of the road: "Oh, thank you for the sugar, bwana! You have my vote." Instead of selling yourselves like prostitutes, you should be joining together, collecting your money. Buy a grade cow or do AI [artificial insemination], and share the profits from that milk. Manufacture and sell stoves and baskets and invest that money together in land and cows. Don't just let it sit doing nothing. Don't let it go to Maji Marefu [a hired Tanzanian witch hunter at that time scouring the villages in search of witchcraft paraphernalia]! Soon you will see your households have developed!

Again, generating development implied cooperation, grounded in love, and so also implied the regeneration of what were understood to be traditional values, but a tradition grounded in women's productive and social work. Ms. Wangui continues:

> But you cannot have development if you do not love each other, and you cannot love each other if you do not love God. Why don't you love each other? Why do you backbite and curse one another? It is because Satan has brought jealousy amongst you to divide you! The eye sees a neighbor having a cow and sending his kids to school, and makes the heart feel hatred! This is what turns development back, and no one is to blame but yourselves!
>
> And what do you women do at barazas? You sit silently! The chief says you and you, you will represent women, and then you sit there and clap when they tell you to clap.

From his expression, it was clear that the chief, who had formerly supported, perhaps even campaigned for, these so-called baboons, recognized this direct attack on his authority over the meeting, and on the paternal structure of call and response. Ms. Wangui was undeterred:

> And where is development!? When things that affect you most of all, my beloved women, are being discussed, you are in your kitchen cooking *ugali*. And if someone comes looking for the owner of the house, you'll hide yourself like there's no one there. Are you nobody, that you cannot represent your own house? Or are you just cooking there until you're chased away by your bwana?!

The tone of Ms. Wangui's speech, and her vanguard call for a development generated by networks of women over and against male politics (*siasa*), drew upon the even older language of the Christian mission, disconnecting that civilizing project from the state while simultaneously invoking understandings of traditional family values and Kidabida. It ensconced Taita in a space and time that was backward, but defined backwardness as synonymous with loyalty to the state, which was equated with wayward, sex-addled men. Ms. Wangui posited motherhood as the foundation for political society, and so grounded politics in an autonomous, natural power that preceded and remained exogenous to the state. At the same time, she urged women to assume control over specifically male forms of value production (cows, land, and the house itself) and to break their nongenerative dependence on abusive husbands, whether or not their husbands were political figures. In this way, she conceptually conjoined wives' unnecessary dependence on unproductive husbands with families' unnecessary dependence on unproductive state figures. Thus, she personalized the state's failure, and development's "turning backward" by arguing that structural decline was caused by the short-sighted selfishness of elite baboons, combined with the habituated passivity of women. She also referenced the demise of marriage and the prevalence of short-term conjugal unions in her suggestion that putative wives could at any moment be "chased away" by their fictive husbands. By extending themselves beyond their individual households—to which male politicians had relegated them with their gifts of sugar, pots, and lamp oil—women could generate a truly sustainable development based on reciprocal horizontal exchanges. Beyond this, Ms. Wangui implied that women had to change their spatial and temporal orientation by grasping a larger, religiously inspired vision in order to avoid jealousy and conflict (epitomized by witchcraft) resulting from preoccupation with the past, as well as the intersubjective.

As mentioned earlier, the emergence of women as major economic, and now political, agents was paralleled in many spheres, including the religious, where women were taking on new roles as prophets (particularly in Pentecostalism). But, importantly, women were being promoted as generators of development at the same time as they were being pursued by men as objects of development. Again, men increasingly depended on the bridewealth generated by their daughters and sisters to reproduce their households in addition to paying for their own bridewealth. Women felt this pressure and often complained that they were treated like cattle. Indeed, many male attempts to generate development, ostensibly for entire communities, in fact hinged on their control of women's sexual and reproductive natures.

For example, at one point the young men in Mgange town requested a permit from the district commissioner to hold a Christmas *disko*, or a dance with an electronic system, in which an outside entrepreneur would be paid for the use of his stereo and amplifier equipment. They said that they hoped to use the money earned from the disko for development projects (there was talk of building a polytechnic, among other projects). Of course, it was clear to everyone that the source of the projected income was the women who, it was hoped, would come to the disko, and in turn draw men hoping to meet them. One young man became very popular for promoting the disko idea: he ran for councilor on a disko ticket, and argued that the disko would be like the warriors' dances of an earlier period. He even went so far as to cite an old Taita folktale about a nighttime raid by Maasai, which was allegedly thwarted because the young male warriors who were the intended victims were dancing with young women in a cave. Diskos were a lifesaving Taita tradition. He acquired the support of the chief and the district commissioner, who eventually granted a permit. The senior men in Mgange caught wind of the disko permit and complained to the district commissioner, with the support of the local Catholic priest. They argued at a baraza that the disko would culminate in mass illicit sex and that, because the proposed site of the disko was a social hall near the Catholic Church compound, church property would become a nocturnal "green lodge" (meaning people would have sex on the grass outside the church) for young lovers: "On the day after, when children see the used *mipira* (rubbers, or balls) on the ground, they will try to play with them, thinking they are balloons!" augured one man. Tellingly, they also argued that a disko would sully the reputation of Mgange's women and drive suitable husbands, and their bridewealth, away. Thus, rather than generating development, the disko would make development impossible, while also encouraging the spread of AIDS and undermining the authority of male household heads over women's bodies and reproductive potentials. Though the disko was never held, the argument was carried on in new registers, as young men argued for their right to use the social hall, and so conceptualize and act on their own visions of development, as they pleased, beyond the control of the church. In turn, the new NGOs opened up a frontier on which struggles among youth and seniors, and men and women, came to be waged around the figure of the sovereign child, brought into the world by woman.

Plan International, the Sovereign Child, and the Public Politicization of Gender and Generation

In the past, you have had promises of development that never came true. You have given your lives and your money to politicians. You have even fought for them violently, and they have ruined you. Now, with Plan, you have something else entirely. You offer your child for sponsorship, and we send the photographs abroad. Money comes to the whole community for the children. That money builds water pumps and schools. It buys cows and medicine. Whatever your new elected Plan leaders decide is needed. What is really new is that it is all for the children. These children, they are bringing you mature people development, and so you become their children. (applause)—A Kenyan Plan representative, speaking to members of the community at a meeting called to reiterate Plan's policy and solicit questions from the public, 1999.

Plan International, one of the largest development organizations in the world, was the most influential and noticeable NGO in the Taita Hills during the course of my fieldwork, and had become one of the major sources of development projects, financial assistance, local employment, and public speculation and hope. Plan is a nonprofit NGO founded in 1937 to assist children afflicted by the Spanish Civil War. The organization, which receives most of its funding from American and European families, claims to have no national or religious affiliation, and it donates about $270 million per year in forty-three countries (see Plan International's Web site at www.plan-international.org). In Kenya during the late 1990s, Plan based its operations entirely around children, funneling manifold activities into two distinct but interdependent arenas: (1) a foster program through which foreign donors "adopted" African children who were selected by Kenyan Plan representatives or, later, elected community leaders, and (2) a community development program in which the number of projects received by a village or town depended on the number of families with children enrolled in the foster program. While most donor money was directed toward the running of the organization and the payment of its employees, each individual donor was said to have adopted a child in an area where Plan was operating.

According to Kenyan Plan representatives whom I interviewed in 2006, these days Plan policy regarding the distribution and accountability of funds is formulated at the home office (the European, not the Kenyan, office), and a complex and rigorous system is in place for insuring that donated funds end up where donors intend for them to be applied.[1] As the Plan representative quoted above remarked, the most original concept about Plan in the late 1990s, from the perspective of most Wataita, was that it articulated a moral foundation for political and economic development around the child, and so it foregrounded an imaginary figure that lay outside of everything that had come to define Kenyan political life, including the politics of ethnicity, the rituals of state, and the masculine idioms in which politics had long been conducted. If an earlier model of Kenyan development operated by projecting a masculine interpretation of family life onto public life, Plan resituated public development in the household itself, and drew attention to alternative, matricentric understandings of the family that state officials like Mbela had overshadowed. In addition to its oft-stated commitment to constructing public development on the foundation of children, Plan distinguished itself from other NGOs in Taita in its commitment to relatively low-cost, sustainable projects designed to improve social and economic life, including household and village sanitation, the subsidization of school fees, the construction of water projects, and the creation of generative sources of income, such as livestock rearing. Plan International came to the Taita Hills in the early 1990s and moved its base of operations away from the government administrative center in Wundanyi to the town of Mgange in 1997, apparently in an effort to escape from government influence and demands and to be closer to the comparatively indigent semi-arid lowland areas.[2]

In retrospect, it is possible to identify a few distinct phases of Plan's operations:

1. An early phase in which Plan employees were directly involved in planning and implementing projects, all of which were designed to benefit individual house-

holds (household granaries, water tanks, and pit latrines being the most common). These projects were available for all households with children enrolled in the foster program, at first for free and later upon receipt of 10 percent of the projected costs from the recipient household.

2. A subsequent phase in which "planning units," composed of local Taita leaders decided which individual households would receive these same projects from Plan, again in exchange for 10 percent of the projected cost from each household. During this phase, Plan representatives mediated the exchange of letters and gifts between foreign donor and local recipient families.
3. A period in which Plan representatives intervened in what they considered to be the corrupt, though democratically elected, planning units, and called for new elections, to which they added stipulations. At this time, Plan also curtailed the policy of funding individual households in favor of large projects designed to benefit entire communities.
4. A final phase in which Plan International exited the community, leaving the planning units, now renamed community-based organizations (CBOs), in charge of the projects left behind, which the CBOs were expected to maintain and augment with the accumulated 10 percent acquired from households over the years.

On a symbolic level, Plan International appeared to augment and eclipse the power of the state, for when Plan relocated to Mgange in 1997, its employees built a massive extension to the chief's office, and subsequently shared the building with the chief. Some argued that Plan sapped legitimacy from the government and drew attention to the difference between false politics and genuine development. As one young man put it at the time, "Now that Plan's office and the chief's office are next to each other, everyone can see the truth clearly. From Plan's office, those people [Plan's employees] can hear the domestic cases taking place outside [in the chief's office]. There are so many cases, why? Because the government has failed to take care of its people! The chief's office tries to resolve these conflicts with meaningless talk. Meanwhile, Plan is next door, and they are solving these problems meaningfully!" This young man's comment was partly directed against senior men's notions about the value of "chewing tongue meat," in which words materialize in relationships and, through them, things, and articulated an interest in rapid and transformative action. But Plan's affiliation with government struck many as contradicting its "nongovernmental" mission, and many speculated that government officials and Plan were engaged in a mutually beneficial relationship aimed at appropriating the public's prospects for development.

Plan's simultaneous remoteness and close proximity fueled local suspicions about its motives, some of which were couched in the idiom of occultism. For despite their global notoriety, Wataita knew of Plan only through its mostly Embu and Meru Kenyan staff, who resided in rented houses near the Catholic Church and who visited many of them on motorbikes at their homes. As a result, Wataita were not aware of transformations in policy taking place at the national level regarding increased local participation in the distribution of resources. And they tended to be unaware of the wrangling between Plan representatives and government officials, for the government administration insisted that Plan use, and pay for, the technical assistance of their development experts (water engineers for water projects, veterinary engineers for livestock projects, etc.). As a result of their removal from these processes, most villagers tended to see any changes in Plan policy as the result of their own efforts or intransigence: they typically argued that Plan was unable to make inroads into their villages because of the rumors that circulated about their intentions, and so had to change policy by employing Taita staff, coming up with planning units, and, later, implementing water projects.

Again, Plan's child-based approach was revolutionary, partly because it rested on a putatively universal cultural concept—mainly, the sacred innocence and prepolitical essence of the sovereign child—whose translation into local parlance yielded unique problems. Plan's very name seemed to be related to the organization's focus on the future and children, which also implied the production of something valuable for future generations. Translated into Swahili as *mpango*, the message, as far as Kenyan Plan representatives were concerned, was clear: development had hitherto taken place haphazardly, or not at all, depending upon the capricious whims of Kenyan politicians and other state figures. Because they were born of ephemeral impulses and desires (the desire to appeal to constituents so as to secure elections, for example), projects never came to fruition. By instead focusing on developing humans who embodied a potential future, Plan representatives hoped that people would sacrifice their own interests for the larger good that children seemed to represent, fostering a sustainable politics morally grounded in the private sphere. Instead, the focus on children fueled ongoing local debate about the legitimacy of patriarchal authority, which many men hold to be grounded in a man's control over women and children.

By basing its development interventions around the child, Plan representatives also asserted that Taita children were worth something to others, and that promoting children (or as some of their Taita critics put it, "selling" children) to wealthy others, who became their providers, would generate prosperity for larger communities. Thus, one family's child would be converted into money, some of which would in turn be converted into projects that would benefit other Taita families, in addition to the original family "giving" its child up for sponsorship. Photographs, supplemented by handwritten letters, enabled Taita children to circulate beyond regional and national borders, becoming objects of concern and desire. For Plan representatives visited households and, upon enrolling family members into the foster program, took photographs of the children (one child from each house), which they then mailed to the foreign families who had adopted them. These representatives then requested that the Taita families write accompanying letters, which they later translated and typed. Most Wataita do not speak English, the language of global interconnection, and they accused the Plan representatives of repressing their voices and requests for aid by writing the letters themselves and omitting key passages that said more than "thank you." Plan representatives defended themselves by arguing that they censored the letters to protect Taita children from foreign criminals and sex addicts who wanted to use Taita children for unsavory purposes.

In general, Wataita appreciated Plan's work, but many bridled at the implicit message that Taita families were incapable of supporting their children. Some men clearly felt sidelined and insulted by Plan's insistence that women be directly involved in the planning process, and argued that Plan's activities would destabilize the patriarchal household. As one thoughtful middle-age man put it,

> You see, if we are saying that development is coming here because of children, really what that means is women. Because women give birth to children. So some say that what they are doing is turning the whole world upside down. And in a way this is true because they are giving more power to women to sit on committees and these planning units [at one point, 30 percent of all elected officials were supposed to be women]. Many men say, "How are we to be ruled by women?" And there is another thing in this: we know that when women are sitting on committees, they will be spending more time away from home, and that is when trouble begins.

Thus, women's involvement in Plan would draw them out of the household and into the public sphere, where their desires would be unleashed and where they would become objects of men's desires, ultimately causing conflict and fragmentation within the household. Another adult man, a former councilor, argued that Plan was insulting Taita men by bringing improvements that most men were capable of providing, while failing to investigate the true nature of Taita problems:

> These people they call themselves Plan, but they have no plan at all! They are cleaning up people's shit when they don't have food to eat! Is that a good plan? They think they are bringing democracy, but they do not talk to the people who know what this community needs. They do not want to talk to politicians, because they distrust politicians, so they end up talking to people who are not even from here. Take this idea of granaries, for example. We don't have enough food for granaries, and our place is too wet for granaries that are outside. [Wataita keep their excess food in the kitchen, above the fire.] This idea of granaries, this is a Kamba [a large, neighboring ethnic group, strongly represented in the District Development Office in Wundanyi] idea! But really it is very insulting to build toilets and granaries for us, as if we do not have men to do this work!

Women tended to take a more positive view of Plan's household improvements, although they sometimes sold the fruits of these improvements to others for cash (especially the water tanks, which were portable). Most were happy for any help whatsoever, and welcomed the possible connection to families from beyond Taita. As one female household head put it, "Plan is saying it is the time of women now! Our children are going to get a better education. They will have the opportunity to go abroad and visit their friends, or their friends from abroad will come to see us here. And they will not come empty-handed. They will carry dollars and sterling pounds, which is good, because who does not want to live well?"

In addition to these concerns, many men also asserted that Plan workers were corrupt, basing their claims on the 10 percent they acquired from households and their control of the transnational exchange of letters and gifts (many suspected them of stealing the gifts that they believed the European families had sent in the mail, with the letters).[3] But according to Plan employees, the 10 percent had a pedagogical message: the offering was intended to demonstrate that Wataita should not expect free gifts, and that each household had to give something of value in order to receive something of value. However, because Plan hired its own contactors, it was easy to suspect that both the 100 percent and the 10 percent were fictive, for Plan workers had, according to some Wataita, entered into profitable arrangements with shady individuals who overquoted prices. Moreover, many claimed that those who bribed the Plan officers rose to the top of Plan's list of families who would receive improvements. According to these increasingly vocal critics, Plan's stated interest in children was belied by the damning fact that many childless families were on Plan's list. As for the alleged bounty from abroad, Plan representatives often explained to people that, in the respective donor countries, the foster parents gave money to an organization that collected all of the donations from all parts of the developed world; it was Plan's responsibility to ensure that this money was equitably disbursed to the beneficiaries' communities so as to avoid some people enriching themselves while others stayed behind.

But in the eyes of many Wataita, Plan representatives were profiting from the good intentions of others, using their literacy as an instrument to fleece people in the name of development. This sentiment was especially strong among the poorest families, who were angered to see people they felt were well off acquiring Plan projects and subsidized school fees. They clearly wanted to develop individual relationships with these invisible foreigners, who no doubt shared the desire to connect with them: why else would they have participated in such a program in the first place? Stories were told about an American family that came to visit Taita, only to be shocked to find their foster child wallowing in poverty.

The photographs seemed to be proof of Plan's self-interested commodification and sale of Taita's future; these globally circulating images of children had acquired an international exchange value of which locals could only guess. As one frustrated senior male put it to me in 1998, "Those people of Plan are so fat from selling photographs of our children to whites that their bellies hang to the ground!" The image of adoption also suggested that foreign families would eventually come to claim the Taita offspring that they had effectively purchased. As one woman, speaking at a baraza where Plan representatives were present in 1997, put it,

> If I sign up my child [in the foster program], how do I know that tomorrow some white people won't come and say, "This is my child"? You see there is no [in English:] *transparency* here, because I do not know these people, and I do not know what you [the Plan representatives working in Taita] are telling them.

> I do not know if they are good people or bad. Nowadays, there are so many things. We hear about devil worshippers. (nervous laughter in the crowd) How are we to know what is true and what is not? And our children are the only wealth we have!

Thus, public concern about Plan's intent ultimately crystallized into a recognizable form: the organization was sinister and occult—a branch of the Satanic Church, the transnational corporation that sold children and organs to families abroad. Soon, many families refused to sign their children up for the foster program, which meant that their villages could not expect larger projects, the distribution of which was dependent on the number of children enrolled in the program. The rumors about Satanism dovetailed with other, similar rumors circulating about the perceived marriage of NGOs and government, such as that of the blood-sucking truck. One rumor had it that NGOs working with the Ministry of Health to provide free condoms to locals were distributing perforated prophylactics to infect the population with the deadly AIDS virus as a prelude to expropriating the land of the deceased.

One Pentecostal preacher named Simon identified Plan as one of several agents in this conspiracy.[4] At outdoor sermons in larger towns, Simon drew intricate chalk diagrams of various forms of birth control ("coils," the sponge, and condoms), showing how these devices upset the normative balance of fluids in the body while also reversing their flow. Drawing on the idea of sex education promoted by NGOs involved in AIDS awareness campaigns, Simon's chalk drawings depicted penises wrapped in sheaths, with backward-pointing arrows dramatizing the dangerous reverse flow of human potential back into the penis, where it would cause sickness. He thus portrayed a drama of thwarted male potency that was suggestive of men's displacement from the production of generative wealth beyond Taita, and their consequent inability to realize their masculinity. Simon also demonstrated that prophylactics were encoded with secret meanings, and he broke the codes by converting the letters in such words as "condom" into numbers following various systems of numerology. Invariably, the numbers were shown to add up to 666, the sign of the Antichrist and the impending Armageddon. In Simon's formulation, the different spiritual and physical potentialities contained in semen (which he described as the soul, material strength, and the legacy of generations) were layered in the seminal fluid and, ideally, these aspects took residence in corresponding "houses" in the female uterus to which, like migrant

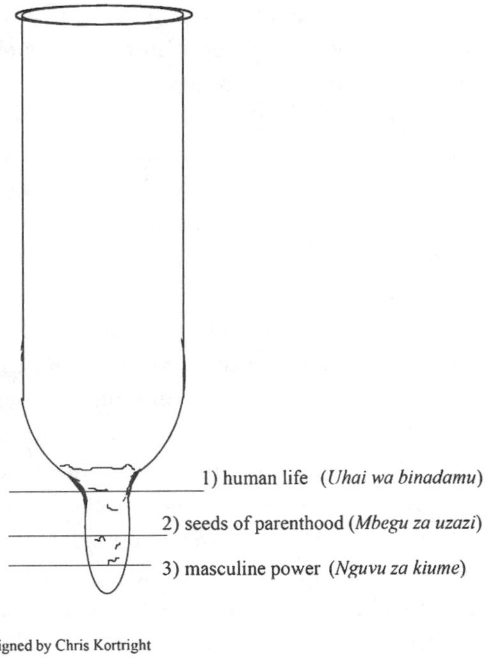

FIGURE 4. What really gets dumped in a pit latrine (originally drawn on chalk on public pavement by Reverend Simon).

laborers, male semen eventually came home to rest (see figure 4). But instead of lodging itself in what Simon drew as an inverted penis (the uterus), semen was being discarded, with condoms, into pit latrines across the nation. He declared that this abominable conflation of bounded substances (semen and feces) was connected to and synonymous with the subversion of national sovereignty: specifically, the control of black Africans by white NGO expatriates with headquarters in Nairobi and abroad.

Plan employees felt compelled to respond to such rumors, and supported democratization of Plan procedures partly in an effort to displace responsibility onto Taita citizens. One afternoon in late 1997, I sat with Cleo, a Taita woman who was also the local Plan officer in charge of all Plan activities in a specific administrative area. Plan was at the time undergoing a change in policy, which Cleo assumed was originating in Nairobi, but which may have also come from the international office abroad. In essence, she was being instructed to facilitate the democratization of Plan's giving practices, and she was enthusiastic about the change.

Plan representatives like Cleo would spend the rest of their time in the area trying to convince people to elect "literate" (meaning English speaking) youth, many of whom were Pentecostals, to the committees, with very limited success. But, as Cleo had hoped, the rumors about Plan representatives' involvement in corruption and, in a related vein, devil worship, dissipated after the introduction of the planning units in 1997, a change that was also made to coincide roughly with the multiparty national presidential elections.

Over time, as power was deposed from Plan representatives to elected leaders, people's rancor shifted to the planning unit representatives, as Cleo had hoped, and focused on their control of desired resources, such as livestock. Plan's efforts to bring development under community control coincided with the implementation of a new dairy cow project, at first intended to benefit women, who would now be able to use the milk to supplement their incomes. This project was particularly symbolic, because it was widely interpreted as the long-awaited fulfillment of a promise made to Taita communities by the government during the 1970s. At that time, Wataita claimed to have been informed by the government that they would receive dairy cows, but at the last minute the "foreign" Kikuyu in the Ministry of Livestock vengefully gave them zebus, which do not give milk, instead. But it soon became clear that the Taita men who chaired the new planning units were taking some cows as payment for their work and using the remaining cows to revitalize defunct, masculine social networks through the exchange of cattle as gifts. One young woman was adamant in her condemnation of the committees: "When the project first took off, almost all of the committee members gave themselves a cow. Also, most of the cows were old, and they were brought in during the time of cold weather. They died right away, and then more were brought in to replace them. But what happened? They were given to the same people who had received the first lot—the committee members! This has made us angry, and so now we want the whole committee to just go!" People complained that the new planning units were more "*karapt*" than Plan alone had been, and that these men were excluding people while completely neglecting the idea of the sovereign child as the foundation for a new political community (an idea that many people, male and female, now asserted without reservation). One senior man from a once privileged family that had fallen on hard times seized upon Plan's idea of the sacred, sovereign child, and complained that the planning units were exacerbating inequality by encouraging those with means to pay for improvements:

> Plan established a law: you have to have a child in the foster program to get anything. They put as many people in the program as possible, because they wanted people to see that there was no shame in it. Even our daughter was invited, to show people that if something new was to happen, everyone would have to be involved. It was a way of bringing people together and saying, "Oh, you think this person is rich, or you think this man is a witch? Well, this family needs our help too! All of these children are Plan's children. Plan is the mother of everyone!" But then, when the PUs were given more power, these people from here identified families like ours, and tried to sell us projects. Even though we were not rich. They knew our large house. But for those who could pay, and did, you can see that it made things more unequal. Because you see there were so many people who got things but didn't have children in the foster program!

Here Plan is figured as a maternal provider who cares for all children, regardless of their family background, and "her" apolitical plan is derailed by a cadre of men seeking to regain their vanquished power and autonomy. But planning unit representatives had their own arguments for giving cows to people whom others called their friends. Some complained that it was impossible to resist the demands of close kin and in-laws; one man explained that the flowery rhetoric of democratization withered under the cold pressures of daily life: "We can talk of democracy forever, but if I still owe bridewealth to my in-laws, it is very difficult for me to not use this opportunity to help them, and to lessen my debt burden." Others argued that villagers deployed the idioms of corruption and law to compensate for the fact that development was not in their hearts. As one retired medical technician who chaired a village planning unit put it, "You people say that time is money, and it's true. You [in the United States] love development, but here I have to look for people who love development. Plan has tried so hard to help people. They built very nice toilets, but our people turned them into homes for their sons. This is because they are not seeing far, into tomorrow. Then Plan decided to make people feel the pinch by making them pay 10 percent, but people made a fuss: 'So and so got his toilet for free,' they said. But do you not see that yesterday was yesterday and today is a new day?"

Thus, debates about development came to be indigenized and linked to historically enduring local conflicts, at the same time as governance became increasingly capillary and somewhat delinked from the state as institutional form. As for the planning units, they continued in this way for four years, and in that time people continued to give 10 percent of the projected costs for various individual projects. The rumors of corruption also continued, and many people complained bitterly among themselves about the lack of accountability, which was embodied in an increasingly compelling fetish: receipts, which the planning unit representatives consistently failed to produce. Young men, many of them Pentecostal converts, bemoaned the fact that Wataita were unwilling to challenge these senior leaders because of their connections to the Catholic Church, and doubted the fairness of the elections that had brought these men into positions of power. They boldly asserted that their elders held onto positions of power by sacrificing their own junior relatives to *majini* (blood-sucking spirit familiars), and began trickling in to Cleo's house to request new elections. Cleo withdrew from these requests and reminded everyone who came to her that they were free to hold reelections at any time or to demand receipts from the elected planning unit leaders. But she eventually changed her position, according to some because she felt ashamed when another European family came to the area to see the fruits of their donations, and left bitterly disappointed. In 2001, she insisted that the chief call a baraza, where she politely insisted that the old leadership should be replaced by younger personnel, both male and female. She explained,

> Beloved people of Mgange, things in Plan have changed. Very soon you will be doing a lot of the work that we are doing ourselves. As you know, the language of work in Plan is English. We are not trying to look down upon our parents who are now old and need to rest [note the shift to the collective "we" and the entailed conflation of Plan with the community]. You sent your children to school so that they can help you deal with the outside world. Now is the time to give them a chance to use that education by running the PU. We have been doing a lot of work, which you are supposed to have been doing, and Plan [now an entity that is outside Taita] is not happy about it. So if you do not bring in young, educated people then I am sorry to say that you will be passed by many good things (*mutapitwa na mambo mengi mazuri*)!

Here Cleo referenced young people's possession of a universal currency (English) that they could use to manage affairs in the way that Plan wanted, in the process acquiring things of value for Taita, but her demand articulated concerns that were entirely local, harmonizing with the interests of youth and women in particular. Importantly, Cleo referred to Plan as a powerful entity that was outside of Taita, which could be happy or sad about things, and implied that development was dependent upon making this organization feel a certain way about Taita people. Plan's symbolic power thus derived partly from the fact that it was both here and there, close and far, high and low, and that it was interested in people's actions and attitudes (the explicit parallel with Pentecostal thought about God is not coincidental). It was an idea that youths and seniors would soon take to heart, deploying the presumed wishes of Plan against one another, while in the process assimilating Plan to themselves.

Cleo's efforts to break the stranglehold of senior men was soon matched by what was widely perceived as an effort to undermine the power of the destructive, elite witches who were also the town's main shop owners. This new hope came to life in a project designed to increase the flow of water from the nearly defunct spring on the hilltop above the school, which had been the site of the failed rainmaking ritual discussed in chapter 5. In this way, Plan now seemed to be submitting to Taita understandings of witchcraft and development, as well as flow and retention, and Plan's popularity increased accordingly. The water project was symbolically loaded, in part because the receding spring Ndolwa had become symbolic of a formerly abundant Taita past. By extending the spring and the network of pipes, the entire community would potentially benefit from this much desired resource, which had formerly been usurped by the town's elite shop owners (prior to this, all water was stored in a tank next to the chief's office, which was also adjacent to the town market). The flow of water from Ndolwa and between households suggested the kind of generative reciprocity that Wataita refer to as "opening" or "flow," and which they counterpose to selfish, witchlike retention. Thus, at stake was a more genuine, collective development than that of the selfishly retentive elites who shared resources only among themselves.

But coming up with the needed funds for the project proved difficult, and Wataita were compelled to engage in a ruse that many would later recollect with pride. The story, briefly told, runs as follows: The Ministry of Water insisted that the government had to be involved in the planning of the project, and the district water engineer led a team in conducting a survey for the pipes and taps. He ultimately presented a bill to Plan, which included transportation and food costs for his government surveyors. Plan in turn requested 10 percent of that money from the community, to be collected by the water committee, consisting of elected representatives. The new arrangement meant that the citizenry, represented by the water committee, owed money to Plan, which in turn owed money to the government for the survey. The water committee did not have this money, but it eventually seized upon an idea: because the government had told Plan and the community that it could choose its own contractor, the civilian water committee decided it would acquire this 130,000 Kenyan shillings from a Kenyan contractor in advance. The contractor would surely be willing to offer this advance, on trust, in exchange for the future contract worth 5.2 million shillings (or about $75,000.00). This illicit plan was successful: the committee found a contractor to agree, and thereby acquired the money they needed to pay the 10 percent to Plan International. Unfortunately, Plan's representatives had interpreted the agreement with the government to imply that the NGO was representing the public, and they had already secured and paid their own, different contractor (contractor number 1), not knowing anything about the water committee's contractor. Now, the water committee was in debt to contractor number 2, who would never actually receive the contract. But once the project was completed, the water committee managed to settle the debt with the money that came in from individual water users who were willing, per the agreement with Plan and the water committee, to pay for individual household access to water.

In the end (it took four years for the project to be completed), and despite a great deal of stress and confusion, everyone seemed happy, and all townspeople had access to tap water for free at public sites. Moreover, it was reasonable to assume that the project was sustainable, as the accumulated fees from individual users, deposited with the planning units, would continue to pay for the maintenance of the pipes over time. Of course, one could frame this story more pessimistically: the episode not only supported the suspicion that the government was useless but it proved its parasitism, as government employees found a way to survive on the backs of the populace. And the project only succeeded because of caprice: an NGO happened to be available at that time, and in the near future it would not. Moreover, because of the state's failings, and the poverty and pessimism of the populace, citizens felt compelled to engage in risky and arguably deceptive ruses in order to secure what they felt they needed. But ultimately community cooperation, which could be called "corruption," had enabled development and defeated witchcraft (the witchcraft of the elite shop owners), and most townspeople recognized that they had managed to initiate and complete something meaningful, thus proving their worth to themselves and future sources of help.

Meanwhile, Plan's newly elected youths began to engage their elders, whose authority and recalcitrance they tended to see as aspects of their witchcraft. The young men who were elected by their villages as representative youths clearly felt that their communities had elected them to ascertain what had happened to the money that the planning units had collected over the years. Later, looking back on that time, one unmarried thirty-year-old man complained, "You find a treasurer, the same guy who was on the church council, has made a thousand transactions and has only recorded three! We wanted transparency!" Another recollected that, when he went to his first meeting, he found an established system in place. The planning unit representatives had developed what they called a "protocol," which included an order for opening meetings and an agenda for discussing future meetings. Early in the meeting, the incumbent planning unit representatives reminded the newly elected youth that Plan wanted the planning units to be directly involved in the translation of letters and the taking of photographs, and suggested that the young men help with this task. The youth grumbled at what they perceived as an attempt, by the seniors, to relegate them to menial, insignificant tasks.

An angry and vocal meeting commenced: at once, the young men demanded to see the accounts, insisting that this was why they had been elected. But the older men and women on the committee refused, invoking proverbs such as, "I wish I knew comes behind" (*Nambe ngamanya yadacha na nyuma*) and "If you shit in a bowl, from what will you eat?" (*Kanye fuwa kujhia hao?*) to express the idea that Plan was powerful and would be driven away by the youths' demands for transparency. By this they implied that they were the employees of Plan, and that any demand for accountability would be interpreted by Plan to mean that Plan's authority was in question. The youth responded by claiming that it was indeed they who were the manifestations of Plan's wishes, that they were actually Plan, and they communicated their desire for equal consideration and democracy by using scabrous proverbs usually reserved for senior men (in particular, "Shit left to sit in your ass overnight will swell"—*Mavi ghikala ghadaba*—meaning that a problem ignored will grow worse with time). For their part, the seniors insinuated that the coveted records had a mystical quality, which they alone could understand. If they were to reveal the accounts too quickly, the youth would misunderstand their meaning and might infer wrongful conclusions from what they saw. The seniors also reminded the youth of their long history of involvement in the Catholic Church and the church's historic commitment to development in the region. The youth in turn responded by reasserting, and aligning themselves with, Plan's secularism, and an emerging future in which development would be unleashed from religious belief. One young man made a speech that sent minor shock waves through the audience; in it, he implied that youth served as patrons for the community by mediating the flow of value from abroad, and argued that this value should circulate openly, regardless of religious affiliation:

> What we want is to separate the church from development! Because this is a multireligious society and we want to help everyone, whether they are Christian, Jew, Muslim, or even devil worshipper! The church is for Sundays, but development is for the living, for everyday. Yes! We are here today, and we have to find our way today. They say, "Give to Caesar what is Caesar's, and to God what is God's." I will give to Caesar what is Caesar's. So if there's anything left for God after we Caesars get ours, maybe I'll give it to him, if I think he deserves it!

The meeting was quickly adjourned. By 2002, the seven youth had left in disgust, while their elders remained outwardly convinced that these youth were uncontrolled and immature, and so unprepared for leadership.

Thus, as Plan relinquished control of the distribution of funds to the civilian population, local social conflicts (such as relations between generations) became explicitly politicized. Meanwhile, public politics was colonized by family politics. Through these arguments, the formerly foreign entity Plan was domesticated, as local groups came to view themselves as embodying Plan's understanding of development—which was, of course, their understanding of development, transplanted onto Plan. As domestic politics were projected to the public sphere, the formerly public-political language of democracy also came to life in the domestic sphere, patterning relationships among socially differentiated family members. This process was only exacerbated after Plan International left Taita, leaving the seniors in charge of the planning units (now renamed CBOs), with youth relegated to the outside. These youth, most of whom presented themselves as at once "saved" (in Pentecostalism) and secular, continued to call for an accounting from their seniors. They also began to form youth groups with a view to securing funding from foreign NGOs, so as to relieve their dependence on their Taita seniors.

Conclusion

The evidence in this chapter demonstrates that Wataita were connecting with foreign institutions in ways that bypassed state institutions, and that forging relationships with foreign households and organizations was an emergent strategy that came to epitomize development, in contrast to earlier models of development centered on the state and long-distance wage labor. To forge a political system that was also a model of and for development outside the state, and in opposition to the culture of Kenyan politics (or siasa), Plan International seized on the image of the innocent child, and so fueled changing power relations centered on the axes of gender and generation while also appearing, at first, to commercialize blood relations. Older men later acquired a positional advantage in this ongoing debate, when they came to manage the planning units, only to find themselves confronted later by young men, who challenged them by claiming literacy, basic knowledge of bookkeeping, and an awareness of what foreign bureaucracies expected. Through these idioms, youth and seniors struggled for control of the planning units and generative resources such as cattle.

While Plan did constitute a new source of wealth and respect, it did not eradicate many of the underlying problems that Wataita felt were impeding development. Moreover, Wataita were only able to acquire what they wanted by engaging with powerful others and submitting themselves to their demands and interests, such as the requirement of 10 percent of the cost of projects or the insistence on written accounts. Many Wataita felt that development on their own terms continued to elude them, and they sought to bring powerful forces under their control, which was synonymous with making them less occult, less like witchcraft. At around the same time as Plan was active in the region, a parallel development intervention was underway, led primarily by the uneducated and aimed largely at educated elites, with a view to transforming Taita society from the bottom up. This witch-finding movement, which came to be known as the Maji Marefu Mission, stylized itself as an NGO, and invoked the idiom of development, but its methods were decisively different from those of Plan International. Maji Marefu's supporters hoped to harness foreign, occult ritual to develop society and economy by acting on people's dispositions, and so their work was more directly concerned with transforming the hegemonic, taken-for-granted values that had come to dominate Taita society at the expense of the imagined moral economy of Kidabida.

CHAPTER SEVEN

Democracy Victorious: Exorcising Witchcraft from Development

In widespread Taita understandings, the simultaneous processes of disintegration and immersion associated with neoliberalism were linked to witchcraft, always already iconic of abusive power that violates and disintegrates social boundaries in systematic ways. New forms of witchcraft were among the things that Taita entrepreneurs and non-Taita merchants brought back with them from far-away towns where witches competed with one another in an effort to attract competitors; moreover, these new forms of witchcraft came to stand for all of the potentially dangerous new things that were entering Taita. In addition, witchcraft was widely deemed responsible for the fact that the practices and institutions that had once allowed certain Wataita to prosper were not working as they ought: jealous witches had sabotaged schools with witchcraft, or they used *majini* (blood-sucking spirit familiars) to prevent people from making it to the city or from getting ahead at work. The state was widely perceived as incapable of safeguarding Taita against these new threats, and so Taita people needed to find a way to unite politically in order to protect themselves and to rebuild dying institutions so they would again become meaningful. In 1998, several villages decided to take matters into their own hands and organize to create a culturally sensitive and sustainable development that took seriously the idea of witchcraft as a reality that resulted ultimately from people's emotional states.

In this chapter, I focus briefly on a "development project" somewhat different than those previously described which sought, in a way, to transcend the failures of all of them. As we have seen, efforts to develop the homestead failed because of internal conflicts over how best to manage social resources (both financial and human). Any attempt to shore up strict boundaries around the home to protect it from outside contention failed, because even at this elemental level there was discontent and disagreement, wrought by forces that raged outside the home. Attempts to revitalize, or at least manage, the past failed because of the self-interests of ritual practitioners and the socially divided nature of the population. Efforts to lure foreign nongovernmental organizations (NGOs) and assert some control over what they were doing in Taita were somewhat successful, but ultimately these organizations left, and even when they did not, the problems of social division and conflict over resources continued. The supporters of the development project I am about to discuss—the Maji Marefu Mission—aspired to go beyond these interventions by dealing directly with the fundamental issue of human frailty. The mission tried to address this issue by eradicating witchcraft in its entirety, and so it posited Taita's problems in terms of an essential evil that could be expunged. But in practice this absolute evil was shown to be eminently social, and the "community" found itself back where it started: divided along multiple lines of social cleavage, finding witchcraft everywhere, but also nowhere in particular (except in Maji Marefu himself).

Why, then, bring up this project at all, especially here, near the end of this book? One answer is that this movement responded in a way to all the others, and so in a sense contained them within itself. For this reason, it represented a kind of advance, for through it Wataita tried to achieve something they had been longing for for some time: they wanted, in short, to create an environment in which people were less afraid, where they felt free to pursue their various projects and watch them come to fruition. Many thought they could achieve this goal by exposing the people whom they were afraid of, thereby reducing their power, and making way for the emergence of a collective disposition that was more amenable to development. Most were, in the end, unsatisfied with the outcome of the project, though they remained convinced of the existence of witchcraft in their midst. Another answer is that, like all of the projects discussed thus far, this one did have positive consequences beyond what was intended, because people initiated a relatively civil undertaking in accordance with their understanding of things, knowing full well the attendant risks. They also invigorated moribund "civil society" institutions while generating a feeling of participatory democracy that extended beyond the moment in question, generally informing people's attitudes about their rights, responsibilities, and expectations.

Witch-finding movements have a long history in Africa, and the Maji Marefu Mission, as this project came to be called, had much in common with them. In Africa, witch-finders are typically recruited to ameliorate an imagined crisis in local social production—such as declining fertility, increased mortality, and falling economic productivity—typically said to be brought about by moral failures in the form of malicious actions by kin and neighbors. In these movements, "modern" rituals and technologies of witch-finding are routinely contrasted, by African participants and their ethnographers alike, to indigenous forms of divination, and the decision to hire a "foreign" witch-finder is typically informed by the presumption that local methods for combating occultism respond inadequately to new social conditions (see Richards 1935; Marwick 1950; Willis 1968; Van Binsbergen 1981; Auslander 1993). Moreover, many witch-finding movements take on the appearance of revolutionary mass action, highlighting endemic social cleavages while at times reversing established social hierarchies (see Marwick 1950; Willis 1968). The transregional and outwardly modern character of African witch-finders is always an important part of their appeal, given that they are hired to wrangle with what are felt to be decidedly new and innovative threats to social order (see in particular Redmayne 1970; Auslander 1993). The Maji Marefu Mission resembled these movements in its ritualized reenactment of the procedures of colonial and postcolonial bureaucracies (including the deployment of administrative titles and honorifics, as well as record-keeping procedures) and in its use of "scientific" divinatory objects with universalizing implications (cf. Auslander 1993; Comaroff and Comaroff 1993, 1999b). Also, like many witch-finding movements, this one resulted in the spectacular public destruction of ritual artifacts associated with the highly particular "traditional" authority of senior males (Richards 1935; Marwick 1950; Willis 1968; Auslander 1993; Comaroff and Comaroff 1999b). While it shared traits with earlier witch-finding movements in diverse parts of the continent, the Maji Marefu Mission also reflected contemporary preoccupations while seeking to transform historically recent events. Most importantly, the "mission" was stylized as a quasi-religious NGO making up for the state's inadequacies while also offering a moral and philosophical alternative to the political culture that had come to characterize postcolonial Kenya.

The Maji Marefu Mission

In 1998, several villages in a location[1] in the Taita Hills in southeastern Kenya pooled their resources to hire a Tanzanian witch-finder by the name of Maji Marefu (Deep Waters) to rid the area of what was widely taken to be an alarming increase in foreign, uncontrollable forms of deadly witchcraft.[2] Maji Marefu's six-month stay in Mgange location generated debate and controversy throughout the Taita Hills, where news and information travels quickly. His public witch-finding activities were limited to two or three sublocations, together comprising about 5,000 people. However, Wataita came from all over the hills to visit Maji Marefu in the house that he rented to privately purchase remedies and protection. Moreover, the social impact of Maji Marefu's work, his authenticity as a witch-finder, and the value of this form of social control and intervention as opposed to others was the subject of open and virulent public controversy throughout the hills and beyond. In many ways, the debate and actions surrounding Maji Marefu's work were more influential than any secrets his group actually uncovered because, through this response to crisis, competing Taita visions of social order became visible and the lines of social and ideological conflict were tightly drawn. I followed Maji Marefu and his group when they worked, frequently sat in his rented house, spoke with a wide spectrum of the population about his visit, and was witness to public gatherings and official assemblies where his visit was discussed and debated. I also paid money to have myself "tied" by him, so that others would not be able to bewitch me.

Maji Marefu was often referred to as Dr. Maji Marefu or Maji Marefu, Professor Emeritus. An unmarried forty-something man with a powerful presence, he had been traveling throughout East Africa with his entourage of young, urban-looking men in urban American "hip-hop" style clothing for many years. His fictive "sons," as they were called, wore oversized athletic and music T-shirts, low-riding baggy jeans, and untied white high-top sneakers; they wrapped long white sashes around their heads and carried crucifixes, calabashes, cameras, and mirrors with them wherever they went. According to most people, Maji Marefu came to be the powerful witch-hunter he now was after he was himself bewitched as a youth by an elder sibling said to have been jealous of his intelligence and education. After a near-fatal bout of fever, God appeared to him in a dream and told him that he was to travel throughout the region ridding communities of the suffering and misfortune caused by jealous people. The soon-to-be Maji Marefu was instructed to journey to a distant lake and to submerge himself in its waters for three days, which he did, ultimately emerging with the power to see witches and to prevent them from harming others through occult means. He thereupon took on the name

Deep Waters, or Maji Marefu, and converted to Islam, though his ritual cleansings included Christian and African elements, including crucifixes, baptisms, and the invocation of water spirits.

Maji Marefu's work consisted primarily of public, house-to-house witch hunts paid for by the host communities, but his group supplemented this community-funded work with private consultations. In these private appointments, allegedly bewitched individuals visited Maji Marefu's rented house to purchase divination readings and cures, as well as relatively benign forms of magic (most commonly, love potions). Most Wataita thought of Maji Marefu much like they thought of any other outside expert or NGO: he was a person possessing foreign technical skill that could be put to work to generate locally sustainable development, and so they sought his input and expertise. As we will see, they also found that, like other NGOs, Maji Marefu was happy to point out Taita's lack of development and to blame this failing on their collective personalities.

Prior to entering Mgange location, Maji Marefu had been living with his fictive sons for several months in the lowland Taita town of Bura; before that, they had worked in the much larger town of Taveta, on the border with Tanzania. Many young men from the highlands area of Taita work in or near Bura (the town is not far from a major tourist hotel), were familiar with Maji Marefu and his work, and brought news of it up to the hills. A widespread rumor had it that, in Taita, Maji Marefu was first hired by the headmaster of a local high school to find the school's stolen automobile; while the police had been stymied, Maji Marefu was alleged to have immediately declared that the vehicle was in Arusha, Tanzania, and to have dispatched his helpers to find it and return it to the school headmaster. This story suggested that public institutions (schools, the police) were increasingly dependent on nonstate authorities like Maji Marefu while depicting Maji Marefu Mission as one among many of the organizations that were slowly taking over the functions of government. It also drew attention to the fact that the movement was specifically aimed at fixing what were widely conceived as improperly functioning institutions, including schools, commerce, and government bureaucracies. Thus, the collective decision to hire this witch-hunter was informed by the overarching sense that the currencies of modern life were coming undone and had changed their meaning, or lost meaning because they had been captured by inscrutable forces.

Maji Marefu had been in the Taita area for over a month when male and female adults in the location's villages gathered in the village councils and development committees to vote on whether they should invite him to "sweep" (*kufagia*) their neighborhoods, house to house. These councils were state-endorsed institutions originally established to iterate government policy, mobilize communities for various development projects and campaigns, and collect money for local improvements. For the most part, these groups followed the long-established precedent for similar development projects: each village council elected a person to chair a subcommittee responsible for all of the practical affairs related to hiring Maji Marefu. Thus, the point of initiation was clearly located at the local, popular level and was accomplished through the remnants of state institutions (village councils), which had been appropriated by locals whose civilian leaders were meticulous about issues of accountability, popular participation, and consent. Thus, in very practical terms, these communities took over the state project of development through those very institutions that were originally intended to bring a modernist model of development into being.

At meetings of the village development committees, Wataita assembled of their own volition to introduce and debate the decision to hire Maji Marefu, and individuals were allocated the responsibility of informing the local state authorities (the chief) and delivering the money to the witch-hunter. During that period, it was invariably the case that any meeting held to discuss development would end in a discussion of Maji Marefu. Different issues were discussed in every meeting, but at none did I hear anyone question the existence of witchcraft. People did question Maji Marefu's veracity (was he "real" or "*feki*"?); whether he might introduce new forms of witchcraft into Taita, rather than bind their place against the ongoing invasion of exogenous witchcraft; and whether he might stir up old conflicts and resentments that were best left to rest. Some even questioned whether ridding Taita of witchcraft might not be fundamentally misguided, for it implied that, after the removal of unfair barriers to trade, a fairer, more productive market economy would emerge in its place. It made more sense to believe that, once witchcraft was removed, everything would stop working; as one woman put it in one of these local meetings, "Majini are in every *matatu* [passenger minivan] and every shop. If we get rid of the majini there will be no goods left in the market!" This comment reflected Taita people's experience of that moment, for their civil service and government were in the process of being downsized and restructured in the interest of fairness and good governance, but very little had emerged to replace the old, admittedly corrupt system.

Ultimately, though, most people asserted that witchcraft constituted an unfair barrier to business and general prosperity, and that removing it would help people to generate development. But they did insist that the ultimate goal was "peace" (*sere*) and that whatever Maji Marefu did would have to be harmless; in part, this reflected a general concern about interference from government and a more or less genuine desire to follow "the law." But it also reflected the underlying desire to return Taita to what was imagined to have been a more serene, harmonious, and happy past while retaining the positive aspects of modernity.

Bringing the Witch Doctor Home

People spoke about Maji Marefu coming months before he actually arrived, and when they did they referred to nothing less than a revolution, a total reconstruction of society, which they feared might be opposed by powerful people threatened by his just work. Many felt that this coming together to revitalize Taita society and economy by expunging dangerous foreign influences epitomized "democracy"; they were concerned that government might interfere and many Wataita were prematurely resentful. It was in this context of ambivalent expectation and general distrust of the Kenyan government that the district officer, Samuel, a non-Taita Kenyan administrator and immediate boss of the district's chiefs, came to a local *baraza*, or public assembly, to speak to people about the issue. Samuel's visit followed a false and ill-fated national election mired by "rigging" (election fraud), intimidation at the polls, and violence: an election that culminated in then President Moi personally reinstating a very unpopular incumbent Taita member of Parliament (MP) in a radio broadcast (see chapter 6). For many, then, the state's and the international community's experiment in multiparty democracy was not working in the way that it ought and, during the baraza many asserted amongst themselves that it was, as one man put it, "time for true democracy."

During the baraza, Samuel warned the assembled public about the possibility of violence and discord coming from Maji Marefu's projected visit. But, he argued, he was not a Taita person, but Somali, and this was an issue that Wataita would have to decide for themselves. "Let me ask you, beloved people of Mgange," he began, "Do you want this Maji Marefu to come here?" The crowd responded with a resounding yes ("*Ndiyo, bwana!*"), and when Samuel decided to embrace the spirit of democracy by proclaiming, "Then let him continue his work!" (in Swahili,

Basi, aendelee na kazi yake), an enthusiastic response—cheering, clapping, and ululations—followed, lasting a full minute. "Provided," he insisted, "that no one is hurt, and no one's rights are infringed. . . . No one should be forced to do something he does not want." Of course, this pretension to respect the right to privacy may seem disingenuous: what witch, or accused witch, would open his or her house to angry, marauding villagers led by a witch-hunter? Indeed, the issue of privacy and household autonomy would later be raised by many former supporters of the idea who later found themselves facing an angry mob in front of their homes, or running away from Maji Marefu in the town market.

Nonetheless, community and government were, for the time being, cooperating and united; both seemed to see in Maji Marefu an opportunity to safeguard Taita from the illicit visible and invisible forces that were depleting local culture, morality, and economy. Indeed, for many, Samuel's reference to Maji Marefu's "work" rather than his "witchcraft" or "Satanism" (appellations to follow) indicated government collusion in the moral and political project of witch-hunting. Certainly, visiting politicians and administrators preached about the dangers of witchcraft often enough, and had long argued that development could not take place without the removal of witchcraft: businessmen were afraid to prosper because they feared making witches angry; wealthy elites who could reinvest in Taita chose to stay in Mombasa because they were afraid of their kin and neighbors; and extension officers and politicians failed to implement development projects because backward witches sabotaged them. In addition to this rhetoric, which saw witchcraft as a threat to governmentality, Maji Marefu seemed to have the implicit backing of powerful national officials and administrators; although he was not a Kenyan, and had no work permits or visa, he was allowed to continue his work for many months while the authorities awaited the results. Some critical observers suggested that local state officials viewed Maji Marefu's visit as an opportunity to extend governmental control and simultaneously enrich themselves at this time when state power was visibly receding under the pressures of neoliberal reforms (an interpretation that resonates with Ciekawy [1992, 1998]). Perhaps, as the Catholic priests often averred in their sermons, local state officials viewed Maji Marefu's visit as a timely fund-raising opportunity—tax collection by other means. For many speculated that administrators received some portion of the agreed-upon 100 Kenyan shillings (or about $1.50) per household that Maji Marefu received from the village committees.

Walking home from the baraza after the district officer's address, I conversed with Eloji, a middle-age man who loudly applauded Samuel for allowing what he really had no choice but to allow anyway. Eloji had a very small *shamba* (agricultural plot), insufficient to satisfy his family's food needs, and so he spent most of his days as a *kibarua* (casual laborer), working on other people's land for small return. Eloji commented that hard work had lost meaning and that wealth acquisition had become a mysterious and an inscrutable process. How, he demanded, could students manage to pass their certificate examinations if they spent every night working, unwittingly, on their neighbors' fields as hypnotized zombies, only to return to school in the morning tired and dirty? He insisted on the need to rid the region of advanced forms of occult practice that local knowledge seemed incapable of combating. Eloji's narrative drew on his own experience of a world of limited opportunities for personal and economic development:

> You know, Wataita have a lot of education. Our people have studied, and yet they do not have jobs. This is because of witchcraft! The rich of Mgange are using witchcraft to develop in wealth (*kuendelea na mali*). They are accumulating land, cows, vehicles without working at all. When they go to the fields, they go at night, and their hoes and *pangas* follow them behind! This is very wrong! We want those who work to benefit from their sweat. These days, a person sweats and sweats and someone else is benefiting while doing nothing. But if Maji Marefu comes, the way will be cleared. We will all develop naturally, based on the work we do!

Eloji drew attention to the corruption of modernity's vehicles (schooling and wage labor in cities), rooting world-historical structural transformations in local attitudes and historical conflicts. Maji Marefu, Eloji continued, offered a "straightening out" (*kughorua*), the kind that older men once performed to great effect (and now to lesser effect) when they stretched out the curled-up intestines of a goat in the act of *βula* (intestines) divination, delving into the convoluted bowels of a community's social relations, and so revealing the conflicts that stretch like an intestine, twisted and opaque, across the social body.

It was certainly timely for Maji Marefu's visit to coincide with national elections, a nationwide debate about the reformation of the constitution and the management of corruption, and a local shift in the distribution and use of transnational patronage, which sidelined state institutions. The popular national discourse about the need for "transparency" in matters of politics and government spending had taken a new, tangible twist, as Taita notions of open circulation and "flow" dovetailed with neoliberal discourse about good governance.[3] For the witch hunt, it was widely argued, was socially accountable, and its findings would be empirically verifiable (although, as we will see, the evidence that Maji Marefu generated turned out to be highly vulnerable to manipulation).

The Problem with Taita

After months of organizing and fund-raising by what came to be called the Maji Marefu committees, the witch-hunter finally arrived in his Nissan pickup truck, accompanied by an entourage of youth in their twenties. He and his numerous sons rented a house in town and went about the business of divining for witches and purportedly curing people afflicted by occult forces. Twice a week, they went on a local crusade, staking out a particular village, or a part of it, and visiting every single home in its domain. One had to run very fast to keep up with them, for no sooner had they suddenly entered a house than they were out and running again, followed by a large fan of young men and children from the villages. When entering a house, they walked right through the main door without asking permission, and they emerged from the kitchen by unhinging the metal sheets that made the roof. They thus popped up from the granary, the most secret and feminine domain of the house, exposing its inner secrets to full public view (see also Auslander 1993). Often Maji Marefu, or more often one of his sons, emerged triumphantly with an item of allegedly occult paraphernalia, exposing it to the crowd and inviting people to take photographs and video pictures. This purgative action came to be known as "sweeping" (kufagia) and, if one viewed their house-to-house migrations from a hillock, that is precisely what it resembled: a rapid movement of people through maize fields, into houses, and up through the roofs. Maji Marefu's public mandate was interpreted by his followers as giving him, and the local youth in his train, the right to commit transgressions that would not be tolerated under normal circumstances, such as trampling maize stalks and invading people's homesteads (see figures 5 and 6).

Over the course of four months, Maji Marefu and his group moved about the location, extracting occult objects (mostly bones, skulls, and gourds—or objects that resembled them from afar) from people's private property, as well as from weakened public institutions like schools and

FIGURES 5 AND 6. Residents watch as Maji Marefu's "boys" search private homes for witchcraft paraphernalia.

churches. While he was sweeping villages, his public relations committee of empowered youth circulated pictures of their "father" throughout the community: here Maji Marefu with his arms hung loosely around a Tanzanian state official, there Maji Marefu with a Catholic priest, here with a policeman, there with a school headmaster. These were smiling, satisfied images suggesting cooperation and positive outcomes among people that mattered. Maji thus appropriated some of the power of these secular and religious authorities while simultaneously augmenting them in several ways. On a stylistic level, highlighted in photographs, he transcended the staid orthodoxy of officialdom, suggesting that he had access to a genuine form of power (and money) that these impoverished, empty figures lacked. What he supplied was, in part, a global, and decidedly hip, element—he and his "gangsta"-clad, Chicago Bulls T-shirt–wearing youth were a small dose of what ailed Taita, and Wataita were, ironically, appropriating this potency to combat the social deterioration brought on by foreign forces.

What Maji Marefu revealed about the condition of formerly meaningful practices and institutions was most compelling, even titillating: in its theatrical aspect, these actions resembled social criticism in that they took symbolically potent, and opposed, images and combined them in ways that caused people to think about what was happening to them, and perhaps to imagine alternatives. A discovered Catholic rosary covered in feces and stuffed in a gourd evidenced a secret, almost atavistic, opposition to the church's mission, but it also gave concrete form to the more nebulous feeling that the church's popularity was indeed waning and that this meant something. Human skulls under a school seemed to express a secret wish that schooling fail, and a general lack of commitment to the project of education; it also implied for many that a particular version of the past was waiting to swallow them up. And a Nissan passenger minivan taxi whose operation depended on majini suggested that a world of apparently open and legitimate commerce was driven by decidedly undemocratic forces. When, after he had been in the region for a month's time, Maji Marefu unearthed what appeared from a distance to be a human arm bone from beneath the soccer field of a secondary school in my host town, he made an observation that was repeated for months and that may have been the beginning of his downfall: "The idiocy of Wataita is that they hate development!" (in Swahili, *Ujinga wa Wataita ni kwamba wanachuki maendeleo!*).

That Wataita could be held personally responsible for bewitching their own development, that their enmity toward each other could derail them from progress and isolate them from a world that was racing into the future, both shamed and inspired them. Indeed, many became all the more convinced that the practices and institutions associated with rectitude, social order, and the good life had been turned into dangerous shells of their former selves by a misanthropic clique. Many more Wataita declared that Maji Marefu's work had made it abundantly clear that nearly everyone was a witch, and that witchcraft and Taita-ness had become synonymous; so much for the "moist" Taita heart. Wataita were living dual lives—one outwardly modern, developed, and harmonious, the other hostile, vengeful, and parochial. Perhaps the most comical example, for Wataita, of this duality were the many headmasters and school teachers—outwardly cosmopolitan and "advanced"—who were shown to be witches harboring concealed stashes of allegedly occult implements. These stories were the object of much hilarious and incendiary discussion, and the carnivalesque mocking of Taita's educated community clearly angered established local elites, who increasingly visited the chiefs' offices to complain about the "witch" who was living in one of their own towns.

In addition to revealing the true backwardness underneath the veil of Taita's modern civility, Maji Marefu's techniques appropriated the state's waning powers of governance. For example, when "patients" arrived at his house, or clinic, to be cured, their names were recorded in a notebook, and the results of their divination were indicated in a second marked "Ministry of Health," with the established price for the cure listed on the right. Maji's fondness for titles and his use of English to draw connections between his own work and contemporary surveillance and information technologies also underscored the technically innovative, even scientific, nature of his work (see also Hasu 1999). His detection methods consolidated this image: As his youth traveled from house to house, they carried mirrors (called *ray-da* or, alternatively, "*mine detekta*") outstretched in front of them, showing the way. Maji Marefu explained to those who asked that his ray-da devices transmitted to him a mild electrical jolt when in the presence of a witch or witchcraft paraphernalia and that he could then discern the image of the witch, who sometimes turned out to be in the crowd of followers. This ritualized appropriation of high technology struck Wataita as very advanced, and they often contrasted it positively to βula, or goat entrails divination, which requires an elder officiate to dig through the dirty innards of a sheep or goat in search of feces and blood clots symbolic of social disruption and blocked flows of social value (see chapter 5). In contrast, Maji Marefu employed diagnostic objects that transmitted and condensed information across long distances, transcending the boundaries and limitations of localized space—in stark contrast to sheep, which were local objects with local owners and were thus thoroughly embedded in Taita social relationships and symbologies. Yet if the modern cadence of Maji Marefu's witch hunt was particularly promising to Wataita, the apparently democratic project of exposing a community's witches was also a form of tyranny, as the sanctity of the domestic household was daily violated by these abrasive children and foreigners.

Over the course of these four months, members of many identifiable social categories (men and women, wealthy and poor, educated and uneducated) were marked as witches; this was, after all, a divided community with many lines of internal division and various subject positions.[4] However, over time, different social factions came to be associated with different kinds of witchcraft of varying degrees of potency. Thus, a poor senior male was found with artifacts pertaining to non-Christian ritual practice, said to be traditional witchcraft, while a middle-age member of the elite had a house filled with hundreds of blood-thirsty majini spirits from Mombasa. Moreover, the accusations of *jini* keeping were often directed at the female heads of matricentric families, who were typically accused of keeping one or two majini, a "fact" that fed into local concern about the commercialization of domestic relations and the involvement of women in illicit forms of trade, such as illegal beer brewing and prostitution, in lieu of men's labor remittances. Maji Marefu revealed these lines of conflict and sources of infiltration, giving shape to already existing local suspicions. Of all of these revelations, Wataita were especially impressed by the sheer quantity of majini kept in Taita, a fact that was further proof, if any was needed, of Taita's infiltration by foreign, commercializing forces.

A Witch to Beat All Witches

Wataita were originally compelled by the fact that Maji Marefu's work was to be public, and so everyone would witness the true dynamics that underlay Taita society—processes of occlusion and blockage that inhibited persons from realizing their projects and capacities. It was said that, at the end of Maji Marefu's stay, all the community's witches would be called to his house by mystical means and would watch as their occult items were burned in a bonfire. However, when Maji Marefu actually arrived in Taita, he and his entourage spent very little of their overall work time going from house to house. The main source of their daily income seemed to come from their private practice, in which individuals came to them for protection or for various charms. This private aspect of Maji Marefu's work was somewhat in conflict with the public demonstrations, for several reasons. First, the fact that people were purchasing cures suggested that Maji Marefu's visit was not eradicating witchcraft at all, but at best introducing new forms of defense that were certain to generate more virulent forms of attack in the future. Second, this private work consisted in a new form of secrecy, in that only buyer and seller knew exactly what was being transacted. This liberalized circulation of occult material was potentially more dangerous than inherited witchcraft because it was available to anyone who could afford it, and Maji Marefu had no obvious loyalties to anyone in the area. Indeed, many people expressed a hope that Maji Marefu would marry and settle locally, the implication being that he would then have a vested interest in protecting the community.

Thus, while in the beginning Maji Marefu's visit had been supported by a wide swathe of the population, young and old alike, as time went on a certain polarizing sociology became discernible, as the witch hunt took on the character of a youth movement directed at the very aged, the comparatively wealthy and powerful, and the female heads of matricentric families. Moreover, the development rhetoric Maji Marefu deployed daily was easily directed against the old, an image assisted by their possession of the symbols of global youth culture (low-hanging denim jeans and video cameras) and their mastery of divinatory objects that resembled global information technologies. Maji Marefu's mission drew attention to endemic generational tension, implying that their elders' diversion of wealth was dependent on, and synonymous with, nocturnal occult activities. As it turned out, the objects and implements Maji Marefu swept from households were very often ritual objects associated with the progression of senior men through the male status hierarchy. Among these were household "shrines" (*milimu*), through which elders and ancestors have long communicated with one another; through these objects, individual households have long been wedded to larger social formations extending over space and across time (cf. Harris 1978). These objects, which once ensured and produced public wealth and prestige, are now widely considered demonic artifacts that allow seniors to keep others behind.

As accusations escalated, and as more people were accused of harboring some form of witchcraft, Wataita became concerned about the social discord that Maji Marefu was fomenting, pitting sons against fathers and neighbors against neighbors, only to leave unscathed and rich at the end of the day. Adult men and women began to suspect that Maji Marefu was making a fool of them, a possibility that religious leaders expanded upon in their weekly sermons against this witch-hunting craze. Moreover, perhaps in an effort to encourage the sense of emergency, Maji Marefu discovered several new witches in a day, marking them with an ash crucifix on the forehead and forbidding them, on pain of death, to return to their sorcery. As one woman protested at a baraza, "He is accusing people without plan or purpose!" (in Swahili, *Anachora watu hivi hivi!*). Soon he acquired telling nicknames, like *Maji Moto* (hot water) and *Maji Magumu* (rough waters), and he came to be known as the *Mchawi wa Wachawi*, the witch to beat all witches. His larger-than-life status took on a nefarious, if predictable, twist: he and his imported youth were ravenous, greedy consumers of local resources, eating countless chickens and eggs in a day (expensive foods, reserved for special occasions). They drowned themselves in beer, regardless of their purported ties to Islam, and were often drunk and disorderly; they took up with local women, some of whom were said to have been impregnated. Moreover, the actual Maji Marefu was almost always gone on some errand in Mombasa or Nairobi, and he left his reckless sons to carry on his work of sweeping in his absence. These empowered youth came to be seen by many as unruly, promiscuous, and immoral, in addition to being paranormally powerful. The mission also charged inordinate amounts for private consultations, some people giving as much as $US100 to have a curse or some other form of sorcery removed from them. Each day people lined up outside Maji Marefu's house, bearing chickens, cows, eggs—whatever they could afford to hand over as payment. They even tried to pay off their debts by becoming his workers, laboring in the kitchen and taking care of the laundry.

Inside the witch-finder's house, visitors sat in the open, receiving instruction in relatively benign forms of magic, like love potions and other beneficent charms. In Maji Marefu's own room, where he saw the afflicted, empty Coca Cola bottles could be found filled with resins and powders, along with numerous gourds and calabashes, fly whisks, magnifying glasses, and small mirrors used to conjure up visual images of witches. Outside, Maji Marefu's younger apprentices milled about, consulting with visitors and customers. Sometimes they gathered to admire the photographs they took of themselves "cleaning households" each week, for the rituals had become spectacles. Young women from the neighborhood, who came to be known as the "wives" of Maji Marefu's sons, filled the kitchen in a seemingly eternal process of food preparation. Sometimes Maji Marefu walked about the house, boasting before the assembled patients of his power and declaring that those who wanted to be healed should "Bring money now!" (*Leta pesa saa hii!*). So much for the mythic charter that suggested his mission was divinely inspired, despite the mission's resemblance to a rural medical clinic.

As people waited for treatment, they watched others receive cures that often seemed abusive. For example, I recall watching an old man sit on a pile of rocks while young men hurled raw eggs at his head; as the yolks dripped down his face, he muttered appreciatively, "True . . . True" (*Kweli . . . Kweli*)—perhaps a better translation is "real." The truth this senior male experienced may have had something to do with his sense that treatment made him impervious after a long period of feeling vulnerable to the jealousy of others. For like the witch hunt itself, the public nature of these cures and the way in which Maji Marefu exposed the formerly esoteric mechanics of indigenous witchcraft to the crowd was part and parcel of the democratization of Taita social life that he purported to effect. However, his cures were themselves a form of occultism, even violence, and many Wataita believed that there was something dangerous about the open proliferation of such practices in public view.

Of course, the members of the Maji Marefu Mission had a different view of their actions. In their discussions with me, they tended to speak as if they were surrounded by witches and that they lived in a constant state of struggle with invisible, local forces that were working to sabotage their divine efforts. As one of Maji Marefu's sons put it to me, "What we are doing is true, and the old man's power comes from God. These people are living in fear, but by the time we leave it will be over. You see what we have found here? The place you are sitting right now, this room you are in, it is filled with dangerous waste! But here it is contained. And we will contain this whole place, because it is God's will. But it will only happen if He sees that these people really want to change." This idea of containment resonated with Taita thought and was reiterated in Maji Marefu's healing rituals, which concentrated, in recognizable ways, on the reconstruction of violated physical borders. For instance, he or his sons would wrap rope around an allegedly bewitched client, surround her with a shield of smoke, and slowly pass an egg over her naked body, pressing it against certain ash-designated points that are understood to be particularly vulnerable to infiltration: in particular, the head, heart, groin, knees, and feet. Here the rope became a shield against sorcery, a method, often referred to as "closing," or *kufunga* in Kiswahili, common among diviners throughout this region. The egg, a locally recognized image of birth and rebirth, was then cast aside or thrown against the victim's head, dispelling the offending disease and allowing for positive regeneration. The egg was equated with the bewitched self; if it cracked open when pressed against the person, it indicated the point where witchcraft had impregnated the body. On the other hand, a whole raw egg thrown and broken against the head of a cured man (as in the case of the old man depicted above) demonstrated the new imperviousness of the reconstituted self.

Despite this culturally resonant talk and imagery, Maji Marefu Mission eventually came to epitomize for locals the practices and behavior they were hired to banish, and their youthful worldliness, once a boon, became proof of their cynical intent. It certainly did not help that Maji Marefu was collecting confiscated occult materials in his house, anticipating a future date when all of the witches would be called to watch as their evil instruments burned in a single conflagration. As the house progressively filled with this "hot" and widely feared cargo, it seemed increasingly clear that Taita was making Maji Marefu more powerful in his witchcraft. Debates raged over whether this foreigner was capable of handling his affairs with transparency, a term that deliberately reiterated the multiparty democratic rhetoric of Kenya's political "opposition." Critics invoked the stuffing of ballots and other forms of electoral fraud when they argued that witches were "rigging" the outcome of the exorcism by buying back their occult materials from the witch-finder. For some, Maji Marefu came to personify the cultural and economic ascendance of Tanzania over Kenya and Taita, for in expropriating local wealth and diverting it, presumably to his home in Tanzania, he enacted in microcosm Tanzania's apparent enrichment at the expense of the Taita economy under neoliberal conditions.

The witch-finder's dangerous implications were highlighted by the threat that seemed to underlay his work, for he would invariably inform all who consulted him that they were bewitched, and that the failure to submit to an expensive cure would culminate in the death of themselves or loved ones. In at least one instance, he publicly threatened to use his occult powers to kill a man who owed him money for a cure. Soon people began to speak ominously about the conditions obtaining in the villages Maji Marefu had left behind: people who had been marked as witches had returned to their forbidden practices with deadly results. Families had been split apart, it was said, and people lost employment and committed suicide; communities were left without transport and everyday comestibles because the majini that had run the vehicles and the shops had been expunged. Certainly Wataita would rue the day that they had invited this foreign witch to come and take the money of a people too foolish and contentious to solve their own problems. Ironically, these doubts and accusations reinforced the general idea that Wataita needed to revitalize local boundaries, develop a self-identity, and encourage a self-sustaining development based on local language and values: the very things whose efflorescence Maji Marefu's visit was supposed to produce.

According to the local Catholic priests, Maji Marefu's "marking" of alleged witches was in fact satanic initiation, the means through which he intended to secretly transform Taita into a branch of the Satanic Church. The priests railed against villagers for their "return" to satanic practices, and they punished the community by silencing the church choir for the duration of Maji Marefu's stay. Some even refused sacrament to those who visited or donated money to the mission, and together the priests brought the archbishop from Mombasa to lend weight to their pronouncements. Wataita had to take a stand, to come out either on the side of Christianity or backward traditionalism, and the priests would force their parishioners to a conclusion by withholding grace. In the beginning, opponents of Maji Marefu, even priests, were publicly shouted down and sometimes threatened by the vast majority (in some cases, villagers left sacrificed goats in front of the church during the night, which the priests claimed was an act of witchcraft). However, by the time Maji Marefu Mission had been at work for two months, the priests' prediction that they would sow disunity and violence seemed vindicated. At least two marked people had committed suicide, a few had lost their jobs, and many more were shunned in various ways, with significant material consequences.

The idea that Taita had been invaded by a gang of witch-criminals was powerfully argued by the town's educated elite, virtually all of whom had been marked by Maji Marefu's group. They complained to state authorities in writing about the police's inability to control this new criminal menace and proclaimed that, in the absence of real government, the backward, criminalized masses were tyrannizing people. This letter, written to a district commissioner, calls for the state to reinstate the very cultural boundaries that Maji Marefu's visit was intended to revitalize.

> Dear Sir,
>
> As from 11th February 1998, a group known as "Maji Marefu" composed of a traditional witchdoctor said to be coming from Tanzania and some members of the community... has been moving into people's homes with the pretext to search homes for sorcery items and charms. In the process, people are being harassed, sometimes beaten and threatened with death, particularly if they do not pay money to the said witchdoctor and the "Maji Marefu" committee....
>
> I would like to inform you Sir, that the named "Maji Marefu" wave has become a great security concern to the lives and property of the people here. More so, given that the ring leader... is a person of very active criminal record who is indeed out of the prisons through the Presidential clemency....[5]
>
> Unfortunately the area Chief and Asst. Chief appear to have failed to contain this state of affairs, possibly out of fear for death.
>
> I do humbly request you to intervene and arrest the situation before it is too late.

Here an ordinary citizen invokes the concepts of security and private property rights to prompt the state, through its local representatives, into action. Another letter, written by an accused witch to the chairman of a town's Maji Marefu committee expands on the theme:

Dear Sir:

> I have gathered from sources quite reliable that on 12th February 1998 . . . you did lead a group of an unknown number of people, accompanied by a sorcerer/witchdoctor by the business name of Maji Marefu to come to my home through my shamba [agricultural plot].
>
> I am made to believe that your missionman the Maji Marefu later cut his way through my fence behind my kitchen and declared that he had seen moving objects (two) come out from behind the house of my parents . . . According to you and your witchdoctor therefore my father is a wizard. Sir, on the basis of this name calling my children were subjected to a lot of harassment by the children of some of your followers, a situation that has likely caused a lot of psychological damage to my children. . . .
>
> The purpose of this letter is therefore to notify you that I am preparing to resort to legal action against you and your Committee for redress of this matter in the court of law as indeed I feel my freedom of worship here has greatly been infringed [that is, his freedom to worship Christianity, which he is contrasting to the alleged paganism/Satanism of the Maji Marefu Committee and the Maji Marefu Mission] and my father is now suffering defamation in addition to your group having trespassed over my legally owned property.

Here, Maji Marefu's mission is said to be a violation of rights to privacy, property, and freedom of beliefs, perpetuated by a gang of opportunists with no material evidence; in sum, a violation of the law and the terms of empirical reason. But the supporters of Maji Marefu were not backward illiterates, and they called forth their own leaders to persuasively argue their points. Thus, the accused respondent to the first letter proved equally adept in rarefied legalese, as he painstakingly described the structure, origin, and rationale for the so-called Maji Marefu committees. This chair of a village development committee, who was also an outspoken defender of multiparty democracy and an aspiring political figure, deployed notions of universal human rights, international law, and the moral preeminence of written constitutions to argue for his community's internationally recognized right to hire the likes of Maji Marefu to locate witches. In so doing, he signaled his membership in an international community of right-bearing citizens while also asserting his village's internationally recognized right to be different—to possess a unique identity and hence a unique method for solving social problems, guaranteed by a law more real than that of the state. First, he lays out the witch-finder's democratically allotted mandate:

> On Sunday 11/1/1998 a Baraza was called for all residents of Xxx village to attend, you inclusive. The agenda of the meeting was "Maji Marefu". After a lengthy discussion, all who attended voted and passed a resolution that they wanted "Maji Marefu" to come and visit every home in Xxx to get rid of any article of sorcery and anything else to do with evil spirits.... An interim financial sub-committee was elected to manage the funds in which I was elected Chairman. Our duty ended with the deliverance of the funds to Maji Marefu on 7/2/1998. From this last activity Maji Marefu had the mandate of all Xxx residents through a majority vote to perform his duty. Thus there is no Maji Marefu Committee.

There was no Maji Marefu committee because Maji Marefu embodied the collective wishes of the populace. Operating under the assumption that witchcraft is real, and not simply an idea, the author goes on to argue that whatever rights this man may have are abrogated if his actions are believed to violate the public good, which the nonexistent Maji Marefu committee seeks to uphold:

> As regards your constitutional rights being infringed as a Christian, I wish to state the following. Like other democratic constitutions, the Kenya Constitution also provides the fundamental rights and freedoms of the individual.... The compulsory search of an Individual's person or property and entry by others on his premises is not permitted.
>
> But here also there are certain necessary exceptions to this rule, e.g.,
>
> i. Searches required in the interest of defence.
> ii. Searches required for public safety and
> iii. Searches required for the purpose of promoting the rights and freedoms of other persons....
>
> I leave it to you yourself to decide into which category your case falls.

These arguments about a Tanzanian witch-hunter invoke constitutions that did not seem to exist at the time, as well as abstract concepts of natural right and democracy that, to an outsider, would seem to have had little real purchase in Kenyan daily life. But these arguments were one of the many avenues through which these abstract concepts and categories were made real for people on the ground. Thus a state condemned in practice was resuscitated in the moral imagination, and legal fictions were held to be more real than social facts. In this debate, the state acted as a nonplayer—at least, until pushed—failing to respond directly to any who addressed it. Yet this absence did not prevent accusers and accused from conjuring it up out of the ether as a jural fiction, and giving more reality to its fetish forms—to the state's representation of itself to itself—than to the actual "working" state as institutional form.

Government officials and NGOs were now rallying against the idea of Maji Marefu. At public barazas, government extension officers warned that the Maji Marefu craze had drawn curious farmers from their agricultural plots and that the community was in danger of missing its next harvest, because of people's failure to plant during the appropriate season. For a while, local authorities deferred on the issue of Maji Marefu's legitimacy, as each office of government passed responsibility for the matter to others, failing to respond to persistent queries concerning the legal status of his work (e.g., "Did Maji Marefu have a work permit?"). The chiefs claimed not to know; they felt that such a decision was beyond their power and did not really fall under the state's jurisdiction. One chief suggested that Maji Marefu was a "traditional healer," and therefore a work permit would have to come from the Kenya African Medical Research Institute, not the local administration. This attention to documentation demonstrated a certain meticulousness with respect to law and state functions, as well as a wariness about the public's perception of events.

But eventually the state, reconceptualized as an authoritative institution, was invoked against Maji Marefu, culminating in his arrest. For after numerous complaints, the district officer gave the order to detain Maji Marefu, and the police entered his rented house during his absence, arresting his five sons for trespassing. The young men spent three days in jail in the large lowland town of Voi and were ordered by the judge to desist from publicly accusing citizens of bewitching each other. Afterward, they were allowed to return to the village, which they did, but to limit their activity to private consultations. And so some elements of this Taita community seemed to partially succeed in domesticating the dangers of globalization by forcing Maji Marefu to submit to the authority of Taita locality—or at least to a local government goaded into action. Furthermore, the local Catholic priest took the opportunity afforded by Maji Marefu's arrest to invite the archbishop from Mombasa to visit Taita. On a Sunday afternoon they called priests from neighboring villages, and

FIGURES 7 AND 8. The priests and the archbishop burn the occult materials collected by Maji Marefu.

hundreds of people watched as together all of the priests broke into Maji Marefu's rented house, gathered the alleged occult materials, and burned them in a public ceremony complete with a Catholic mass (see figures 7 and 8). In so doing, the priests hoped to reestablish the Catholic Church's monopoly on Taita spiritual life, although in burning the confiscated paraphernalia they also reaffirmed the reality of witchcraft and the truth of Maji Marefu's accusations. Nonetheless, in their sermons, the priest and archbishop depicted themselves as steering Taita toward enlightenment, implying that this condition entailed the victory of Christianity over what they referred to as traditional occultism. Some irony was evident in this depiction, because in private the priests held that the burned items were not witchcraft and were in fact the customary ritual implements of elder men. This dissonance they regarded as pure serendipity, arguing that their destruction would hasten Taita's evolution toward full Christian rectitude and away from the secret practice of traditional religion.

Conclusion

As noted earlier, Wataita have long sought to retain a sense of Taita uniqueness while appropriating needed things and values from outside, and this particular strategy is the product of colonial and postcolonial history, combined with Taita's particular social geography. The insight of the Maji Marefu "project" lay in its attempt to resolve the problem of particularity and universality that has long been central to Taita experience and history. The people who hired Maji Marefu sought to preserve aspects of Taita's particularity against foreign threat (and thus against a kind of universalization), and in order to protect this particular they felt that they needed access to a universal, and so chose to hire a group that (1) claimed to be able to expunge all forms of witchcraft regardless of where they were from, (2) resembled a foreign NGO and a government bureaucracy, and (3) employed universalizing techniques and technologies that referenced science as an idea. Of course, there was nothing truly universal about the Maji Marefu Mission, as its provenance and symbolic usages were highly particular. But through this controlled and powerful amalgamation of local and foreign capacities, old and new, Wataita sought to control the terms of their connection to the world while reconceptualizing schools, Christianity, and roads as aspects of their cultural and historical heritage as Taita people, rather than as foreign interventions (see also White 2004 and Ngwane 2004 on this paradoxical temporal aspect of neoliberal rupture).

Again, the event revealed that, for Wataita, development was not synonymous with the universal, but rather entailed managing the particular and the universal and creating a productive synthesis of both, thereby transcending the distinction. But such transcendence turned out to be impossible because of the irreducibility of particularity and because Maji Marefu's revelation of multiple layers of difference came to be seen as divisive. The paradox of Maji Marefu's work was that his approach to development was to act on local dispositions and to regard these dispositions in terms of absolutes, which then dissolved in the face of multiple lines of social cleavage. As a result, Wataita began to conceptualize Maji Marefu as a threat to development and conjured up a legal-bureaucratic order based on literacy that was at once universal (based on allegedly universal ideas of human rights, for example) and particular (literacy and education were aspects of Taita's historical-cultural heritage). His visit thus suggested that the forms and procedures of the state have become a conceptual resource for emerging publics at the same time as the formerly localized discourse about witchcraft has been projected to the national level. In the end, the Catholic Church used the experience to assert its own challenged universality against two particular threats, one foreign (Maji Marefu) and the other domestic (senior men and their rituals).

Perhaps then it was not so much that Maji Marefu failed, but that his success created a paradox, in that by demonstrating the ubiquity of witchcraft, he left people with no alternative solutions and a great deal of resentment (cf. Niehaus 2001). In this sense, the promising idea of witch eradication was constrained by material reality—the fact that the accused still had to live with their accusers and that, in the absence of a genuine transformation of social conditions, people had no other means of relieving tensions born of economic blight. Thus they were certain to return to their bewitching, risking the threat of Maji Marefu's deadly curse. Yet Maji Marefu's mission also spoke tellingly of the power of ideas to construct reality. Here the notions of sustainable local development, moral modernity, and rational statehood that were finally deployed against him suggest something in the making. Wataita resurrected these otiose fragments and assembled them against the witch-finder, the new personification of their demons, who in turn proved that they already inhabited, at least conceptually, the modernity they so desperately sought—this despite their disconnection from the global flows of wealth and power. On the other hand, the theatrical dimension of Maji Marefu's work deployed metaphor and performance to demonstrate the absurdity of things, thus inciting people to reflect on taken-for-granted associations and assumptions, such as the equation of schooling and school-educated elites with development. This aspect was carnivalesque and anarchic, for in a spirit of ironic laughter and relativism the absurdity of elite pretension was performed before a bemused public.

CHAPTER EIGHT

Conclusion: Tempopolitics, Or Why Development Should Not Be Defined as the Improvement of Living Standards

That twentieth century development discourse depoliticized politics is only part of its problem. Perhaps the more important problem is that it tried to make a politics out of the perpetuation of simple life itself, and in this way identified people's animal nature as the beginning and end of their humanity. In doing so, development discourse has defined the people of the world subsequently known as "third" as animal objects of pity, contempt, and experimentation. This dynamic was made very clear to me early on in my research when a development-oriented Peace Corps volunteer responded to my offhand comment that Taita people were fascinating by asserting that everything they did was a mere adaptation to circumstance: "They're poor. What's so fascinating about that?" she demanded. But as critic of contemporary human rights discourse and liberal "ethics" Alain Badiou (1992) has argued, what defines human beings, and what must be at the heart of any genuine politics, is not their biological life but their occasional refusal of life: their capacity to reject the relentless daily rhythm and logic of "things as they are" in pursuit of something immortal, or that which defies experience and sense—that is, their ability to follow through on a new, dangerous idea.

In his writings on the African postcolony, Achille Mbembe has referred to the everyday, tautological flows of interests, posturings, mimicries, necessities, and abuses as the "banality of power," but his analysis offers little alternative to this convivial mire of abuse and deceit, and his sophisticated work risks lending itself to an admittedly partial reading: namely, that it is indeed the animal nature of Africans that determines their existence (Mbembe 1992). The evidence provided in this book, if read in the optimistic mode that I think it should be read, suggests that Wataita, and Kenyans as a whole, conceptualized development as a refusal of the norms of daily life and saw refusal as the prerequisite for a genuine improvement of their lives. If the postcolony is a "system of signs," as Mbembe (2001, 102) suggests, then Kenyan development work appropriates its most compelling and conflictual—indeed, its master—trope, and tries to make it real through practical actions.

The Pentecostal searching for some new truth, the young men who came up against established authority structures and demanded an accounting, the townspeople who thought that, by hiring a witch-hunter they could exercise control over established forces that were running them into the ground, the ritual specialists who felt they could curb an unfettered modernity by redeeming the past, their critics who took their mandate seriously and took them to task as poseurs, and the young women who felt themselves possessed (whether because that was the only way they felt they could express themselves or because their actual possession by others in real life erupted from their bodies in this particular form) all found themselves irritated by a truth until they felt something needed to be done, and many (though by no means all) of them did so against the noise of public opinion and the bruteness of daily life. The articulation of an inchoate truth, and not the perpetuation of life itself (or the nihilistic, and totally uninteresting if taken only by itself, improvement of living standards), catalyzed their actions. Admittedly, many of their efforts were derailed by the realities of daily life: people were taken advantage of, or they found their efforts to be misguided in their implementation, or they found themselves misunderstood, and became cynical, alcoholic, or corrupt. But none of these obstacles kept people in general from reaffirming their genuine human, immortal life in their stubborn decision to try something else, very often taking advantage of the implosion of the state and its attendant model of development.

But how do we know that these acts of refusal do anything more than reproduce dominant logics (the politics of the belly, the regime of the phallus, or some other such hegemony)? Indeed, at various points in the text I have suggested that the things that people did in the name of change often ended up reinscribing them in a new regime of power relations, which I have identified as neoliberal. Pentecostalism glorified the transcendent individual and encouraged entrepreneurialism in the wake of state downsizing and formal sector decline. The pervasive interest in identifying a heritage that was flexible and useful harmonized with capitalism's need for flexible, partly rooted, and largely mobile people, who could be both at home and away from home depending on the needs of capital (which is to say, the requirements of brute life in itself). The idea that development was the responsibility of individuals made it a function of choice and personal grit, and so drew attention away from political abuse and economic inequality. The notion that people were responsible for governing themselves and that they should therefore take over the state's function of regulating and accounting for their practices by themselves transformed all people into human resources and arguably extended government into new dimensions of life, such as the household and intergenerational relations: read kinship.

All of these notions can be convincingly argued, but the problem is that such analyses presume a temporal trajectory that extends into the future and whose outcome can be predicted. What I have identified is a dialectic of refusal and reconstitution that is inchoate and ongoing. As Foucault (1990) argued, the potential exists in any act of resistance for the transformation and reconstitution of power, and these processes of resistance and realignment are simultaneous. Outcomes cannot be known, except to say that, in facilitating new collaborations with power, each act of resistance also extends beyond itself and suggests a line of action that builds upon the initial refusal, in relation to new elaborations of power and governance. I hold, in short, that in any specific African context, an intensity of moral debate and action, coupled with efforts to construct viable moral and social boundaries, can mitigate the impact of violence, greed, and death from outside. We discern inchoate change whenever we closely examine how people live on the ground and how people have worked to make sense of and control putatively rationalizing processes, such as state and market expansion and decline. It is only through such close ethnography that we can see politics in Africa as an exciting moral drama in which original efforts to produce social justice and development are fueled by the injustice and maldevelopment of corrupt regimes, and flourish because of the incompleteness of any single governing authority.

Thinkers such as Mbembe, Bayart, and Chabal and Daloz have worked to identify African forms of power and governance that are different from those that emerged in modern Europe, offering such concepts as "the politics of the belly," "the criminalization of the state," "the post-colony," and "the necropolitical" to argue for a political history of Africa grounded in African experiences. In particular, their analyses demonstrate the Eurocentrism of such concepts as "biopower," or governance aimed at "the administration of bodies and the calculated management of life" (Foucault 1990, 140). However, these authors also rely on ideal-typical arguments that, like all typologies, allow the part to stand for the whole, because the models do not always emerge from close, ethnographic analyses of grounded, everyday practices. Therefore they are hard pressed to account for a great many things that are happening in the social field, where people work to construct moral and social order out of conflict and to bring powerful exogenous forces under control for the social good. Moreover, in many ways Europe remains central to their analyses, and Africa continues to be understood in largely antithetical terms: for example, Mbembe offers the concept of a postcolonial necropolitics, or the organization of life and meaning around the pursuit of death, partly to suggest an alternative to the idea of biopolitics, and suggests that the emergence of biopolitics and necropolitics were historically coeval and depended on one another (in this, to be sure, he offers a great advance by suggesting a political economy of extraction that would make sense of the emergence of European biopolitics in ways that Foucault did not). The reflexive orientation to Europe is also suggested by the underlying theme of scarcity in most of these works: as Mbembe puts it, "the post-colony is characterized above all by scarcity" and this condition accounts for the "tendency to excess and lack of proportion" (Mbembe 2001, 130) in African life and politics (theatrical self-inflation, violence, publicized virility, and gluttony). Similarly, Bayart's (1993) politics of the belly is largely an adaptation to scarcity and to the fact that Africans have been compelled to negotiate undemocratic and complexly interlaced institutions, such as slavery, indirect rule, and, more recently, governments that are losing their power to control as the result of bankruptcy. In *Africa Works*, Chabal and Daloz (1999) similarly argue that the apparently dysfunctional features of African politics function in a situation defined by scarcity by producing dependency on political patrons, who have an interest in perpetuating disorder so as to expand their own position by building client networks.

I take seriously the contention of all of these scholars that we must completely rid ourselves of the prevailing discourse of lack that characterizes African studies by keeping our eyes closely fixed on the positive, future-oriented actions of people on the ground. In closing, I suggest that part of what is unique in African social and political life is the degree to which it is dominated by a tempopolitics and a tempomorality that has come to shape meaningful action, which sometimes goes under the name "development." Colonial tempopolitics depended entirely on the idea of African backwardness and on the hegemony of the notion of unlinear progress; furthermore, it was focally concerned with managing world history as it appeared to be reenacted, at breakneck speed, in particular places. I refer here to the problem, to which late colonial Kenyan administrators and academics endlessly drew attention, of introducing superstitious neolithic peoples who had "not yet advanced to the stage of the wheel" to the mid-twentieth century without creating anomie and criminality. Late colonial development projects were, in part, experiments in the regulation of historical time, which simultaneously tried to fix people in particular times (such as the traditional past) or to move them through historical time in a regulated manner. For colonial officials, resistance to state-managed development was a symptom of overly rapid mutation or atavistic indolence in the face of the inevitable, and was synonymous with "witchcraft and savagery." So colonial officials tended to address resistance to their project from within the idiom of witchcraft (hence the colonial government's decision to hire witch doctors to cleanse Mau Mau insurgents of their oath of loyalty as a prelude to reintroducing them into "normal" society; see chapter 1), and thus originated the state governmental practice of deploying witchcraft as a field of knowledge in an attempt to govern threats to its sovereignty. Now, diverse local communities deploy concepts of witchcraft as a field of knowledge to catalyze and safeguard their emerging sovereignty, sometimes against the state and some times in collusion with it.

In Kenya and many other colonies, the state's efforts to govern through the regulation and normalization of historical time, and of people in historical time, took place in and through concrete spaces and took the form of trying to control the movement of Africans in space. These governing and development efforts had the effect of creating the appearance of multiple historical times existing in what was in fact a single spatiotemporal arena. Thus, understandings of natural temporal process, separate development, and the intrinsic opposition between tradition and modernity undergirded the colonial and postcolonial political orders and the emergence of the dual forms of governance (i.e., subjection and citizenship) to which Mahmood Mamdani (1996) and others have drawn attention. Colonial and postcolonial tempopolitics participated in the idea of biopolitics in its stated effort to manage populations and to thereby depoliticize governance, by making sure that change, or modernization, occurred at the "correct" rate. However, the real substance of this tempopolitics, on the ground, emerged from the fact that "true" biopolitics never emerged in the colony or the postcolony and that authoritarian indirect rule and exclusion came to be the primary instruments of governance, augmented by educational systems that castigated tradition and promised a select few salvation from incarceration in spaces of exception that were equated with the past. The fact that Africans were excluded from full participation in the life of the city meant that they were compelled to continue and extend their links with rural kin in ways that seemed, to Africans, to be reproducing the past under new conditions.

Structural adjustment programs disrupted colonial and postcolonial tempopolitics by sabotaging the power of chiefs and undermining the moral and economic effectivity of schools while simultaneously precipitating a rapid set of changes that were not easily regulated by the established spatial control mechanisms (such as national territorial boundaries and the regulatory power of "traditional" ritual and political authorities). Globalization and neoliberalism catalyzed new eruptions of tempopolitics, as the spatialized past becomes a useful conceptual and economic resource as well as a potential source of moral and political sovereignty. Neotraditionalist movements and other such experiments in autochthony have emerged in the fissures of the old tempopolitics, resisting old teleologies and positing new ones while still staying firmly grounded in dominant historical narratives and in the overall commitment to managing the flow of historical time and people in time. These movements (such as Mungiki) reject dominant assumptions about the positive value of particular temporal trajectories and assert new models of progress that emerge from a retracing of abandoned temporal avenues or a close inspection of how current ones became corrupted.

Understanding tempopolitics offers us an entry point into understanding African actions as part of this ongoing struggle over the meaning and value of history, which takes place under changing structural conditions. Indeed, many scholars have drawn attention to African tempopolitics in various ways. To take one example, James Ferguson (1994) has shown how senior Lesotho men, forbidden from remaining in apartheid South Africa, invested in livestock in an effort to forge social networks with other men upon retirement; their sons and wives often drew attention to their putative traditionalism in the hopes that they would convert some of this livestock into money. In doing so, all of these people were participating in tempopolitics by simultaneously resisting and reinscribing the dominant form of time management set in force by the apartheid regime (where apartheid literally means separate development, or multiple, mutually exclusive, historical trajectories in a single time). These dominant temporal logics were perpetuated and challenged in terms of historical time (the way things used to be done in the past versus the way they should be done in the present day). Similarly, Zambian migrant laborers in the 1990s felt as if they were submitting to the past when they returned home from a city that had failed them, and were forced to learn how to hold themselves accordingly; thus they experienced economic decline and social restriction in terms of backward temporal movement, but not always in a negative way (Ferguson 1999). None of this is meant to say that a single African tempopolitical form or trajectory exists. In Congo, for example, the extractive logic of rapid expenditure dating back to the colonial period has led to total annihilation (or, over the longue duree, cycles of liminal destruction and temporary reaggregation around evanescent resources), which orients people toward fantasies of permanence and long-term continuity (roads, houses, minerals) in opposition to a cannibalistic politics that, in destroying everything enduring, creates the sense of an eternal present.

The witch figures significantly in tempopolitics, or efforts to manage the flow of historical time to create alternative futures, partly because witches meddle in time, imploding spatial and temporal constraints in ways that are destructive to everyone. They also preempt inchoate life from developing in a natural way when they kill children or prevent childbirth in exchange for rapidly extinguished cash and when they prevent other people from carrying out their various life projects to fruition. Controlling witchcraft therefore also implies establishing control over temporal processes within a particular space in order to have development. We can thus begin to understand the futures that people work to create on the ground by interpreting these representations of the forces that sabotage their visions of order. The idea of the witch operates in tandem with others, such as that of the criminal, with which it often overlaps. The concept of witchcraft is a fecund source of the political imagination because it is both fluid and fixing, responding to new situations while locating badness in particular places and in particular kinds of activities. In this way, witchcraft directs and orients the search for truth even if Western observers see it as based, ultimately, on a falsehood. Moreover, in the process of controlling witchcraft, Kenyans also work to bring the embattled and often absurd sign "development" under social control, all the while creating communities and networks around the idea.

Notes

Preface

1. Kenyatta's government agreed to purchase settler land at inflated prices, borrowing from the British to do so (cf. Leys 1978).

Chapter One

1. I have placed Ferguson in this category because of his groundbreaking, partly deconstructive work on development in his *The Anti-Politics Machine: "Development," Depoliticization, and Bureaucratic Power in Lesotho* (1994). But this is no doubt too reductionist: Although in this book he criticized what he called "the development apparatus" in Foucauldian terms, he was also among the first to point out that Africans on the ground remain very interested in development. His chapter on the bovine mystique, for example, shows how socially differentiated groups of people in Lesotho (senior men, youth, and women, for example) appropriate and redeploy the terms of development institutions (such as the idea of backward senior men) in their material and symbolic struggles to acquire the support of developers. In many ways, this book continues Ferguson's line of inquiry, in a somewhat different register.

2. A perfect example is James Scott's *Seeing Like a State*, which was published in 1998.

3. A number of scholars have picked up this theme and begun to examine development as an indigenized and domesticated discourse that has taken on a new life in postcolonial societies, partly detached from its original historical antecedents (see, for example, Stacey Leigh Pigg on Nepal 1992). But in general scholars seem uncertain as to what to make of the indigenization of development, for the idea of a derivative discourse and elite false consciousness continue to plague academic understandings of the issue. Laura Ahearn's (2001) analysis of

Nepalese youths' love letters is the most interesting and relevant exception I know of, for she examines how the concept of romantic love, something not ordinarily associated with development, has been the vehicle of modernization, and Western values, in Nepal. What makes Ahearn's analysis most compelling is the suggestion that social change occurs at the level of people's emotions and desires in ways that the actors involved do not suspect or plan, and that the multiplication of these private feelings and relationships has the capacity to tear through, and transform, entrenched social hierarchies and codes of conduct.

4. Most Kenyans today say that witchcraft is a kind of devil worship, but it can equally be said that devil worship is a kind of witchcraft, as Kenyan ideas about devil worship simply reference a more advanced and modern form of witchcraft.

5. The psychologist J. C. Carothers drew a parallel between Mau Mau occultism in 1950s Kenya and European occultism in the 1600s: what motivated both early modern Europeans and late colonial Africans to worship Satan was "a desire to achieve some personal aim which they could not achieve within the righteous social framework of their time" (Carothers 1954, 15).

6. See, for example, Carothers (1954, 16): "Jomo Kenyatta is very certain to have made some study of European witchcraft; he had the opportunity, and it is easy to imagine more than one incentive. . . . The writer thinks, especially in view of the separate application of certain types of oath to different sectors of the population, that the broad outlines of the oath were conceived by highly sophisticated persons."

7. This anxiety owed much to the British historical experience of lost pastoral innocence, which now seemed to be repeating itself in late colonial Africa (cf. Williams 1977).

8. This system was especially open to corruption, and much Harambee money went unaccounted for (Holmquist 1972, Haugerud 1995, Throup and Hornsby 1998), such that today most Kenyans view Harambee as a great idea that was poisoned by unscrupulous politicians. Like most development strategies, it did not generally serve to ameliorate social inequities, and often entrenched them. In addition, the Harambee system helped the Kenya African National Union to consolidate its power, as individuals who alienated themselves from the sources of power found themselves cut off from public funds and correspondingly unable to contribute large gifts to harambees.

9. Nyayo, or footsteps, was originally coined by President Moi when his position was challenged from within the government, to communicate that he did not intend to deviate from the development and political strategies of his predecessor, the late Jomo Kenyatta. However, as Angelique Haugerud (1995) reminds us, the term took on new meanings as the state became more repressive after the abortive coup of 1982.

10. In truth, Kenya's economic crisis had begun in the 1970s, when falling prices for coffee and the rising cost of oil resulted in progressive indebtedness.

Chapter Two

1. Wataita had different perspectives on the origin and meaning of these pet names. Most people who professed to know anything about the subject claimed that the current usage began relatively recently, within the past twenty or thirty years, and that prior to that the terms were used only between blood brothers and affinal kin. People had different explanations for the change: some claimed that nearly everyone was related to everyone else anyway, and people had increasingly forgotten how exactly, and to whom, so it was no use being too stringent about rules. Others claimed that the usage changed as the result of wage labor in cities, as Wataita came to live in predominantly Taita neighborhoods and used the terms to identify each other as fellow kinsmen sharing a bond of ethnicity. In this case, young men were using names such as Aβongo, or man of brain, that were formerly reserved for senior men, who were the only people actually allowed to eat brain. And so it was a somewhat transgressive act that cut against established custom, as well as the institution of blood brotherhood between senior males.

2. This interpretation of the social referents of these objects is mine, not Grace Harris's.

3. This process of ethnic identification was encouraged by (1) Wataita's progressive territorial incarceration and administration as an ethnic entity by governing and church authorities and (2) the influence of an emerging class of educated Christian youth who mobilized ethnicity to make political claims (see Bravman 1998 for an overview).

4. Land consolidation was first proposed by the Kenyan government during the height of the Mau Mau insurrection, in 1954, as an aspect of the Swynnerton Plan, and was an explicit response to that crisis. The plan was designed to create a middle class of African farmers with individual rights over property in the Kikuyu-dominated Central Highlands. The plan's architects hoped that individual tenure would create a prosperous buffer class between the masses of African farmers and European Kenyans, and that this class would have a vested interest in developing good relations with the colonial regime.

5. I had the opportunity to visit one village preconsolidation (1990) and post-consolidation (in 1998).

6. "Medicines" is translated as *βugunga* in Taita language or *dawa* in Swahili. They are products composed at least partly of local herbs, created by specialists to achieve a certain goal, which is construed as positive.

7. While official government statistics put the unemployment rate at between 45 and 50 percent, my own observations suggest that it is much higher, probably well over 90 percent.

Chapter Three

1. In *vuturi*, a man loans livestock to another person, who cares for it and has use of its products but gives the offspring to the original owner.

2. In truth, most bridewealth in Taita today takes the form of currency, but many Wataita nonetheless see the substitution of money for livestock and produce in marriage exchanges as potentially problematic. They attempt to domesticate its effect by staggering payments and exchanging numerous meaningful objects along with the currency.

3. Taita fathers have been receiving more money for educated daughters since the 1930s (see, for example, Bravman 1998, 194).

Chapter Four

1. I use the present tense here to refer to this partly fictive type that Wataita refer to when they speak about the past, and how their society and morals have changed.

Chapter Five

1. However, the elders' appropriation of meat for themselves was probably not a deviation from the past, for Grace Harris wrote of the 1950s that those involved in a rainmaking ritual returned to their homes with the ritual material and performed a shortened version of the same ritual, involving the tossing of food about the compound and numerous acts of kutasa (Harris 1978, 130–31).

2. The skull is placed in a cave, or ngomenyi, alongside other skulls belonging to childbearing men and women of the lineage.

Chapter Six

1. According to the high-level employees with whom I spoke, Plan underwent a number of structural transformations after 2002, apparently with assistance from external consultants following complaints by donors concerning the distribution of funds. Thus, everything that I have written about Plan, unless otherwise noted, pertains to the period before 2002, and especially the period 1997–1999, when I was living in Taita and Plan retained its coastal headquarters there. Notable dimensions of the narrative, including the focus on children via the child foster program, have changed significantly, and it is my understanding that the foster program, which had originally been the foundation for everything Plan did, no longer exists, as money is channeled directly to the popularly elected community-

based organizations (formerly called planning units) and there is apparently full transparency and accountability concerning the source and distribution of monies.

2. While Plan had some Taita employees, most of its staff seemed to be either from Embu or Meru in central Kenya, where Plan had formerly been based before moving to Taita, for Plan's policy was to relocate once it had established what its employees hoped were self-sustaining civil society institutions.

3. This was probably untrue, because Plan representatives in Taita did not receive gifts directly from foreign families; the donations went directly to the national office in Nairobi, and so there seemed to be no opportunity for theft. The basis for the rumor lay in Plan's policy of compelling Taita families to write letters to their donor families updating them on the foster children's progress. Plan employees were not allowed to transfer the Europeans' addresses to the Africans, and vice versa, or to allow Taita and foreign families to communicate directly with one another.

Chapter Seven

1. A location is an administrative area composed of sublocations, which are in turn composed of small villages. Several locations, taken together, constitute a division. The Taita Hills is one division in the district of Taita-Taveta in Coast province, Kenya.

2. Maji Marefu is a translocal East African figure whose work has been discussed by others, including Paivu Hasu (*Desire and Death*, 1999), who has a section on Maji Marefu in her PhD thesis about the cultural construction of AIDS in Tanzania.

3. See also Auslander (1993) on the intermingling of multiparty democracy movements and witch-finding in 1980s Zambia.

4. It is difficult to know exactly how Maji Marefu identified the witches in a community. I only met two or three cynical people, all of them nonlocal priests or ministers living in the area, who claimed that community members were informing Maji Marefu about their suspicions. Nearly everyone vehemently asserted that Maji Marefu simply "saw" those with hearts capable of bewitching. However, it may be that, as more and more people came to his private consultancy for witchcraft remedies and related to Maji Marefu the particulars of their lives, and as his "sons" continued to fraternize with people in the community in bars after hours, they began to develop a picture that corresponded with local opinion.

5. This is a reference to the popularly elected local chairman of this village's Maji Marefu Committee, the group responsible for raising community funds and forwarding them to Maji Marefu. Though this chairman had spent twelve years in a Kenyan prison for reasons that were somewhat obscure, he campaigned for an influential opposition politician and considered himself an amateur lawyer.

References

Ahearn, Laura, 2001, *Invitations to Love: Literacy, Love Letters, and Social Change in Nepal* (Ann Arbor: University of Michigan Press).

Anderson, Davis, 2002, Vigilantes, violence, and the politics of public order in Kenya, *African Affairs* 101 (405): 531–55.

Appadurai, Arjun, 1996, *Modernity at Large: Cultural Dimensions of Globalization* (Chicago: University of Chicago Press).

Apter, Andrew, 2005, *The Pan-African Nation: Oil and the Spectacle of Culture in Nigeria* (Chicago: University of Chicago Press).

Arce, Alberto, and Norman Long, 2000, *Anthropology, Development and Modernities: Exploring Discourses, Counter-tendencies and Violence* (London: Routledge).

Arendt, Hannah, 1958, *The Human Condition* (Chicago: University of Chicago Press).

Ashforth, Adam, 1999, *Madumo: A Man Bewitched* (Chicago: University of Chicago Press).

———, 2005, *Witchcraft, Violence, and Democracy in South Africa* (Chicago: University of Chicago Press).

Aubrey, Lisa, 1997, *The Politics of Development Cooperation: NGOs, Gender and Partnership in Kenya* (London: Routledge).

Auslander, Mark, 1993, "Open the wombs!": The symbolic politics of modern Ngoni witchfinding, in *Modernity and its Malcontents*, J. Comaroff and J. L. Comaroff, eds., 167–93 (Chicago: University of Chicago Press).

Badiou, Alain, 1992, *Ethics: An Essay on the Understanding of Evil* (New York: Verso).

Barkan, Joel, 1993, Kenya: Lessons from a flawed election, *Journal of Democracy* 4 (July): 85–99.

Barkan, Joel, and Njuguna Ng'ethe, 1998, Kenya tries again, *Journal of Democracy* 9 (2): 32–48.

Barkan, Joel, ed., with John Okumu, 1979, *Politics and Public Policy in Kenya and Tanzania* (New York: Praeger).

Baudrillard, Jean, 1992, *The Illusion of the End* (Stanford, CA: Stanford University Press).

Bayart, Jean-Francois, 1993, *The State in Africa: the Politics of the Belly* (London: Longman).

———, 1999, The "social capital" of the felonious state, in *The Criminalization of the State in Africa*, by Jean-Francois Bayart, Stephen Ellis, and Beatrice Hibou, 32–48 (Oxford, UK: James Currey).

———, 2005, *The Illusion of Cultural Identity* (Chicago: The University of Chicago Press).

Bayart, Jean-Francois, Stephen Ellis, and Beatrice Hibou, 1999, *The Criminalization of the State in Africa* (Oxford, UK: James Currey).

Behrend, Heike, and Ute Luig, eds., 1999, *Spirit Possession: Modernity and Power in Africa* (Madison: University of Wisconsin Press).

Benjamin, Walter, 1968, *Illuminations: Essays and Reflections* (New York: Schoken Books).

Berman, Bruce J., 1991, Nationalism, ethnicity, and modernity: The paradox of Mau Mau, *Canadian Journal of African Studies* 25: 181–206.

Bloch, Ernst, 2000, *The Spirit of Utopia* (Stanford, CA: Stanford University Press).

Blunt, Robert, 2004, Satan is an imitator: Kenya's recent cosmology of corruption, in *Producing African Futures: Ritual and Reproduction in a Neoliberal Age*, Brad Weiss, ed., 294–328 (Leiden, Netherlands: Brill).

Boddy, Janice, 1989, *Wombs and Alien Spirits* (Madison: University of Wisconsin Press).

Bornstein, Erica, 2005, *The Spirit of Development: Protestant NGOs, Morality, and Economics in Zimbabwe* (Stanford, CA: Stanford University Press).

Bravman, Bill, 1998, *Making Ethnic Ways: Communities and their Transformations in Taita, Kenya, 1800–1950* (Portsmouth, NH: Heinemann).

Brokensha, David, and Peter D. Little, eds., 1988, *Anthropology of Development and Change in East Africa* (Boulder, CO: Westview Press).

Burke, Timothy, 1996, *Lifebuoy Men, Lux Women: Commodification, Consumption, and Cleanliness in Modern Zimbabwe* (Durham, NC: Duke University Press).

Carothers, J. C. 1954, *The Psychology of Mau Mau* (Nairobi: Government Printer).

Chabal, Patrick, and Jean-Pascal Daloz, 1999, *Africa Works: Disorder as Political Instrument* (Oxford, UK: James Currey).

Chambers, R., 1983, *Rural Development: Putting the Last First* (New York: Longman).

Ciekawy, Diane, 1992, *Witchcraft Eradication as Political Process in Kilifi District, Kenya, 1955–1988*, PhD diss., Columbia University.

———, 1998, Women's "work": The construction of witchcraft accusations in Coastal Kenya, *Women's Studies International Forum* 22 (2): 225–35.

Cohen, David, and Atieno Odhiambo, 1992, *Burying SM* (London: James Currey).

Comaroff, J., and J. L. Comaroff, 1991, *Of Revelation and Revolution: Christianity, Colonialism and Consciousness in South Africa* (Chicago: University of Chicago Press).

———, eds., 1993, *Modernity and Its Malcontents*, (Chicago: University of Chicago Press).

———, eds., 1999a, *Civil Society and the Political Imagination in Africa* (Chicago: University of Chicago Press).

———, 1999b, Occult economies and the violence of abstraction, *American Ethnologist*, 26: 2.

———, 2000, Naturing the nation, *Hogan International Social Science Review* 1 (1): 7–40.

———, 2001, Millennial capitalism: First thoughts on a second coming. In *Millennial Capitalism and the Culture of Neoliberalism*, John Comaroff and Jean Comaroff, eds. (Durham, NC: Duke University Press).

Cooke, Bill, and Uma Kothari, eds., 2001, *Participation: The New Tyranny*? London: Zed Books.

Cooper, Frederick, 1988, Mau Mau and the discourses of decolonization, *Journal of African History* 29: 313–20.

———, 1996, *Decolonization and African Society* (Cambridge, UK: Cambridge University Press).

Cooper, Frederick, and Randall Packard, 1997, *International Development and the Social Sciences: Essays on the History and Politics of Knowledge* (Berkeley: University of California Press).

Corfield, Frank, 1960, *Origins and Growth of Mau Mau* (Nairobi: Government Printer).

Cowen, Michael, and Robert Shenton, eds., 1997, *Doctrines of Development* (London: Routledge).

Crush, John, ed., 1995, *Power of Development* (New York: Routledge).

Dahl, G., and G. Megerrsa, 1992, The spiral of the ram's horn: Boran conceptions of development, in *Kam-Ap or Take-Off: Local Notions of Development*, G. Dahl and A. Rabo, eds., 157–74 (Stockholm: Stockholm University).

Dahl, G., and A. Rabo, eds., 1992, *Kam-Ap or Take-Off: Local Notions of Development* (Stockholm: Stockholm University).

Daily Telegraph, 2004, Iconoclasts turn their fury on Kenya's colonial past, *Daily Telegraph*, December 16, 1.

Davis, Mike, 2006, *Planet of Slums* (London: Verso).

De Boeck, Filip, 2004, On being "shege" in Kinshasa: Children, the occult, and the street, in *Reinventing Order in the Congo*, Theodore Trefon, ed. (New York: Zed Books).

———, 2005, The apocalyptic interlude: Revealing Death in Kinshasa, *African Studies Review* 48 (2): 11–32.

De Sardan, Jean-Pierre Olivier, 2005, *Anthropology and Development: Understanding Contemporary Social Change* (London: Zed Books).

Devarajan, Shanta, David Dollar, and Torgny Holmgren, 2001, *Aid and Reform in Africa: Lessons from Ten Case Studies* (Washington, DC: Development Research Group, World Bank).

Diouf, Mamadou, 1997, Senegalese development: From mass mobilization to technocratic elitism, in *International Development and the Social Sciences: Essays on the History and Politics of Knowledge*, Frederick Cooper and Randall Packard, eds., 291–313 (Berkeley: University of California Press).

———, 2003, Engaging postcolonial cultures: African youth and public space, *African Studies Review* 46 (2): 1–12.

Donham, Donald, 1999 [1990], *History, Power, Ideology: Central Issues in Marxism and Anthropology* (Berkeley: University of California Press).

Douglas, Mary, ed., 1970, *Witchcraft Confessions and Accusations* (London: Tavistock).

Downs, R. E., and S. P. Reyna, eds, 1988, *Land and Society in Contemporary Africa* (Lebanon, NH: University Press of New England).

Edelman, Marc, and Angelique Haugerud, eds., 2005a, *The Anthropology of Development and Globalization: From Classical Political Economy to Contemporary Neoliberalism* (Malden, MA: Blackwell Publishing).

———, 2005b, Introduction: Development and globalization. In *The Anthropology of Development and Globalization: From Classical Political Economy to Contemporary Neoliberalism*, 1–75 (Malden, MA: Blackwell Publishing).

Escobar, Arturo, 1988, Power and visibility: Development and the invention and management of the Third World, *Cultural Anthropology* 3 (4): 428–43.

———, 1995, *Encountering Development: The Making and Unmaking of the Third World*, (Princeton, NJ: Princeton University Press).

Evans-Pritchard, E. E., 1993 [1937], *Witchcraft, Oracles and Magic among the Azande* (Oxford, UK: Clarendon).

Fairhead, James, 2000, Development discourse and its subversion: Decivilization, depoliticization, and dispossession in West Africa. In *Anthropology, Development and Modernities: Exploring Discourses, Counter-tendencies and Violence*, Alberto Arce and Norman Long, eds., 100–112 (London: Routledge).

Feldman, Allen, 1991, *Formations of Violence: The Narrative of the Body and Political Terror in Northern Ireland* (Chicago: University of Chicago Press).

Ferguson, James, 1993, De-moralizing economies: African socialism, scientific capitalism, and the moral politics of "structural adjustment," in *Moralizing States: The Ethnography of the Present*, Sally Falk Moore, ed., 78–92 (Arlington,VA: American Anthropological Association).

———, 1994, *The Anti-Politics Machine: "Development," Depoliticization, and Bureaucratic Power in Lesotho* (Cambridge, UK: Cambridge University Press).

———, 1999, *Expectations of Modernity: Myths and Meanings of Urban Life on the Zambian Copperbelt* (Berkeley: University of California Press).

———, 2006, *Global Shadows: Africa in the Neoliberal World Order* (Durham, NC: Duke University Press).

Ferguson, James, and Akhil Gupta, 2002, Spatializing states: Towards an ethnography of neoliberal governmentality. *American Ethnologist* 29 (4): 981–1002.

Finnemore, Martha, 1997, Redefining development at the World Bank, in *International Development and the Social Sciences: Essays on the History and Politics of Knowledge*, Frederick Cooper and Randall Packard, eds., 203–28 (Berkeley: University of California Press).

Fleuret, Anne, 1988, Some consequences of tenure and agrarian reform in Taita, Kenya, in *Land and Society in Contemporary Africa*, R. E. Downs and S. P. Reyna, eds., 136–58 (Lebanon, NH: University Press of New England).

Fleuret, Patrick, 1985, The social organization of water control in the Taita Hills, Kenya, *American Ethnologist* 12 (1): 103–18.

Fortes, Meyer, ed., 1962, *Marriage in Tribal Societies* (Cambridge, UK: Cambridge University Press).

Foucault, Michel, 1980, *Power/Knowledge: Selected Interviews and Other Writings* (New York: Pantheon).

———, 1990, *A History of Sexuality*, vol. I (New York: Random House).

———, 2003, *Society Must Be Defended: Lectures at the College de France (1975–1976)* (New York: Picador).

Fox, Jonathon, 2003, Advocacy research and the World Bank: Propositions for discussion, reprinted in *The Anthropology of Development and Globalization: From Classical Political Economy to Contemporary Neoliberalism*, Marc Edelman and Angelique Haugerud, eds, 306–313 (Malden, MA: Blackwell Publishing).

Frank, Andre Gunder, 1991, The underdevelopment of development, *Scandinavian Journal of Development Alternatives* 10 (3): 5–72.

Fukuyama, Francis, 1992, *The End of History and the Last Man* (New York: Avon Press).

Furedi, Frank, 1989, *The Mau Mau War in Perspective* (London: James Currey).

Gardner, Katy, and David Lewis, 1996, Beyond development?, in *Anthropology, Development, and the Post-Modern Challenge* (London: Pluto Press).

Garland, Elizabeth, 1999, Developing bushmen: Building civil(ized) society in the Kalahari and beyond, in *Civil Society and the Political Imagination in Africa*, J. Comaroff and J. L. Comaroff, eds., 72–103 (Chicago: University of Chicago Press).

Gellhorn, Martha, 1959, *The Face of War*, ch. 5 (New York: Simon and Schuster).

Gertzel, Cherry, 1970, *The Politics of Independent Kenya, 1963–1968* (Nairobi: East Africa Publishing House).

Geschiere, Peter, 1997, *The Modernity of Witchcraft: Politics and the Occult in Post-Colonial Africa* (Charlottesville: University Press of Virginia).

Geschiere, Peter, and Francis Nyamnjoh, 2001, Capitalism and autochthony: The seesaw of mobility and belonging. In *Millennial Capitalism and the Culture of Neoliberalism*, Jean Comaroff and John L. Comaroff, eds. (Durham, NC: Duke University Press).

Giles, Linda, 1999, Spirit possession and the symbolic construction of Swahili society, in *Spirit Possession: Modernity and Power in Africa*, Heike Behrend and Ute Luig, eds., 142–65 (Madison: University of Wisconsin Press).

Gledhill, John, 2001, Disappearing the poor? A critique of the new wisdoms of social democracy in an age of globalization, *Urban Anthropology and Studies of Cultural Systems and World Economic Development* 30 (2): 124–56.

Gluckman, Max, 1954, The magic of despair, *The Listener*, April 29.

Graeber, David, 2001, The Globalization movement: Some points of Clarification, Reprinted in *The Anthropology of Development and Globalization: From Classical Political Economy to Contemporary Neoliberalism*, Marc Edelman and Angelique Haugerud, eds., 169–73 (Malden, MA Blackwell Publishing).

Grillo, R. D., and R. L. Stirrat, eds., 1997, *Discourses of Development: Anthropological Perspectives* (Oxford, UK: Berg).

Gupta, Akhil, 1998, *Post-Colonial Developments: Agriculture in the Making of Modern India* (Durham, NC: Duke University Press).

Hansen, Karen Tranberg, 2000, *Salaula: The World of Secondhand Clothing and Zambia*. (Chicago: University of Chicago Press).

Harbeson, John, Donald Rothchild, and Naomi Chazan, eds., 1994, *Civil Society and the State in Africa* (Boulder, CO: Rienner Publishers).

Harper, Richard, 2000, The social organization of the IMF's mission work: An examination of international auditing. Reprinted in *The Anthropology of Development and Globalization: From Classical Political Economy to Contemporary Neoliberalism*, Marc Edelman and Angelique Haugerud, eds., 323–34 (Malden, MA: Blackwell Publishing).

Harris, Grace, 1957, Possession 'hysteria' in a Kenya tribe, *American Anthropologist* 59 (6): 1049–66.

———, 1962, Taita bridewealth and affinal relationships, in *Marriage in Tribal Societies*, Meyer Fortes, ed. (Cambridge, UK: Cambridge University Press).

———, 1978, *Casting Out Anger: Religion among the Taita of Kenya* (Cambridge, UK: Cambridge University Press).

Hasu, Paivu. 1999, *Desire and Death: History through Ritual Practice in Kilimanjaro*, PhD diss., University of Helsinki.

Haugerud, Angelique, 1995, *The Culture of Politics in Modern Kenya* (Cambridge, UK: Cambridge University Press).

Hayter, T., 1971, *Aid as Imperialism* (Harmondsworth, UK: Penguin).

Hobart, Mark, ed., 1993, *An Anthropological Critique of Development* (London: Routledge).

Hoben, Allan. 1982. Anthropologists and development, *Annual Review of Anthropology* 11: 349–75.
Holmquist, F., 1972, Implementing rural development projects, in *Development Administration: The Kenyan Experience*, G. Hyden, R. Jackson, and J. Okumu, eds. (Nairobi: Oxford University Press).
Hyden, G., R. Jackson, and J. Okumu, eds., 1970, *Development Administration: the Kenyan Experience* (Nairobi: Oxford University Press).
Jaffrelot, Christophe, 1993, *Les Nationalisms hindous: Ideologie, implantation, et mobilization des anees 1920 aux anees 1990* (Paris: Presses de la Fondation Nationale des Sciences Politiques).
Karp, Ivan, 1989, Power and capacity in rituals of possession, in *Creativity of Power: Cosmology and Action in African Societies*, W. Arens and Ivan Karp, eds. (Washington, DC: Smithsonian Institution Press).
———, 2002, Development and personhood: Tracing the contours of a moral discourse, In *Critically Modern: Alternatives, Alterities, Anthropologies*, Bruce Knauft, ed. (Bloomington: Indiana University Press).
Kenya Daily Nation (KDN), 1999, Kirima alleges devil worship a foreign ploy, *Kenya Daily Nation*, August 15.
Kenya Human Rights Commission (KHRC), 2004, *The Manufacture of Poverty: The Untold Story of EPZs in Kenya* (Nairobi: KHRC).
Kenyatta, Jomo, 1964, *Harambee! The Prime Minister of Kenya's Speeches, 1963–1964* (Oxford, UK: Oxford University Press).
Kioi, Samuel Ng'ang'a, 1999, Devil report is unrealistic, *Kenya Daily Nation*, August 27.
Kitching, Gavin, 1980, *Class and Economic Change in Kenya: the Making of an African Petite-Bourgeoisie, 1905–1970* (New Haven, CT: Yale University Press).
Knauft, Bruce, 2002, ed., *Critically Modern: Alternatives, Alterities, Anthropologies*. (Bloomington: Indiana University Press).
Kulick, Don, 1992, "Coming up" in Gapun: Conceptions of development and their effect on language in a Papua New Guinea village, in *Kam-Ap or Take-Off: Local Notions of Development*, G. Dahl and A. Rabo, eds., 10–35 (Stockholm: Stockholm University).
Kwamboka, Evelyn, 2004, Mau Mungiki trains killers, *East African Standard*, March 8.
Leakey, L. S. B., 1953, *Mau Mau and the Kikuyu* (London: Methuen).
———, 1954, *Defeating Mau Mau* (London: Methuen).
Lensink, Robert, 1996, *Structural Adjustment in Subsaharan Africa* (New York: Longman)
Leys, Colin, 1978, *Underdevelopment in Kenya: The Political Economy of Neocolonialism, 1964–1971* (Berkeley: University of California Press).
———, 1996, *The Rise and Fall of Development Theory* (Bloomington: Indiana University Press).

Little, Peter, and Catherine Dolan, 2000, Non-traditional commodities and structural adjustment in Africa, reprinted in *The Anthropology of Development and Globalization: From Classical Political Economy to Contemporary Neoliberalism*, Marc Edelman and Angelique Haugerud, eds., 206–16 (Malden, MA: Blackwell Publishing).

Lonsdale, John, 1990, Mau Maus of the mind: Making Mau Mau and re-making Kenya, *Journal of African History*, 31: 393–421.

———, 1992, The moral economy of Mau Mau: Wealth, power, and civic virtue in Kikuyu political thought, in *Unhappy Valley: Conflict in Kenya*, vol. 2, Bruce Berman and John Lonsdale, eds. (London: James Currey).

Mamdani, Mahmood, 1996, *Citizen and Subject: Contemporary Africa and the Legacy of Late Colonialism* (Princeton, NJ: Princeton University Press).

Marwick, Max. 1990. *Witchcraft and Sorcery: Selected Readings* (New York: Penguin).

———, 1950. The Bwanali-Mpulumutsi anti-witchcraft movement, in *Witchcraft and Sorcery: Selected Readings*, ed. Max Marwick (New York: Penguin).

Marx, Karl, 1977, *Capital*, vol. I (New York: Vintage Books).

Mathiu, Mutuma, 2001, Welcome to Kenya, the IMF's little colony, *Kenya Daily Nation*, May 20.

Mbembe, Achille, 1992, The banality of power and the aesthetics of vulgarity in the postcolony, *Public Culture* 5: 1.

———, 2001, *On the Postcolony* (Berkeley: University of California Press).

———, 2003, Necropolitics, *Public Culture* 15 (1): 11–40.

Meyer, Birgit, 1998, "Make a complete break with the Past": Memory and postcolonial modernity in Ghanaian Pentecostalist discourse, *Journal of Religion in Africa* 28 (3): 316–49.

———, 1999, Commodities and the power of prayer: Pentecostalist attitudes toward consumption in contemporary Ghana, in *Globalization and Identity: Dialectics of Flow and Closure*, Brigit Meyer and Peter Geschiere, eds., 151–76 (Oxford, UK: Blackwell).

Meyer, Birgit, and Peter Geschiere, eds., 1999, *Globalization and Identity: Dialectics of Flow and Closure* (Oxford, UK: Blackwell).

Ministry of Planning and National Development, 1994, *Taita-Taveta District Development Plan: 1994–1996* (Nairobi: Government Printer).

———, 1998a, *First Report on Poverty in Kenya, Volume 1: Incidence and Depth of Poverty* (Nairobi: Government Printer).

———, 1998b, *First Report on Poverty in Kenya, Volume 2: Poverty and Social Indicators* (Nairobi: Government Printer).

———, 1998c, *First Report on Poverty in Kenya, Volume 3: Welfare Indicators Atlas* (Nairobi: Government Printer).

Ministry of Planning and National Development and the Institute of African Studies, University of Nairobi, 1986, *Taita-Taveta District Socio-Cultural Profile*, Gideon Were and Robert Soper, eds. (Nairobi: Government Printer).

Mitchell, Timothy, 2002, *Rule of Experts: Egypt, Techno-politics, Modernity* (Berkeley: University of California Press).

Miyazaki, Hirokazu, 2004, *The Method of Hope: Anthropology, Philosophy, and Fijian Knowledge* (Stanford, CA: Stanford University Press).

Mkangi, G. C., 1983, *The Social Costs of Small Families and Land Reform: A Case Study of the Wataita of Kenya* (Oxford, UK: Pergamon Press).

Moi, Daniel arap T., 1986, *Kenyan African Nationalism: Nyayo Philosophy and Principles* (London: Macmillan).

Moore, Henrietta, and Todd Sanders, eds., 2001, *Magical Interpretations, Material Realities: Modernity, Witchcraft, and the Occult in Postcolonial Africa* (London: Routledge).

Munn, Nancy, 1986, *The Fame of Gawa* (Chicago: University of Chicago Press).

Musil, Robert, 1995, *The Man without Qualities* (New York: Picador).

Muthai, Wahome, 2000, Grazing cows in the lecture theatre, *Kenya Daily Nation*, August 27.

Mutua, Makau, 2000, A scandal that could topple Kenya's shaky democracy, *Boston Globe*, June 17.

Mwachofi, Kirisha wa, 1998, in *Mwanedu*, March 15.

Mwachofi, M. M., 1977, *Land Reform in Taita: A Study of Socio-Economic Underdevelopment in a Kenya District*, BA thesis, University of Nairobi.

Mwai, Muthui, 2000, What makes Mungiki tick? *Kenya Daily Nation*, October 23, 2.

Nazzaro, A. A., 1974, *Changing Use of the Resource Base Among the Taita of Kenya*, PhD diss., Michigan State University.

Ngugi wa Thiong'o, 1987, *Devil on the Cross* (London: Heinemann).

Ngwane, Zolani, 2004, "Real men reawaken their fathers' homestead, the educated leave them in ruins": The politics of domestic reproduction in post-Apartheid rural South Africa, in *Producing African Futures: Ritual and Reproduction in a Neoliberal Age*, Brad Weiss, ed., 167–92 (Leiden, Netherlands: Brill).

Niehaus, Izak, 2001, Witchcraft, power and politics: From colonial superstition to post-colonial reality? In *Magical Interpretations, Material Realities: Modernity, Witchcraft, and the Occult in Postcolonial Africa*. Henrietta Moore and Todd Sanders, eds., 184–205 (London: Routledge).

Njau, Muteji, 1999a, Posh lifestyles of the Satanists, *Kenya Daily Nation*, August 5, 1.

———, 1999b, Satan a threat to Kenya's schools, *Kenya Daily Nation*, August 6, 1.

Nyamnjoh, Francis, 2001, Delusions of development and the enrichment of witchcraft discourses in Cameroon. In *Magical Interpretations, Material Realities: Modernity, Witchcraft, and the Occult in Postcolonial Africa*. Henrietta Moore and Todd Sanders, eds., 28–49 (London: Routledge).

Ogembo, Justus Mozart H'Achachi, 1997, *The Rise and Decline of Communal Violence: An Analysis of the 1992–1994 Witch Hunts in Gusii, South-Western Kenya*. PhD diss., Harvard University.

Olowu, B., 1999, Redesigning African civil service reforms, *Journal of Modern African Studies*, 37 (1): 1–23.

Ombuor, Joe, 2000, Is devil worship real in the country? *Kenya Daily Nation*, March 27.

Parker, Ian, 2004, *Slavoj Zizek: A Critical Introduction* (London: Pluto Press).

Pels, Peter, 1998, The magic of Africa: Reflections on a Western commonplace, *African Studies Review* 41 (3): 193–209.

Pigg, Stacey Leigh, 1992, Inventing social categories through place: Social representations and development in Nepal, *Comparative Studies in Society and History* 34 (3): 491–513.

Piot, Charles, 1999, *Remotely Global: Village Modernity in West Africa* (Chicago: University of Chicago Press).

Presidential Commission of Inquiry, 1995, *Report of the Presidential Commission of Inquiry into the Cult of Devil Worship* (Nairobi: Government Printer).

Rahneman, Majid, 1997, Towards post-development: Searching for sign posts, a new language, and new paradigms, in *The Post-Development Reader*, Majid Rahneman and Victoria Batree, eds., 377–403 (London: Zed Books).

Rahneman, Majid, and Victoria Batree, eds., 1997, *The Post-Development Reader* (London: Zed Books).

Rao, Vijayendra, and Michael Walton, eds. 2004, *Culture and Public Action: A Cross-Disciplinary Dialogue on Development Policy* (Stanford, CA: Stanford University Press).

Redmayne, Alison, 1970, Chikanga: An African diviner with an international reputation, in *Witchcraft Confessions and Accusations*, Mary Douglas, ed., 103–28 (London: Tavistock).

Reno, William, 1998, *Warlord Politics and African States* (Boulder, CO: Lynne Riener).

Richards, Audrey, 1935, A modern movement of witch-finders, in *Africa* 8: 448–61.

Rival, Laura, ed., 1998, *The Social Life of Trees: Anthropological Perspectives on Tree Symbolism* (Oxford, UK: Berg).

Rowlands, M. J., and J.-P. Warnier 1988, Sorcery, power, and the modern state in Cameroon, *Man* 23: 118–32.

Sachs, Wolfgang, ed., 1995, *The Development Dictionary* (London: Zed Books).

Schmoll, Pamela, 1993, Black stomachs, beautiful stones: Soul eating amongst Hausa in Niger. In *Modernity and its Malcontents*, J. Comaroff and J. L. Comaroff, eds. (Chicago: University of Chicago Press).

Scott, James, 1998. *Seeing Like a State: How Certain Schemes to Improve the Human Condition Have Failed* (New Haven, CT: Yale University Press).

Shaw, Carolyn Martin, 1995, *Colonial Inscriptions: Race, Sex, and Class in Kenya* (Minneapolis: University of Minnesota Press).

Shaw, Rosalind, 2002, *Memories of the Slave Trade: Ritual and the Historical Imagination in Sierra Leone* (Chicago: University of Chicago Press).

———, 1989, *Bitter Money: Cultural Economy and Some African Meanings of Forbidden Commodities* (Washington, DC: American Anthropological Association).
———, 1994, Land and culture in tropical Africa: Soils, symbols, and the metaphysics of the mundane, *Annual Review of Anthropology* 23: 347–77.
Shipton, Parker, 1988, Kenyan land tenure reform: Misunderstandings in the public creation of private property, in *Land and Society in Contemporary Africa*, R. E. Downs and S. P. Reyna, eds. (Lebanon, NH: University Press of New England).
Siegel, James, 2006, *Naming the Witch* (Stanford, CA: Stanford University Press).
Simon, P., Wim vanSpenger, Chris Dixon, and Anders Narman, 1995, *Structurally Adjusted Africa: Poverty, Debt, and Basic Needs* (London: Pluto Press).
Simone, AbdouMaliq, 2004, *For the City Yet to Come: Changing African Life in Four Cities* (Durham, NC: Duke University Press).
Sivaramakrishnan, K., 1998, Modern forestry: Trees and development spaces in South-west Bengal, in *The Social Life of Trees: Anthropological Perspectives on Tree Symbolism*, Laura Rival, ed., 273–96 (Oxford, UK: Berg).
Smith, James H., 1998, Njama's supper: The consumption and use of literary potency by Mau Mau insurgents in colonial Kenya, *Comparative Studies in Society and History* 40 (3): 524– 48.
———, 2001, Of spirit possession and structural adjustment programs, *Journal of Religion in Africa* 31 (4): 427–56.
———, 2006, Snake driven development: Culture, nature and religious conflict in neoliberal Kenya, *Ethnography* 7 (4): 423–59.
Smith, M., 1994, *Hard Times on Kairiru Island: Poverty, Property, and Morality in a Papua New Guinea Village* (Honolulu: University of Hawaii Press).
Stewart, Pamela, and Andrew Strathern, 2004, *Witchcraft, Sorcery, Rumors, and Gossip* (Cambridge, UK: Cambridge University Press).
Stiglitz, Joseph, 2001, Thanks for nothing. *Atlantic Monthly* 288 (3): 36–40.
———, 2002, *Globalization and Its Discontents*. (New York: W. W. Norton).
Taussig, Michael, 1980, *The Devil and Commodity Fetishism in South America* (Chapel Hill: University of North Carolina Press).
Taylor, Chris, 1992, *Milk, Honey, and Money: Changing Concepts in Rwandan Healing* (Washington, DC: Smithsonian Institution Press).
Taylor, Darren, 2005, In a situation like this, who cares about human rights? Inter-Press Service, http://www.ipsnews.net/.
Tenbruck, F., 1980, The dream of a secular ecumene: The meanings and limits of projects of development, *Theory, Culture, and Society* 7 (3): 193–206.
Throup, David, 1985, The Origins of Mau Mau, *African Affairs* 84: 399–433.
———, 1988, *Economic and Social Origins of Mau Mau* (London: James Currey).
Throup, David, and Charles Hornsby, 1998, *Multi-Party Politics in Kenya: The Kenyatta and Moi States and the Triumph of the System in the 1992 Elections* (Oxford, UK: James Currey).

Trefon, Theodore, 2004, ed., *Reinventing Order in the Congo: How People Respond to State Failure in Kinshasa* (London: Zed Books).

U.S. Department of State, 1994, *Kenya: 1995 Country Report on Economic Policy and Trade Practices* (Washington, DC: U.S. Department of State).

Van Binsbergen, W. M. J., 1981, *Religious Change in Zambia: Exploratory Studies* (London: Kegan Paul International).

Wallis, M., 1982, *Bureaucrats, Politicians, and Local Communities in Kenya*, Manchester Papers on Development, no. 6, Paul Cook, ed. (Manchester, UK: Manchester University).

Wamue, Grace, 2001, Revisiting our indigenous shrines through Mungiki, *African Affairs* 100: 453–67.

———, 2004, The Mungiki movement: A source of religio-political conflict and peace-building in Kenya. Unpublished ms. presented at the Religion, Conflict and Peacebuilding in Africa conference in Jinja, Uganda (Kroc Institute for International Peace Studies, University of Notre Dame).

Weiss, Brad, 1996, *The Making and Unmaking of the Haya Lived World* (Durham, NC: Duke University Press).

———, 2001. Getting ahead when we're behind: Time and value in urban Tanzania. American Anthropological Association conference paper.

———, 2002. Thug realism: Inhabiting fantasy in urban Tanzania, *Cultural Anthropology* 17 (1): 93–128.

———, ed., 2004, *Producing African Futures: Ritual and Reproduction in a Neoliberal Age* (Leiden, Netherlands: Brill).

Werbner, Richard, ed., 2002, *Postcolonial Subjectivities in Africa* (London: Zed Books).

West, Harry, 2005, *Kupilikula: Governance and the Invisible Realm in Mozambique* (Chicago: University of Chicago Press).

White, Hylton, 2004, Ritual haunts: The timing of estrangement in a post-Apartheid countryside. In *Producing African Futures: Ritual and Reproduction in a Neoliberal Age*. 141–166, Brad Weiss, ed., (Leiden, Netherlands: Brill).

White, Luise, 2000, *Speaking with Vampires: Rumor and History in Colonial Africa* (Berkeley: University of California Press).

Williams, Raymond, 1977, *The Country and the City* (New York: Oxford University Press).

Willis, R. G., 1968, The Kamcape movement, in *Witchcraft and Sorcery: Selected Readings*, Max Marwick, ed. (New York: Penguin).

Wilson, Monica, 1951, Witch-beliefs and social structure, *American Journal of Sociology* 56: 307–13.

Woost, Michael, 1997, Alternative vocabularies of development? In *Discourses of Development: Anthropological Perspectives*, R. D. Grillo and R. L. Stirrat, eds. (Oxford, UK: Berg).

Index

Note: in this index, β is alphabetized as b.